MORE GRAMMAR TO GET THINGS DONE

Complementing Crovitz and Devereaux's successful *Grammar to Get Things Done*, this book demystifies grammar in context and offers day-by-day guides for teaching ten grammar concepts, giving teachers a model and vocabulary for discussing grammar in real ways with their students. Through applied practice in real-world contexts, the authors explain how to develop students' mastery of grammar and answer difficult questions about usage, demonstrating how grammar acts as a tool for specific purposes in students' lives. Accessibly written and organized, the book provides ten adaptable activity guides for each concept, illustrating instruction from a use-based perspective. Middle and high school preservice and inservice English teachers will gain confidence in their own grammar knowledge and learn how to teach grammar in ways that are uniquely accessible and purposeful for students.

Darren Crovitz is Professor of English and English Education at Kennesaw State University, USA.

Michelle D. Devereaux is Associate Professor of English and English Education at Kennesaw State University, USA.

MORE GRAMMAR TO GET THINGS DONE

Daily Lessons for Teaching Grammar in Context

Darren Crovitz and
Michelle D. Devereaux

Routledge
Taylor & Francis Group

NEW YORK AND LONDON

NCTE National Council of
Teachers of English

First published 2020
by Routledge
52 Vanderbilt Avenue, New York, NY 10017

and by Routledge
2 Park Square, Milton Park, Abingdon, Oxon, OX14 4RN

Routledge is an imprint of the Taylor & Francis Group, an informa business

© 2020 Taylor & Francis

The right of Darren Crovitz and Michelle D. Devereaux to be identified as authors of this work has been asserted by them in accordance with sections 77 and 78 of the Copyright, Designs and Patents Act 1988.

All rights reserved. No part of this book may be reprinted or reproduced or utilised in any form or by any electronic, mechanical, or other means, now known or hereafter invented, including photocopying and recording, or in any information storage or retrieval system, without permission in writing from the publishers.

Trademark notice: Product or corporate names may be trademarks or registered trademarks, and are used only for identification and explanation without intent to infringe.

Library of Congress Cataloging-in-Publication Data
Names: Crovitz, Darren, author. | Devereaux, Michelle D., author.
Title: More grammar to get things done : daily lessons for teaching grammar in context / Darren Crovitz and Michelle D. Devereaux.
Description: New York, NY : Routledge, 2020. | Includes bibliographical references and index.
Identifiers: LCCN 2019034602 (print) | LCCN 2019034603 (ebook) | ISBN 9780367194741 (hardback) | ISBN 9780367194819 (paperback) | ISBN 9780429202711 (ebook)
Subjects: LCSH: English language—Grammar—Study and teaching (Secondary) | English language—Study and teaching (Secondary)
Classification: LCC LB1631 .C776 2020 (print) | LCC LB1631 (ebook) | DDC 428.00712—dc23
LC record available at https://lccn.loc.gov/2019034602
LC ebook record available at https://lccn.loc.gov/2019034603

ISBN: 978-0-367-19474-1 (hbk)
ISBN: 978-0-367-19481-9 (pbk)
ISBN: 978-0-429-20271-1 (ebk)

Typeset in Sabon
by Apex CoVantage, LLC

Darren's Dedication:
To my family.

Michelle's Dedication:
To my husband and our two girls.

BRIEF CONTENTS

CONTENTS

TABLES

FIGURES

ACKNOWLEDGMENTS

Like any book, this one wouldn't be around without some important people helping out.

Holly Hoover and her magnificent high school students were the first to engage with these ideas. Thank you for your kindness and patience, and for the feedback that has made this work better.

We leaned hard on Chris Palmer, our supersmart linguist friend, when we got lost in the details. Thanks, Chris. We're also grateful to Rob Montgomery, Clarice Moran, Harmony Dalgleish, and Ande Nesmith, who offered suggestions on portions of this book. Our community of colleagues at Kennesaw State University are also a part of this work. Thank you to Michelle Goodsite, Jen Dail, Steve Goss, Keith Botelho, Ralph Wilson, Bill Rice, and Sheila Smith McKoy for their support. Thank you to Andrea Marshbank, Kim Van Es, and Chris Parsons for their engagement with and support of our work.

Our editor at Routledge, Karen Adler, has been a great partner in this effort. Thank you to Karen and her team, who offered insightful guidance on the scope and shape of this book. At NCTE, Kurt Austin has been a constant supporter of our work.

Finally, massive thanks to the preservice and inservice teachers in our courses, who kept us grounded on a central question: "But how do you actually *teach* grammar?!?" Their consistent questioning led us toward answers. Because of them, this book exists.

CHAPTER 1

What Is This Book About?

Since you're holding a book about how to teach grammar, well, we're guessing that some of the following statements probably ring true for you.

- There's something wrong with the way that grammar instruction has been traditionally taught.
- "Teaching grammar in context" makes sense, but it's harder than it sounds.
- Close study of language concepts should probably be centered on actual examples of language use.
- Monday looms—you need to tackle grammar, and you don't know how to come at this subject confidently for your students' benefit.

Let's talk about each one of these, and how what follows in this book can help you approach grammar and language instruction from a position of principle, intentionality, and confidence.

1. **There's something wrong with the way that grammar instruction has been traditionally taught.**

We all know what traditional grammar instruction looks like. See if you recognize this general process:

1. *A teacher notices a common issue in student writing: comma splices, noun/pronoun agreement, sentence fragments, or something similar.*
2. *To address this issue, the teacher plans a targeted grammar lesson, drawing upon grammar and usage resources and reviewing the related rule with students.*
3. *Students get a set of practice exercises that reinforce the rule, often in the form of a worksheet.*
4. *Going forward, students correctly apply the rule in formal writing situations.*

Steps one through three should sound pretty familiar. Step 4 should not. Let's change that final one so it matches reality:

4. *Going forward, students continue to demonstrate the same issue in their writing as they did previously.*

If you've been a student in American public schools, chances are you've experienced this process a number of times. If you're a teacher, you've probably tried it out as well, maybe thinking that with a little extra attention, with a little bit of your own instructional effort and flair, things might turn out differently. Alas, the result is almost always the same. Students don't seem to take up this kind of stand-alone grammar instruction in any sustained, applied way.[1]

Let's think about that for a few moments. Research shows that the isolated, teacher-orchestrated mini-lesson described above *doesn't help students become better users of language*. We think this is kind of a big deal, and it really calls into question why this approach is still so prevalent in classrooms. Weaver (1996) wrote about this type of grammar instruction 20-plus years ago and provided a dozen reasons why teachers keep going back to it. Here are three reasons we find particularly convincing:

- **Traditional grammar lessons look like conventional schoolwork.** It's highly unlikely that a teacher will be admonished—by parents, administrators, or anyone else—for conducting a typical grammar lesson like the one described above. This process actually fits many people's preconceptions about what an English classroom should look like: students somehow learning how language works through direct instruction of terminology and rules accompanied by drills. It looks like school as we traditionally imagine it.
- **Teachers don't have the confidence or experience to approach grammar another way.** This one makes total sense to us because we've felt the same way ourselves. Our initial efforts with grammar instruction were superficial rather than thoughtful. Most of the time, we were able *to completely avoid* grammar instruction if we wanted to. Without preparation and a willingness to try something different, it's simply safer—and less face it, easier—to stick with what we prefer to teach. Maybe you feel the same right now. We get it. Teachers' professional lives are forever at the mercy of new demands on their time and initiative. If you didn't get a firm foundation in your teacher preparation program, grammar instruction can sit on the backburner indefinitely.
- **Teachers—most of them, at least—don't enjoy grammar.** Most of us (there are exceptions, of course) didn't get into teaching for a love of grammar. A deep affinity for books and reading did it for us, followed later by personal epiphanies about the power of writing. If we thought about grammar at all, it was mostly in implicit ways. We recognized good writing when we read it, and sometimes we were even able to produce such prose ourselves. But the nuts and bolts of the language—what grammar concepts are called, the technical rules for their use, the identification and analysis of sentence parts—yeah, not so much. For reasons we explore a little later, grammar hasn't been a particularly pleasant subject for most people, and that goes for teachers as much as students. Since many English teacher preparation programs don't spend a great deal of time on how to teach grammatical concepts in

---

1. It's not all bad news. Students sometimes show improvement in one specific way: they get better at doing isolated grammar exercises (Hillocks, 1986). We'll leave you to ponder the educational merit of this outcome without any concurrent improvement in writing.

a comprehensive and effective way, it's rare for teachers to have the opportunity to reposition their own perspective and attitudes toward language study.

Let's move on to the next item on our list of things-you-might-suspect-about-grammar.

2. "Teaching grammar in context" makes sense, but it's harder than it sounds.

For several decades, teachers have been advised to "teach grammar in context" as an alternative to stand-alone grammar lessons and units. In a nutshell, grammar in context means that we approach grammar as both an integrated component of language arts skills (i.e., reading, writing, speaking, etc.) as well as an important aspect of students' day-to-day language experiences.

For example, imagine that we've created a unit around the theme of civil disobedience. There are obviously a variety of texts—canonical, young adult, informational, current events–related, etc.—that we might use to explore this theme. Likewise, there are many ways for students to show what they've learned (i.e., through a traditional literary analysis essay, applied multimodal projects, etc.). The notion of grammar in context means that we've also thought of what grammar moves we might purposefully integrate within this unit. That is, what grammar concepts might go well with the theme of civil disobedience? What concepts might we encounter in the texts we're studying? Perhaps more compellingly, how do concepts of authority, obedience, protest, and conflict resonate in students' everyday lives, and how might their own language use be leveraged in such explorations?

Maybe the idea of a unit that fully integrates the different subdomains of English language arts is common sense. Shouldn't we always be weaving reading with writing, analyzing with creating, speaking with listening, viewing with visually representing? And shouldn't students' lives be a fertile source for language discussion and analysis?

Well, of course. Yet, the reality of the English classroom is that such harmony often remains an unachieved ideal. There are a lot of potential obstacles to this unified vision (such as scripted curriculum, mandated texts, standardized pacing guides, testing regimes, departmental/school culture, and so on), and making it happen takes added time and effort, especially if it's not already the norm. When the existing course curricula feels predetermined or already well-established, change is difficult.

"Grammar in context," then, is really related to integrating the many domains of English language arts. If that larger work has yet to happen—if we haven't figured out a unifying thread or theme for a unit, or thought about how students might best experience the complexities of that theme; if instead we're just trying to get through the week, and what's happening next Monday morning is pretty much a mystery, let alone what's happening next month—well, "grammar in context" can feel like a tough ask.

Some teachers interpret "grammar in context" narrowly. For example, it may mean discussing a particular grammar concept by pulling a sentence for analysis from a book or a student essay. And while this is certainly a piece of grammar in context, it isn't the whole story. Alternately, "grammar in context" can mean something like *a mini-lesson on whatever grammatical issue I see regularly in student writing*, which takes us back to the not-so-effective approach that opens this chapter. Unfortunately, it doesn't do much good if we just stop there. The call to "teach grammar in context" is only the first step in a much larger project (and our hope is that this book helps you understand and conceptualize that broader work).

3. **Close study of language concepts should probably be centered on actual examples of language use.**

Focusing on real-world language use may seem sensible. *Of course we should use our students' language and lives in our classrooms!* However, when we begin digging into this statement, we realize that this idea is actually contested linguistic terrain, with different camps staking out turf. Questions of language purpose (*whose* purpose) and language emphasis (*which* emphasis) take center stage. For example, should we only emphasize traditional language expectations for academic purposes (that is, Standardized English)? Or, instead, should we focus on language in real-life communication situations? Is it possible to do both?

These questions and the arguments around them are difficult to parse and here's why: we can't separate *language* from the people who use it and the places in which it is used. We also can't ignore the power dynamics bound to language use or the beliefs behind language use. For an easy example, think of language use and social media. People regularly call out others online for unorthodox spelling, syntax, or usage. However, this "calling out" isn't done as an act of compassion; instead, it's often about discrediting the grammar offender's personal views. The act of correcting others online is inevitably wrapped up in power and privilege.[2]

Beyond questions of *which* English (or, more appropriately, *whose* English), real-world examples of language use have a potential pitfall: there's no answer key at the end of the book. If we use student-created sentences or sentences we find on a billboard or sentences from social media, we have to be our own answer key. And this can be super scary if we're unsure of our own grammar knowledge. However, take heart—gradations exist. On one extreme, students might create sentences on the spot and immediately examine them for specific grammar moves. But this can be *very* intimidating for a teacher, as spontaneous language events inevitably mean dealing with a lot of gray areas. If you're not confident about certain grammar concepts and what they do, this may not be the best place to begin.

Don't worry. There are other approaches. Rather than handling grammar questions more-or-less randomly as they appear in student writing, we might consider first deciding *what* grammar concept to focus upon (including *why* this concept is important to discuss). Then we can locate real examples *beforehand*, understand the nuances of that grammar move ourselves, and *then* bring it to the class. Obviously, this version has its own limitations. First, this option takes more time than using an example in a book or something a student just wrote. Second, students may still ask questions you can't answer. But we think the benefits are worth the trouble. When students understand that language is living, that it is malleable, that it can be used for specific purposes in specific ways, they are learning the skills and tools they'll need to be powerful players in their worlds, and we think the time and investment toward this is energy well spent.

---

2. We think this discussion of people, place, power dynamics, and language is so important that we've dedicated an entire section to it in Chapter 2.

4. Monday looms—you need to tackle grammar, and you don't know how to come at this subject confidently for your students' benefit.

We've all had this feeling. And while this book isn't a perfect solution to the what-to-do-with-grammar-on-Monday-morning blues, we hope that it provides you with some solid models for how to approach specific grammar topics with both confidence and direction. With that in mind, let's take a look at what this book tries to do.

WHAT THIS BOOK DOES AND HOW IT'S ORGANIZED

Chapter 1: We're here right now. As you can see, we're looking at some of the reasons you might pick up a grammar instruction book. Within those reasons, we've touched on why teaching grammar can be a real challenge—more on that in Chapter 2. Rest assured, we'll emerge from this discussion with a focus on the positive, as the rest of this book works to make grammar instruction easier and more purposeful.

Chapter 2: We offer some grounding for what we call a "grammar reset." If we're going to tackle grammar concepts without repeating the same cycle of frustration and failure, we'll probably want to rethink some assumptions and clarify a few goals. Doing so helps us establish a base for why we're doing what we're doing—a foundation of principle and practicality, if you will—that informs our weekly, daily, and in-the-moment moves with grammar.

Chapter 3: We consider the realities of "grammar in context" in the English language arts classroom. Since the connections between word, sentence level, and paragraph/passage grammatical decisions are vital to the development of meaning, we organize this chapter into three sections: text-based grammar in context, writer-based grammar in context, and specific ideas for what we call reality-based grammar in context.

Chapter 4: This is the heart of the book. In this chapter, we look at ten grammar concepts and provide ten days of activities for each. These plans are anchored on the guiding principles discussed below.

Incremental Growth

One of the more frustrating implications of traditional grammar instruction is the idea that a language deficiency[3] can be neatly addressed with direct exposure to formal rules and some practice with those rules. In reality, there's no "quick fix" for getting more proficient with language options. It takes sustained effort over a long time to get better with words, sentences, and passages. Improvement is incremental, often not linear, and based on personal relevance. We try to honor these truths in the lesson ideas we present, but don't get the wrong message here. Yeah, you might see some legitimate growth in how students understand a grammar concept after a week's worth of focus, but in all likelihood, you'll need to be thinking in longer terms. This is gradual stuff.

---

3. And it's almost always viewed this way—that is, through a deficit lens: we have to stop and work on grammar now because these students *can't do something that they should already be able to do*. Frustration and negativity are threaded through the experience from the start.

Guides, Not Scripts

We get pretty specific in detailing day-to-day lessons in Chapter 4, right down to how you might phrase ideas and discuss concepts with students, and how you might respond to their possible misconceptions and questions. Some parts of these lessons can look like *scripts*—a series of things that a teacher is supposed to say in order for a lesson to go well. But we hope that you don't take them up this way. They're suggestive guides: what *could* be said, not what *should* be said.

But why include such material, you might be thinking, *if there's a concern that teachers might just treat these remarks as the "right" way to teach?* Our thinking is this: we've spoken with a lot of teachers who simply struggle with how to talk about grammar concepts with students in ways that (a) aren't full of alienating technical terms and (b) actually help students grasp the ideas. We include examples of what a teacher *might say* to help concretize the process. Anybody can look up the definitions and rules of a grammatical concept. But how to talk about that concept in ways that can actually help adolescents learn? That's altogether different. We need some models, and that's what we've tried to provide.

Reciprocal Teaching and Learning

A lot of us are wary of forays into grammar instruction. We end up feeling compelled to act like experts when we don't feel confident with our own knowledge of the material, and so we lean hard on textbook rules and exercises with predictably poor results.

But there's a different way to imagine our roles as teachers. Teaching reciprocally means being open to learning ourselves, both from our students and through the process of teaching. This can be challenging (and downright intimidating) since most conventional classrooms are organized with the teacher as the source of knowledge and the students as recipients. Other learning environments—craft workshops, art studios, apprenticeships, internships—might help us conceive a different approach. To varying degrees, these quasi-real-world spaces might act as models for what grammar instruction might become: a democratized and socialized process of learning, where the instructor is still positioned as an authority, but an authority rendered through applied demonstration, individual guidance, openness to innovation, and an inductive stance toward inquiry.

The materials in Chapter 4 are anchored on this ethos: that exploring, questioning, and grappling with grammar concepts and how those concepts involve people, places, and power is both interesting and worthwhile. There's a divergent quality to the conversations that we imagine, and this is on purpose. We think investigating the richness of language should be a positive, if not invigorating, experience. There's something freeing about teaching from a position of genuine curiosity instead of simply adopting a pose of presumed (and sometimes phony) expertise.

From Downright Overwhelming to Teachable

Recently, Michelle and Darren were interviewed for *The Suggestion Box*, a podcast designed to give teachers practical ideas for their classrooms. The first question the interviewer asked was "How did you learn grammar?" After listening to the interview, Michelle realized her answer may have scared some teachers: "It was me spending hours, and hours, and hours, and hours with grammar books." And while that answer may seem scary, it's the truth. But in the larger sense, that's what teaching is, right? We spend hour upon hour thinking about something so that we can teach it in an accessible and purposeful way—so that we *distill* the knowledge we've gained. That's what we hope we've done in this book. We've spent a lot of time with grammar, trying out these ideas to see what works. We hope we've distilled our understanding for you here. Our hope is that you then further shape the ideas in this book to help your own students in ways that are uniquely accessible and purposeful for them.

REFERENCES

Hillocks, G. (1986). *Research on written composition*. Urbana, IL: NCTE.
Weaver, C. (1996). *Teaching grammar in context*. Portsmouth, NH: Heinemann.

CHAPTER 2

Language Study Reset

Shifting the Grammar Focus

A METAPHOR TO GET US STARTED

Before we really get into the nuts and bolts of grammar, let's take a short side trip into the realm of physics.

You don't need to be a science expert to know that inanimate objects (rocks, houses, a picnic basket) don't move unless something else makes them move, that letting go of something heavy means that it reliably falls downward, that physical things occupy particular locations in space. Weird things start happening, however, when we look at really large things (like stars, galaxies, and the universe) and really small things (like electrons). In these realms, a "commonsense" view of the physical rules of the world doesn't always apply. Stuff starts happening that seems illogical and looks instead like *magic*.

If we want to study something tangible—a flea, let's say—we have a whole scientific method for how to do this. We can look at it under a microscope, dissect it to understand its biology, watch what it does on a dog, track it as it crawls or jumps, and so on. The same goes for any familiar object, from voles to volcanoes: observation is often the first step toward understanding. Totally normal, right? But when we try to examine an extremely small thing, such as an electron or some other subatomic particle, something completely mysterious happens: the act of looking at the thing *actually changes the nature of the thing*.

This is rather mind-blowing, since we're used to the act of looking at inanimate objects as a neutral activity.[1] But it's true: when scientists attempt to pinpoint the location of an electron, the act of observing the electron suddenly changes its location. Why this happens relates to the nature of light and is shrouded in hard-to-grasp phenomena. Metaphorically, it's as if the electron somehow senses the attempt at observation and reacts to confound that effort. The best that scientists can tell is where an electron *probably is* at any given time. Can we agree that this whole business is just wild?[2]

Okay. Now let's try to draw a rough parallel to grammar.

---

1. We *do* know that observing self-aware things (like people and some animals) can affect behavior. Social scientists call this the Hawthorne effect, and it makes sense: if you know you're being watched, that knowledge can affect how you act (think Jumbotron Fan-Cams at sporting events or formal observations of your student teaching).

2. Modern physics (i.e., quantum theory and Einsteinian relativity) is full of this kind of mind-boggling stuff.

Grammar is happening right now, everywhere, constantly, in every moment of communication around the world. It's the framework for making ourselves understood when we use language, providing invisible patterns in our minds for combining words into statements, sentences, and passages. This framework is immensely flexible: we're able to use language to make our way through all sorts of situations, each with their own unique demands.

In the vast majority of our language interactions, we employ grammar reflexively, automatically. We're using words and phrases and sentences without a whole lot of conscious, premeditated thought, relying instead on the immediate cues of context: who we are speaking with or writing to in the moment, what that person needs, and what we ourselves want to accomplish. Language is the primary way we negotiate life in a social world, and we employ grammatical moves almost instantaneously in most day-to-day situations. As is probably clear, you certainly don't need an advanced degree in linguistics to be an adept user of language. Most five-year-olds are well on their way to becoming master manipulators with words, and by the time they hit the high school classroom, students are deeply practiced in shaping how others perceive events (if not reality itself) through language.

But as with the mysterious electron, when we begin to examine grammar as a subject—when we *observe, analyze, and discuss how grammar works*—everything changes. Grammar transforms from a natural, embodied, and contextual skill that we've intuitively mastered into something strange and hard to understand. Something we're really good at doing naturally becomes a mystery. That's unsettling.

Our metaphor may not be perfect. After all, grammar is not a "thing" that exists out there in the physical world but rather something that we do or enact. But what happens to both particles and participles when we suddenly try to examine them is worth thinking about.

Shifting Our Lens

If we're going to teach grammar in ways that matter, we're going to have to shift our lens a little. Clearly, the grammar instruction of yore isn't working. And, like most things, teaching isn't just about delivery but also about our beliefs and understandings of the materials we're delivering. Below, we discuss some truths about language and language instruction that we need to grapple with to be ready to move toward effective instruction. Shifting our lens is never easy, but thinking through the understandings discussed below may ease the transition.

Understanding 1: We Aren't Teaching Grammar; We're Teaching Language

Grammar has become a bit of a catch-all in the classroom—from the rules of how to punctuate a compound-complex sentence, to the hows and whys of varying sentence structure, to the correct use of the apostrophe. But grammar is actually only one part of a much larger system of language. We want to pause here and parse out some important definitions.

Grammar

According to linguists (the folks who study language), grammar is simply "a description of language structure" (Kolln & Gray, 2013, p. 1), meaning that it's the internally understood patterns that all first-language speakers use to communicate on a daily basis. By this definition, if you can understand the message of a speaker, then the speaker has been "grammatical." You're never going to hear anyone say *the is book counter the on* because that syntax doesn't align with any structure in English (meaning it's not grammatical); instead, first language speakers will say *the book is on the counter* (with variations such as *the book's on the counter*—both of which are, by definition, grammatical).

We want to emphasize an important point here: *all* dialects are grammatical, which means that all dialects, including Standardized English,[3] follow particular patterns and rules. For example, linguists agree that *him and me went to the store* is as grammatical as *he and I went to the store* because both constructions are understandable and follow an underlying structure for making sense—that is, they're grammatical. While the first example may not follow *usage* rules for Standardized English (which we'll get to next), both follow the English language structure of subject-verb-object.

Usage

We hate to break it to you, but you haven't been teaching grammar all this time, you've been teaching *usage*: "The arbitrary rules of language that have been deemed correct by mainstream groups" (Crovitz & Devereaux, 2017, p. 2). Usage rules aren't stable—they change as the language expectations of society change.

Let's dig into an example here for clarity. Have you ever wondered why we don't use *thee* or *thou* anymore? Well, social expectations changed, so the "rules" changed with them. Long ago, *thou* was the subject case and *thee* was the object case. *You*, meanwhile, was originally considered plural in the 1100s, but by the 1300s, it had become the formal version of *thou* (due to the French influence on English from the Norman Conquest). In the 1700s, with the emergence of a middle class (thanks, Industrial Revolution), folks didn't want to commit a faux pas by using the informal when the formal was more appropriate. The solution? Just use the formal *you* all the time. With that adjustment, the use of *thee* and *thou* died out (Fogarty, 2014). This is usage at work. As society changes, our language rules change—or rather, our *usage* rules change.[4]

Mechanics

When we teach punctuation, spelling, or capitalization, we're teaching mechanics. If you've assigned a speech to your students, you can't really grade for mechanics. Think about it. When someone is speaking, how would you know if a certain word is capitalized or not? How would you know if a speech is punctuated properly? You can't "hear" a misspelling or a misused semicolon. Mechanics belongs to the realm of written language, where we can see how a writer has employed these conventions.

---

3. The variation of English that we teach in English language arts classrooms goes by many names, including *Standard English*, *Academic English*, and *Language of Wider Communication*, to name just a few. For this book, we've decided to use *Standardized English* because this term emphasizes "that standardization is a process enacted on language rather than an inherent property of a particular dialect of English" (Metz, 2019, p. 71).

4. For a fun video that looks at how usage rules change, see "Adam Ruins Everything: Why Grammar Rules Aren't Always Exact" (August 14, 2017). Retrieved from https://www.youtube.com/watch?v=fu5XDrdD7KM

Okay, now that we've provided a few definitions, we can move on with our original point: we need to shift our lens from grammar instruction to language study. As the physics metaphor earlier suggested, dealing with any kind of minutia, in language or the universe, can be tricky. Rather than just honing in on a participle—the definition, its form, its function—what if we also pull the lens out a little and explore the *nature of participle use*: Why are participles used and for what purpose? What can they do for us out there in the world? How do they influence meaning and shape how we understand reality? Why might I use a participle instead of a regular ole adjective? Shifting our instructional lens from grammar to language study affords us several benefits:

1. *Language study* aligns with all levels of the profession, kindergarten through college, and it's right there in how we describe the field: "English language arts."
2. *Language study* offers a better template to explore the region between a single word and a larger passage. Studying the *language* of a sentence (or a line, stanza, or paragraph) presumes a specific *user of language* (a writer, speaker, or composer) and thus a specific rhetorical situation. With its morass of rules and conventions, grammar as a conventional classroom focus often leads in the opposite direction: toward a realm of abstract, supposed truths (where the author's intentions and options are minimized or ignored) rather than contextual fit.
3. A *language study* approach invites us to view privileged dialects such as Standardized English or Academic English as forms of *foreign language*, which they are since no one is raised as a native speaker of either one. The power these dialects possess is socially granted rather than inherent, and a language study approach can expose assumptions of morality and privilege to help students crack these useful codes.
4. Starting from a linguistic perspective (rather than the often-alienating nomenclature of grammar) acknowledges that students themselves are legitimate *experts with language* in their own right (Devereaux & Crovitz, 2018, pp. 19–20).

By opening the classroom to language study, we can better grapple with the nuances of the English language, create a more democratic space for all voices, and really dig into what language is and what it can get done in the world.

Understanding 2: Language Is Really Weird, and We Have to Anticipate, Plan for, and Build on That Weirdness Rather Than Pretend That It Doesn't Exist

Check out this social media graphic.

> COFFEE HELPS ME PERSON.
> PERSONING IS HARD WITHOUT CAFFEINE.

Figure 2.1 Personing Is Hard

Ah, so true, you might be thinking. Or maybe you're an herbal tea fan, in which case your reaction is more like, *Yeah, not so much.*

Whatever your response, it probably wasn't, "I don't understand this message because it uses the word *person* in an unorthodox way."

Ponder this. Almost every time *person* appears in communication, it's going to be used as a noun, right?[5] And now here it is, suddenly showing up as a *verb*.[6] Strangely enough, our reaction is not confusion or outrage: *What in the world is happening?!? Person is a noun, not a verb! This is a terrible grammatical violation! Call the language police!* Far from it. We understand what's being conveyed here easily, despite the non-standard usage. That's because of a very important fact that we somehow tend to forget about in classrooms: **First and foremost, language use is about shared meaning rather than rule following.** Yes, adhering to conventions can be a major part of creating shared understandings. But formal grammar rules are not the first consideration. Conveying meaning is.[7]

There's always been a pretty wide disconnect between how language actually happens in the world (what linguists call *pragmatics*) and how we typically study language in an English classroom. The immense variability, creative richness, and constant evolution of the English language—its weirdness, basically—make it a poor fit for approaches to teaching and learning that emphasize rules over conventions and formula over contextual fit. If we imagine the richness of language as a kind of vibrant, evolving ecosystem[8] constantly producing new forms of life, then what happens in a classroom is more akin to factory farming: pruning and paring away exuberant wilderness until we're left with rows of neatly cropped plants producing genetically engineered results. Students spend their time learning how to produce a few specific species (the five-paragraph essay, the literary analysis paper, etc.) while all other kinds of language use are treated as worthless (i.e., weeds to be removed) or irrelevant (i.e., unworthy of cultivation).

This phenomenon is especially apparent in grammar instruction. A traditional approach holds that students need to master a set of established rules, which, of course, seems logical. But most English teachers have experienced teaching a grammar rule only to be confounded by actual language-in-use examples that don't conform to that rule. Let's consider the *person* example from earlier. In a traditional lesson on nouns, what would happen if a student mentioned the examples of *person and personing* as described above?[9] The typical teacher reaction might be to dismiss such anomalies with unpersuasive rationales such as the following:

1. *That's slang and doesn't count.*
2. *Professionals, experts, or other specialists are allowed to break the rules. Students aren't.*
3. *You have to know the rule before you can break it.*
4. *I can't explain it, so let's just get back to practicing the "rule" anyway—even though it's clearly not a rule but something else.*

---

5. Heck, it's right there in one of the age-old definitions of a noun: "a person, place, or thing."
6. Technically, a *verbal* (as a *bare infinitive* in the first example and a *gerund* in the second), although even this interpretation is up for debate.
7. See our definition of *grammar* earlier in this chapter.
8. We're switching up our metaphors. Roll with it.
9. Or "adulting," which is perhaps more common.

None of these are convincing. In fact, they all demonstrate a turning away from legitimate linguistic inquiry, conveying the idea that curiosity about and creativity with language is to be discouraged—which is just sad.

Responses like these are reinforced by the materials usually employed in grammar instruction. Typical textbooks, grammar guides, worksheets, and other common resources employ a subtle tactic: present a bunch of examples and exercises for students that suggest the universality of a particular grammar rule while avoiding examples that contradict it or introduce inconvenient complexities. There are reasons behind this phenomenon,[10] but they all sidestep a central truth: actual language use is too complex, too messy—too weird, again—to deal with in formulaic, lockstep fashion.

The weirdness of language means that we may have to shift some very basic assumptions about how people learn, and thus, how we teach. For folks outside of education, the process of student learning can seem absurdly simple: *You just tell kids the things they're supposed to know, and then they prove they've learned it on a test. What could be simpler?* Not accidentally, those who subscribe to this version of learning find it pretty easy to locate blame when studies show issues in student achievement: *The problem must be the teachers or the schools—they're simply not providing students with the information they should learn and know.* There are similar reductions in traditional grammar instruction, though blame here lands on students: *Well, we've taught the grammar rules over and over and still the students can't write or speak properly, so either they need more intense worksheets and drills, or they're just lazy.*

Can you identify the common faulty assumptions in these visions of teaching and learning? The "transmission" view of teaching described above only works if we pretend that students are passive vessels waiting to be filled with knowledge (and that possessing discrete bits of information in our skulls is what it means to be educated). Similarly, the grammar-as-rules-to-be-learned approach is based on a mechanistic view of students: just tell 'em the rule, make 'em practice it, and you're done. Language teaching and learning suffers from these inaccurate stereotypes, wrongly professing the complex as simple. Taking up these stereotypes means devaluing both the creativity of students and the endless flexibility of language-in-action.

If it's not abundantly clear, the narrowing of what and to whom we teach is about power (or rather, disempowerment). When we dismiss or downplay examples of language at work in the world in favor of a set of abstract truths about language, we're telling students that truth and power have already been established—and that questioning what's important or relevant or appropriate based on their own experiences isn't worth considering. That's not a good look for principled teaching, and it won't do much for engaging students either.

Finally, be wary of arguments that presume a logic to language. Words aren't like numbers, and English often won't be logical. Even those old English classroom mnemonics turn out to have limited utility, and the Internet is full of examples: like "i" before "e" except after "c"—except when *Keith weighs a feisty heist on a weird beige foreign neighbor's sleigh*. English is odd, "but it can be understood through tough thorough

---

10. Here's one reason: textbook companies like to market their products as time-saving, problem-solving cure-alls for teachers, which means that the materials themselves can't dwell too much on elements that might actually *increase the complexity* of topics for students. In other words, they can't get too real.

thought though." Had enough? Here's one more, maybe our favorite given its playful contrast between authority and freedom:

With the English language, they're our know rules.[11]

We need an approach to language instruction that embraces rather than dismisses weirdness. We think it's possible. And there's even a little etymological support for a more encompassing view. *Weird* originally meant something close to "having the ability to control fate," and that provides a pretty good gloss on more constructive ways to view the potential of students and their ability to wield the inherent power in the language that they use.

Understanding 3: For Almost Everyone, Grammar Instruction Has Been Contaminated by Negative Experiences. We Can't Move Forward Until We Address This Significant Problem

The vast majority of teachers and students find grammar instruction boring. That's no shock. Worse, many people bring negative vibes with them to this subject. A traditional emphasis on grammar rule-following comes with an inevitable focus on errors and correction, on what students have done wrong, and on what they don't know how to do. Attach grades to this scenario, and you've got a recipe for negative association. And then extend this process over years of schooling, and the message that many students inevitably take up is depressing and self-defeating: *I'm not good at this. I don't know this. I'll never understand this. Why bother?*

We're talking here about a pretty big psycho-emotional obstacle to learning, and this goes for teachers as well. For many of us, the negative associations we have with grammar as a subject are deeply entrenched—and we're professional English language arts teachers! We're supposed to feel confident about this supposed area of expertise! Fact is, few of us do. Now imagine what it's like for students, encountering yet again a fruitless, tedious topic that only serves to emphasize their confusion, lack of awareness, and oh-so-evident shortcomings.

When we raise the topic of grammar with students, it comes laden with long-accumulated emotional residue that can't be ignored or casually dismissed. We think this negative-grammar-experience syndrome deserves explicit attention because unless we're able to speak honestly with students about what we're dealing with here, our efforts to clear the slate and start fresh with language study are unlikely to work.

There's a terrible irony at work in a lot of conventional schooling. By the time students graduate, many have reached a depressing conclusion: they hate learning, reading, and writing, and are resolved to stay away from these activities in the future. When such beliefs are the result of years in school, something has gone very wrong. Candid discussions about what schooling typically does with language learning—and how we might imagine another way—might get students considering something different about what classrooms can be for.

---

11. As compared to "There are no rules." Get it? Google "English is weird" for lots of other examples.

Now is probably as good of a place as any to note a few caveats and disclaimers, just in case we've triggered a bit of skepticism from readers inclined toward a more "old school" perspective. Here we go.

- A discussion of grammar concept definitions and rules has its place.
- Practice with grammar concepts can be useful and productive.
- Repetition serves a legitimate educational end, though in the case of language study, *repetition* should equate more to "multiple exposures to a concept in context" rather than just drilling a rule in isolation.
- By all means, English language arts teachers should have a solid grasp of common grammar and usage concepts. You can't teach concepts that you don't know well yourself.[12]
- And yes, Standardized English is **essential for all students to master,** not as the "right way" to speak and write, but because it's the primary dialect of conventional power and achievement pathways in mainstream society.

Understanding 4: Language Is Bound in People, Places, and Power Structures, and If We're Going to Talk About Language, We Have to Understand and Respect These Connections

How do we go from resistance and negative association to something different? Where can we begin, knowing that there is no quick fix, and that shifting attitudes is never an easy task?

We recommend starting with frank and open conversations that deal with why grammar and language study got so poisoned in the first place, which means dealing with a host of linguistic, cultural, and political tensions:

- How has grammar been dealt with in your experience? What kinds of activities stand out in your memory?
- Are these memories positive, negative, or some combination? Why?
- How do you feel about grammar now? What influences your thinking?
- How do you notice grammar in your everyday life? When does it show up, if ever?
- Have you ever been corrected, mocked, or scolded for how you use English?
- Should all people in this country learn Standardized English? Why or why not?
- What does Standardized English mean to you?
- How do you use language in ways that are different from school expectations?
- How do you use language skillfully outside of school?

To be clear, some people have had positive experiences with language and grammar study, and these episodes are worthy of discussion too. What does talking about these questions—and others like them—do? Ideally, it helps students understand their feelings about language in the classroom. Even for students who have found success through

---

12. Our previous book, *Grammar to Get Things Done: A Practical Guide for Teachers Anchored in Real-World Usage*, is designed to be a low-risk, high-application resource for teachers looking to learn more about grammar and how to teach it constructively.

conventional approaches to language study, a likely implicit theme to emerge from these talks is this: multiple forces conspire to portray students in deficit-laden terms, emphasizing what they *can't do with words* rather than *what they can*. In Chapter 4, we provide specific examples of how you can start these conversations with students with a variety of grammar concepts.

If we really work toward shifting our language instruction, seeing students in terms of what they *can do*, we're also forced to grapple with some bigger questions about power, place, and people. Language can't be separated from the people who use it (and people's families and communities and histories and cultures and traditions and, well, their very ideas of self). And when we begin to grapple with some of the complexities of real-world language use, we're also forced to grapple with some of the false tenets of language instruction.

Somewhere along the way, many English language arts teachers (ourselves included) are taught that our job is to uphold and honor Standardized English at all costs against the evils of language change. We've been taught that good language is good and bad language is bad. But these false tenets of language are problematic because they don't honor the fact that language is fluid, malleable, and, perhaps most importantly, human. Adhering to Standardized English in some contexts becomes (mistakenly) a measure of someone's positive upbringing, class, or worth. These types of examples and questions are important to bring into a classroom that truly studies language. We can't get beyond these judgments without addressing that they exist and hold a strange power in our world. If we're going to talk about language, we need to do so within a context of actual language use that asks questions about power, intent, and impact.[13]

Understanding 5: We Need to Stop and Really Think Carefully About What Terminology We Want Students to Learn and Be Able to Justify the Reasoning Behind It

While we hope some students in our class fall in love with language and go on to become authors, poets, editors, and English teachers, that's just not going to happen for everyone. Your students will do amazing things, but rarely will they need to know the difference between a transitive and intransitive verb, or the various ways that a preposition can function in a sentence. That's just trivia.[14] What they *will* need to know, however, is how to craft powerful prose, how to use language in ways that matter, and how to communicate effectively with diverse groups of real people.

So, this leads us to an important question: what terminology should you include in your lessons, and for what reason?

Michelle's been teaching grammar classes for years, and every semester, students make the same mistake—they write an absolute phrase when they mean to write a participial phrase, and vice versa (which are understandable mistakes; in their most basic forms,

---

13. We delve further into this in Chapter 3. Also, please see the Appendix for an annotated bibliography of resources about language variation and language ideologies in the classroom.

14. And not even *fun* trivia—we've never heard reference to such distinctions at any Trivia Night, ever.

the only difference between the two is a noun). When this happens, Michelle gets to ask that important question: what terminology and for what reason?

As preservice teachers, her students need to know the difference between an absolute and a participle,[15] but how important is it that their future students know the difference? Yes, there are differences in what participial phrases and absolutes do (a participial phrase modifies a noun and an absolute phrase modifies an entire clause), but really, both phrases modify the sentence (either in part or whole) and can be used to include more detail without getting bogged down with too many adjectives (see Chapter 4). If we're really interested in students improving their writing, do we want to focus our time and attention on the esoteric differences between absolutes and participles, or do we want to spend our time experimenting with how these modifiers can bring vivid detail to student writing?

Most of the vocabulary of grammar doesn't reflect what particular grammar concepts actually do. *Gerund, clause, infinitive*: these words provide no insight into how these concepts function in a sentence or passage. Terms such as *conjunctive adverb* or *coordinating conjunction* do a better job of suggesting a particular action, but these phrases will sound distant and alien to many students. Since memorizing official terms isn't the point of grammar instruction, let us suggest a different approach: because we're reenvisioning grammar and language instruction, then we should also reconsider these labels as well.

That statement may trigger the grammar purists out there, so let's pause for a quick story.

Years ago, Michelle read a long-forgotten article about a veteran teacher who loved teaching *The Scarlet Letter*. He'd taught the novel for decades and reveled in rereading it and reteaching it each year. Lo, in the middle of year 23, he had an epiphany: the significance of *hats* in the story. Yes, hats! He was thrilled. Hats mattered! Who wore which hat at what time had a secret meaning. He could not wait to teach this to his students.

You've likely guessed how this turned out. His students were bored out of their gourds. Their apathy, in turn, made the teacher pause. He *loved* this stuff and had been so excited to discover the hat motif. How could these students not care?

We think there's a takeaway here for grammar instruction. You may *adore* grammar terminology, dream about gerunds and appositives, love teaching the nuances of participial phrases and absolutes. But we have to ask the question: are you really just teaching about *hats*?

In Chapter 4, we help you begin thinking about renaming grammar concepts according to what those concepts are *doing* on a functional and rhetorical level. We won't ruin any surprises. But as you keep reading, we encourage you to think about how grammar terminology played a role in your own schooling—and whether memorizing such labels was really time well spent.

Understanding 6: Believe It or Not, It's Okay If You Don't Know All the Answers. We Have to Be Comfortable in Our Not-Always-Knowing

Michelle remembers vividly her first year of teaching. She was petrified of not knowing an answer. She lived in fear of the inevitable: a student asking her a question about a preposition or a comma and—*yikes!*—the answer wouldn't be there. It. Was. Terrifying.

---

15. Research has shown that teachers need to know more grammar terminology and usage than their students (Myhill, Jones, Watson & Lines, 2013).

However, she also remembers the first time she admitted not knowing. It was her third year of teaching (that magical time when the stars align and you suddenly feel that you can actually call yourself a teacher). During a class change, a student approached her and asked whether a question mark should go inside or outside of quotation marks. Michelle realized that she had no idea. She took a deep breath, and hoping the heavens wouldn't open up and smite her, said, "I don't know, but let's go find out." Together, they walked across the hall to a veteran teacher who quickly and easily explained the rule,[16] and both Michelle and her student left feeling a little smarter.

Every time after that, it became a little easier for Michelle to admit she didn't know.

We understand that this can be a scary thing to confront, admitting that you don't know the answer. Such a posture turns the traditional power dynamics of the classroom upside down. But if you're really going to teach language in ways that matter, you're going to have to get comfortable with a different model than teacher-as-knowledge-provider. We're talking about dialogic teaching, which isn't a teaching method but a process in which students and teachers co-construct knowledge (Freire, 2007). This means you don't have to be the *expert*—you just have to be a good facilitator. You get to question and wonder alongside your students. Which grammatical move is most effective and for what reason? How can I best convince my reader of my position, and what grammar moves can help me do this? If I want to add more description but don't want to bog down my writing with adjectives, what can I do?

In this model of teaching, you don't have to have all the answers, because you, along with the students, are learning too.

Sounds pretty fantastic, doesn't it? We think so.

REFERENCES

Conover, A. (2017, August 14). Why grammar rules aren't always exact. *TruTV*. Retrieved from www.youtube.com/watch?v=fu5XDrdD7KM

Crovitz, D., & Devereaux, M. D. (2017). *Grammar to get things done: A practical guide for teachers anchored in real-world usage*. New York, NY and Urbana, IL: Routledge, NCTE.

Devereaux, M. D., & Crovitz, D. (2018). Power play: From grammar to language study. *English Journal, 107*(3), 19–25.

Fogarty, M. (2014, December 12). Why did people stop saying "thou"? *Grammar Girl*. Retrieved from www.quickanddirtytips.com/education/grammar/why-did-people-stop-saying-thou

Freire, P. (2007). *Pedagogy of the oppressed*. New York, NY: The Continuum International Publishing Group Inc.

Kolln, M., & Gray, L. (2013). *Rhetorical grammar: Grammatical choices, rhetorical effects* (7th ed.). Boston: Pearson.

Metz, M. (2019). Principles to navigate the challenges of teaching English language variation: A guide for nonlinguists. In M. D. Devereaux & C. C. Palmer (Eds.), *Teaching language variation in the classroom: Strategies and models from teachers and linguists* (pp. 69–75). New York, NY: Routledge.

Myhill, D., Jones, S., Watson, A., & Lines, H. (2013). Playful explicitness with grammar: A pedagogy for writing. *Literacy, 47*(2), 103–111.

---

16. To be honest, this particular teacher was a little huffy and self-righteous in her explanation of the rule, conveyed with a "how could you not know the answer to this question" attitude. But Michelle knew that was the teacher's problem, not hers.

CHAPTER 3

Grammar in Context
Texts, Writing, and Real Life

When Michelle was a preservice teacher, she heard a common refrain about language study.

"Just teach grammar in context," more experienced teachers would tell her.

Michelle's response (similar to most beginning teachers, we'd bet) was, "Huh?"

What does that look like? What does in context *mean? I'm supposed to use writing? And books? How exactly do I do that?*

And while Michelle was too early in her career to know, what she also might have asked herself was, *How on earth do I talk about language in ways that matter*? Because that's what we think "grammar in context" really means—talking about language in ways that aren't just abstract and academic, but in ways that matter to both us and our students.

In this chapter, we've put together some ideas about how to integrate language instruction into a larger curriculum. Think units and novels and personal connections. Think grammar in real-world contexts.

TEXT-BASED GRAMMAR IN CONTEXT

Here's a term you've probably heard before: *mentor sentence.*[1] Sometimes mentor sentences are pulled from students' writing; other times they come from the novels and other works you read as a class. Mentor sentences can be great tools, but sourcing sentences from your reading curriculum is only the first step. That mentor sentence you've selected probably needs a larger context than "this is language used in a book that we just happen to be reading right now."

In this section, we're hoping to walk you through a larger grammar in context— beyond mentor sentences (though it will include mentor sentences), beyond Daily Oral Language[2] (though it could include Daily Oral Language), beyond worksheets and

---

1. Here's a quick definition. A mentor sentence is a sentence from actual written work that serves as a model or example. Just what it's an example of (a solid thesis statement, a vivid description, an engaging use of unorthodox grammar) can vary.

2. Daily Oral Language is a form of grammar instruction in which the teacher gives students a sentence with either several errors or one error repeated several times. Students must identify and correct the errors, rewriting the sentence so that it follows Standardized English usage rules. For an interesting discussion about Daily Oral Language, see Mark Pennington's blog post in the **References** at the end of this chapter. For an interesting response to his take on Daily Oral Language, read the comments as well. As you will can see, grammar instruction can indeed be divisive.

handouts (which aren't automatically a problem). When we talk "grammar in context" here, we want to pull the lens *way back* to consider how the novels that we read, the themes that we discuss, and the grammar that we teach can all work synchronously—and how that synchronicity can help students use language in powerful ways to achieve powerful goals.

Text, Theme, and Grammar

In our first grammar book, we argued that thematic units could include grammar instruction aligned with unit themes. Since then, we've gotten a lot of questions as to what such planning looks like. So, let's dig into thematic grammar instruction a little bit more.

Thematic grammar considers how authors use language (and for what purpose) and considers, in turn, how students can learn similar language moves to get things done in their own worlds. To make this more concrete, we offer a step-by-step list to help you consider what thematic grammar might look like in your own classroom.

Step 1: Grammar Does Things

First of all, you need to have a somewhat solid understanding of what grammar concepts do in use. We understand that this might be a tall order, particularly if you're new to the "grammar in context" game. To help, we've created a shortcut sheet (in the Appendix)—a list of grammar concepts and what they're useful for in context. Keep in mind that this resource is based on our understanding of what grammar does.

Step 2: The Novel and the Theme

Once you've spent some time with the grammar shortcut sheet and have a sense of which grammar concepts do what things, next, think about a text you'll be teaching and the relevant themes that text explores. For the purposes of an example in this chapter, we'll consider *Harry Potter and the Sorcerer's Stone*, which has many possible themes such as *choices*, *family*, and *power*.

Step 3: What Grammar Concept Is Going to Benefit My Students and What Grammar Concept Is Found in the Novel?

This is where things start getting sticky, and you'll need to be patient with yourself. If you're new to this type of thinking, it may take a couple of tries before you get it right. First of all, take heart. Every good book has multiple grammar moves you can examine. For example, Michelle downloaded *Harry Potter* and found excellent examples of hyphenated adjectives, hyphenated nouns, dashes, participles, absolutes, appositives, and very interesting uses of conjunctive adverbs.[3]

---

3. Common conjunctive adverbs like *instead*, *however*, *anyway*, and *finally* are used throughout the book; however, the more formal conjunctive adverbs, like *therefore* and *otherwise*, are used only by Dumbledore. This makes sense since he is an erudite, venerable character. Other formal conjunctive adverbs, such as *consequently*, *furthermore*, and *henceforth*, are not found in the book at all.

Step 4: Making a Decision

You've got your potential themes and many possibilities for grammar topics. Now you need to consider the following:

1. Which grammar concept will help your students become better writers, readers, thinkers, and communicators?
2. Which grammar concept best speaks to the themes you've identified, taking into account the interests of your students? (Some might love talking about *power*, while others may be more interested in different ideas of *family*.)

Let's work in a hypothetical space for a moment. We're teaching a group of eighth graders *Harry Potter* (Rowling, 2015), and we want to teach a unit with thematic grammar. First of all, it's eighth grade, and whew! We can all remember that's a rough time. Lots of choices to make—how you want to identify yourself, who's a friend and who isn't, who you want to be. A thoughtful discussion of *choices*, we imagine, would be useful and relevant to most adolescents, particularly those who are about to leave the safety of middle school for the larger and more confusing world of high school.

But which grammar concept is going to help students understand the implications of *choice* better? We also need to consider the grammar moves that students might need help with in their writing. For instance, eighth graders might reasonably still need help controlling *coordinating conjunctions*. Let's think on that idea for a moment.

We probably don't need to introduce students to FANBOYS. Our hypothetical eighth graders have been working with FANBOYS since third grade. What they probably haven't done, though, is to consider how authors use *and*, *but*, and *nor* rhetorically to set up situations where real things are happening in language. As a taste of what we have for you in Chapter 4, here's how we set up these little coordinating conjunctions:

- And: *signals that something is being added, extended, or emphasized*
- But: *signals that a contrast, obstacle, or limitation is coming*
- Nor: *signals a negative contrast with a previous statement or situation*

Do these reenvisionings of *and*, *but*, and *nor* pair well with discussions of *choice?* Sure, and you can obviously find examples of these uses in *Harry Potter*. But, beyond this, you can help students explore how these words do things in their own worlds.

In Chapter 4, you'll find ten days of lessons focusing on coordinating conjunctions. It's highly unlikely that you'd use all of these lessons "as is." You'll choose what works for your students, use your own flair, perhaps focus only on *and*, *but*, and *nor*. But you're also going to add examples from the novel that help reveal how coordinating conjunctions connect to the idea of *choice*. And maybe you've prepared a few scenarios that connect the use of coordinating conjunctions to students' choices in their own lives. And of course, you'll integrate those discussions throughout the unit, with a final assignment that asks students to use this strengthened grammar concept in a meaningful way.

These are the steps you might consider when preparing for "thematic" grammar instruction. We understand that this may be challenging, especially thinking it through the first few times. Isolated exercises can seem easier, but they won't help students get better with language. Grammar practice needs to be wrapped in a framework that considers theme, text, and intention to become meaningful. Just for good measure, we've included a few more examples of thematic grammar in Table 3.1.

Table 3.1 More Examples of Thematic Grammar

Book	Grammar Concept	Theme	Reasoning
The Hate U Give by Angie Thomas	Participles and Participial Phrases	Racism	How is something described? How does that change or alter or affect our understanding of that thing?
Night by Elie Wiesel	Appositives	Identity and Power	How is naming or renaming a marker of power? How are names attached to identity?
The Color Purple by Alice Walker	Fragments	Self-Discovery	The process of self-discovery isn't easy or fluid—fragments help us demonstrate the difficulties involved
1984 by George Orwell	Colons and dashes	Control	Clarifying and defining something—who gets to define and clarify? How is defining and clarifying a marker of power?
I Am Malala by Malala Yousafzai	When, where, and why dependent clauses	Women's Rights	How do the when, where, and why help us understand women's rights in Malala's world and our own?

WRITER-BASED GRAMMAR IN CONTEXT

The second broad area for considering grammar in context comes from your students' own writing.

Good language arts teachers have pretty much always examined student work and adjusted their instructional plans accordingly. As we described in Chapter 2, however, this response often takes the form of *isolated remediation* of problems rather than using student writing as the foundation for planned language study. We all know that students tend to struggle with grammar. But when we see these struggles manifest in their work, we tend to react with a combination of surprise, exasperation, and impatience. Grammar becomes a problem to fix, and the most expedient solution is a remedial lecture and drill. There's certainly nothing wrong with practicing grammar daily, but when this activity is formalized into a rote, standardized package, teachers and students resign themselves to a familiar but joyless process with minimal returns.[4]

---

4. Cynical devil's advocate response: "Still, no one's really gonna get called out by an administrator for sticking with traditional approaches in an English classroom, amirite?" Us: "Who wants to lead a professional life characterized by cynical devil's advocacy?"

If we can clear the decks of these old-school reactions to grammar, maybe we can start fresh. Here are a few principles to replace those initial remedial responses:

1. Students—all of them—can already do things with language.
2. Even students who struggle with some elements of written expression are simultaneously demonstrating what they can control.
3. Sentence-level errors are normal and to be expected.
4. Patterns of errors (or error avoidance) might suggest future areas for attention, but . . .
5. . . . we should base new learning on a solid foundation of confidence, ability, and mastery. That is, we should begin with what students can do and move forward from there.

That last point is pretty important, so let's unpack that a little bit with this series of questions.

- Where are your students now in terms of what they can do in their writing?
- What do they seem to have mastered?
- What are they confident about?
- How can this existing knowledge serve as the platform for new experimentation?

We think these questions align with commonsense notions of how humans learn anything. Every time we learn something new, we have to fit that new skill within a web of existing knowledge. Eventually, through practice and failure and more practice, we form new strands of that knowledge web. All of your students come to class with a web of language understanding. Of course, there will be complexities. Your students are not homogenous or standardized. A few will have mastered sentence-level tactics that trouble others. There will be outliers of understanding and competence in various directions. Truly, part of beginning this work is understanding where your students already are in their grammar understanding.

Beyond this, a key facet of this work is your own positioning as a teacher. Students aren't dummies. They can figure out a teacher's attitudinal stance toward a subject, and they'll take their cues from your dispositions. If you approach language study as a necessary evil or an occasion for frustration—an annoying distraction from the "regular" curriculum—getting even minimal compliance is a best-case scenario with students. When the adult in the room is projecting a distinct lack of enthusiasm for the work at hand, why would we expect more from students?

What's that? You say you don't really like grammar all that much yourself, so it's hard to get pumped to teach it? Well, we've been in that place ourselves. For a long time, we avoided grammar instruction as much as possible, and when forced, we went about it with reluctance and distaste—and a fear of being outed as phonies. Our own pivot on the subject came with the revelation that grammar instruction should actually be a constructive experience anchored on how language is actually used. But we first had to confront our own assumptions in order reposition ourselves in the classroom.

Table 3.2 Where to Next?

If Students Can Do This . . .	You Might Teach This Next . . .
Capitalize initial words and include end punctuation	Sentences and nonsentences
Write simple and compound sentences	Complex sentences, noun/appositive phrases
Use *and*, *but*, *or*, and *so* confidently	Conjunctions used rhetorically; *nor*, *yet*, and *for* used functionally
Write in paragraphs with logical progression of sentences	Dashes, colons, and semicolons for particular effects
Recount events chronologically	Participles and absolutes used to dramatize events
Write paragraphs in support of a point	Conjunctive adverbs to emphasize particular elements
Use adjectives for description	Hyphens to create compound adjectives and nouns
Claim credit or avoid blame	Active and passive voice to manipulate meaning
Argue a point based on personal experience	Nominalization to argue a larger concept, policy, or position

You don't need to be a grammar expert to teach grammar. You do have to be willing, however, to learn and take some risks. Fear of not knowing some obscure grammar rule usually sends teachers to lecture notes and PowerPoints, handouts and drills. *Talking with students* is a far better way to begin and sustain meaningful language study. *How does this sentence sound to you? What do you notice here? What's interesting about how this is written? What other options are available?* These kinds of questions emphasize curiosity and attention over correction and inadequacy.

Of course, a positive demeanor is just a start. You've asked your students to do some writing, you've read through their work, you've noticed their strengths and challenges. You have a solid sense of what they can already do. Where to next?

Table 3.2 below offers some suggestions. Your decisions will be based on a lot of factors, including your future units, the texts you plan to read, and the ways in which your students will demonstrate their learning.

Having recognized what students can do well, you next need a specific plan for moving forward purposefully. That's what Chapter 4 is all about.[5]

REALITY-BASED GRAMMAR IN CONTEXT

Language absolutely saturates our lives, mediating our experiences in the world. Think about it. Almost every moment that we're awake involves exposure to and interaction with words, especially now that our phones are a crucial means of managing our networked lives. It's a challenge even to imagine life situations that *don't* have an embedded element of language. The best we can think of are solitary technology-free

---

5. And our previous book.

experiences in nature, a minimalist hike or camping in a deep forest or mountain wilderness or desert landscape. Even then, we're unlikely to fully escape language as a lens on experience. If we don't encounter trail signs or use a map, there are still the labels on our clothing, gear, and food. And then, of course, we have the running monologue of our language-driven thoughts (which practices such as meditation seek to temporarily disable). To strip away language as a filter for experiencing the world definitely takes some work.[6]

The richness and unending variety of language use around us suggests another avenue for how we might organize language study, what we're calling reality-based grammar in context. The idea here is that we commit to anchoring aspects of grammar study on the language that surrounds us. Many teachers already incorporate real-world language use in their classrooms in some form; bulletin boards on which students are invited to post interesting wordplay, puns, or vocabulary-in-action are fairly common. But we're talking about taking this approach further, about building out mini-units around this reality-based focus.

Easy to say, you might be thinking. But harder to do. No doubt. So, let's parse this out a little with a few intentions and examples to show the thinking, the processes, and the applications that would make reality-based grammar units a viable option. After that, we'll delve into some practical advice for making reality-based grammar in context an actual thing in your classroom.

What's the Goal?

Language curiosities are cool, and we love talking about them. But if we're going to make reality-based grammar in context a sustained part of our teaching, we need some guidelines. In Table 3.3 you'll find one possible statement of purpose for anchoring language study on real-life language situations, a mission statement of sorts, both for yourself and others.[7]

Table 3.3 The Purpose of Reality-Based Grammar in Context

The purpose of reality-based grammar in context is to use engaging real-world language situations to reveal context-specific conventions, patterns, and assumptions as a way for students to
• realize their own language awareness, understanding, and abilities
• see language episodes and varieties as systematized and "rule-governed"
• leverage unconventional usage rhetorically and stylistically

Know that this articulation works for us—yours might certainly be different. What this statement provides is a systematic means of exploring some interesting language context out there in the world. Let's take a look at some examples.

---

6. Maybe we're just as much *homo lingis*—"man the language user"—as we are *homo sapiens*. Discuss among yourselves.

7. As in those moments when a skeptical colleague or administrator asks, "Why are you doing *that*?"

Example 1: Netflix Show Summaries

Netflix and other streaming services are now common platforms of media entertainment. Regardless of which service you select, the "dashboard" interface is fairly universal and pretty familiar to most of us: a visual scroll of viewing options often categorized by genre (e.g., Romantic Comedies, Cooking Shows, Sci-Fi Thrillers, Socially Conscious Documentaries, etc.).

Select any film or television show, and you'll get a new screen that contains a brief summary of what you're about to watch. These blurbs might seem like simple and straightforward kinds of texts, but they're actually pretty sophisticated. Let's take a look at a few examples, using the "mission statement" above as a guideline for possible pedagogical uses.

Avengers: Infinity War
Invader. Annihilator. So-called savior. As Thanos moves ever closer to omnipotence, the fate of the universe rests with the Avengers.

Stranger Things (Season 3)
A lost boy. A government lab steeped in secrets. And a dark force that turns a town upside down.

Black Panther
He's a warrior. A superhero. And a good man. But it's hard for a good man to be king. Doing what's right will take all his power.

Bird Box
Stay silent. Stay alert. Stay blindfolded. As a terrifying force lies in wait, a mother leads her children on a harrowing journey.

The Ballad of Buster Scruggs
Saloon shootouts, vigilante justice, covered wagons on the trail. Saddle up for six Wild West tales, Coen brothers–style.

These film summaries do a lot of work with just a few words. No doubt you've already noticed some of the conventions in these examples. Identifying common moves might be the first step for students, but just as important will be speculating about *purpose* and *effect*. So, we might first begin with a list of the elements that we notice. Then we can think about possible purpose and effect, as in Table 3.4.

Of course, not every movie or TV blurb uses the conventions highlighted in the examples above. Let's take a look at a few more.

My Next Guest Needs No Introduction (with David Letterman)
He revolutionized late-night. Now he's diving deeper in a series packed with heart, laughs, and extraordinary people.

Tidying Up with Marie Kondo
In a series of inspiring home makeovers, world-renowned tidying expert Marie Kondo helps clients clear out the clutter—and choose joy.

Table 3.4 Conventions, Purposes, and Effects

Convention	Possible Purpose or Effect
Sentence fragments leading off	Raises dramatic stakes; crystalizes memorable images; echoes dramatic film genres
Triplet phrases	The power of "threes" in language and culture; pace and rhythm; establishes conflicting forces; may suggest beginning, middle, end
Repetition of specific phrases	Plays on known-new contract;[8] emphasizes importance
Specific concrete nouns and noun phrases	Calls to mind specific, evocative visual images
Complex sentences beginning with *as* dependent clauses	Suggests dramatic action as several events, forces, or characters converge
Unconventional conjunction use	Adds dramatic emphasis
Imperative sentences	Directly involves audience in drama; playful invitation to join in the action or gird oneself for events
Present/future tense (instead of past)	Suggests immediacy and suspense (literally, drama that is "hanging or looming over"); injects audience into the moment

Dumplin'
She's taking a stand in a swimsuit and gown. And she's not doing it alone. Because everybody—and every body—deserves a chance.

The Princess Switch
Stacy makes delicious confections. Her look-alike has royal connections. Swapping lives gives both a taste of what they're missing.

No doubt you're noticing some particular grammar moves in this second set: we see triplets again, alliteration, and some interesting uses of dashes and hyphens, among other tactics. As students gain a sense of the appropriate style of this mini-genre of writing, they can put into practice what they've learned. Given a show or movie title they know, can they write summaries that come close to what's actually published? Can they demonstrate knowledge of the form and substance of such writing, and can they capture some of the stylistic flourishes (that is, grammar concepts employed rhetorically) that get viewers to press "Play"?

You might find some students taking a skeptical pose with this work: why bother thinking carefully about a piece of casual language that we might scan and dismiss dozens of times in a sitting? And yet, these summaries are clearly crafted by professionals

---

8.   See the **Glossary**

facing a pretty tough challenge. With limited space[9] and in just a few careful phrases, they must craft a compelling message that summarizes a story, highlights its appeal, and hooks a potential audience—in just a few seconds!—so that a browsing viewer chooses this show over a thousand other options. Such constraints actually *raise* the stakes. There can be no slack in such writing—every word and phrase must be precise and punchy, and you can bet that a lot of streaming revenue depends on this specific stylistic economy.

Example 2: Rhetorical Grammar on Social Media

Like it or not, social media dominates many students' lives. If we acknowledge this reality at all, it's either to constantly police the classroom for illicit cell phone use or, less commonly, to use this avenue as a way for students to demonstrate what they can do. We want to build on this latter piece—we propose that students might serve as analytical experts for the moves made on platforms and in genres with which they're most familiar.

One way to start might be to invite students to provide insight about what they know about the idiom in these online spaces. For example, ask students to choose an example from the list below (or supply their own) and provide a 'splainer about how to employ this option fluently in digital realms.

- amirite
- bruh
- be like
- chef's kiss
- ima let you finish
- you might want to sit this one out
- stanning
- I'll see myself out[10]

The goal here is to move beyond "this is what this means." We want students to do more, taking on the role of the teacher. How is *amirite* used in a passage for maximum effect? What's a poor example versus an effective example? How is irony communicated through this tool? You don't need to be an expert on these matters, just curious and willing to explore alongside your students.

Beyond idioms, the texts that proliferate on social media platforms offer their own potentials. Just about every Internet meme has its own internal rules, a protocol that must be followed for the form to work (in terms of *humor, satire, irony,* or *critique*). So-called *image macros*—a common meme variation comprising a single-frame combination of image and text formatted in a specific, rule-governed way—offer ways for

---

9. None of these examples, for instance, are longer than 140 characters, the length of an old-fashioned tweet.

10. This list will age fairly quickly, so if you're reading this book even two years after its initial publication, we suggest going to your students for new idioms.

students to reveal their linguistic dexterity and understanding, especially if they're positioned as experts explaining how these texts work.

Example 3: News Articles

Used to be, people had opinions about *news subjects*. Now, many have opinions about the *news itself*—there's too much of it, it's biased, it's too focused on superficiality, it's distorted by partisan agendas, and so on. We mention this complexity to point out that bringing with news articles for language analysis can be loaded territory if not done carefully.

We would argue, however, that in an era when "fake news" is a real thing, we have a responsibility to teach students how to think critically about the information they encounter. Bottom line, our job as teachers is to get our students to *think*. (Note: not to get students to *think like us*.) We're after ways to get them thinking about the world as they experience it. A thoughtful and directed study of grammar can help you do this.

The days are probably gone when "current events" news articles can be viewed neutrally. We may have to challenge ourselves these days, seeking out news sites we might not otherwise visit—the most liberal of news sources along with the most conservative, fringe, and alternative outlets, along with established newspapers and networks. You might take advantage of resources such as AllSides (www.allsides.com) to find the same story from multiple sources. After years of looking at news stories with grammar in mind, we've found several consistently employed grammar concepts that we think are worthy of classroom study.

Noun Phrases and Appositives

Different news sources name (or rename) nouns differently, often reflecting underlying stances and ideologies. For example, consider the noun phrases (bolded) in these news stories:

1. **The Kentucky high school student** seen in a viral video standing face-to-face with **a Native American protester** at a Washington rally spoke out for the first time Sunday evening, claiming in a statement that he and his classmates were taunted by a group of African-American protesters and saying that he and his family had received death threats (Chamberlin, 2019).
2. More video emerged on Sunday of the viral moment between **a Native American man** and **a student wearing a "Make America Great Again" hat**, complicating an incident that has already been cast as yet another parable of the nation's heavily divided politics and growing racial tension (Visser, 2019).
3. The viral video of **a group of teenage boys** appearing to taunt **Nathan Phillips, a Native American veteran**, as he played a drum during the Indigenous Peoples March is another reminder of the racism and intolerance that plague the country (Rosser, 2019).

4. New video and dueling narratives emerged Sunday about an encounter between **a Native American leader** and **a group of Kentucky high-schoolers** in Washington that went viral and drew widespread condemnation this weekend (Albert, 2019).

Some sources choose to focus on a single student (described as "a high school student" in one and "a high school student wearing a Make America Great Again hat" in another). Others decide to focus on "teenage boys" while another names "a group of Kentucky high-schoolers." Likewise, Nathan Phillips is named differently in each news source, referred to as a "protestor," "man," "leader," and "veteran." All of these noun phrases might be factually correct. Each, however, tells a different story. Do the sources of these stories matter? It may be more important (at least initially) for students to note these naming differences and hypothesize about how they affect our understanding of those involved in this event.

Participial Phrases

There are a surprising number of participial Phrases used in news stories, and they do a surprising number of things. Participial phrases can act as a bridge between two sentences, as in this example:

> Yutu is the latest in a series of tropical cyclones that have intensified incredibly quickly, **strengthening from a category 1 to category 5 storm in under a day.** Some forecasts have the storm maintaining that strength for at least another day.
>
> (Mack, 2018, n.p.)

Or they can set a tone by revealing a writer's position on a subject:

> DeSantis also positioned himself as the candidate of a purring economy, **hammering Gillum's plans** to raise corporate taxes **and jumping on Gillum** when the mayor criticized Republicans for passing Trump's tax bill.
>
> (Smiley & Flechas, 2018, n.p.)

In the example above, the participles *hammering* and *jumping on* suggest aggression and perhaps even bullying behavior. We might ask students why a writer might seek to position a political candidate in such a manner, when less charged synonyms (e.g., *questioning*, *rebuking*) might be available.[11]

Verbs

Surely finding "verbs" in a discussion of grammar in news stories isn't surprising. Journalists tend to be fond of action verbs, using them to paint vivid pictures and incite powerful reactions. However, if you choose to dig into the world of verbs in the news, we might suggest taking a small slice of a very large verb pie: article titles.

---

11. See **Absolutes and Participial Phrases** for a deeper discussion of participles in news stories

You might begin by examining several titles about the same event, such as the following:

- Trump **warns** Nancy Pelosi to "be careful" after Democrats signal they won't accept his shutdown offer (Smith, 2019, n.p.)
- Trump **proposes** wall-for-DACA in bid to end US government shutdown (Holland & Wolfe, 2019, n.p.)
- Trump **offers** DACA protections in exchange for border security funding (Fantis, 2019, n.p.)

The different tones of these three verbs tell three very different stories: Trump warns, Trump proposes, Trump offers. Each verb seeks to convey a sense of a "truth" about President Trump's actions. Why would news sources use these different verbs when discussing the same story? Is one or more inaccurate? Can they all be correct?

Some sources may also use titles as a form of clickbait with word choices that seem to sensationalize rather than simply report. For example, contrast the verbs used in these two renditions:

- Missing journalist Jamal Khashoggi **believed killed, dismembered** at Saudi consulate in Istanbul, report says (Chamberlin, 2019, n.p.)
- Jamal Khashoggi **Died** In Consulate In Istanbul, Saudi State TV Reports (Sullivan & Kennedy, 2018, n.p.)

These two headlines are about the same story, but the verbs used emphasize different aspects. Why? What are the implications behind these word choices? By studying such differences, students become more critical consumers of information. While the universe of grammar concepts in media is more than we can possibly study, beginning with nouns, participles, and verbs can help students begin to grasp rhetorical decisions.

Example 4: Leveraging Language Diversity

If we're talking about real-world language study, we need to take into account the ways students speak with those most important to them: their families and friends, of course, but also the extended networks of people in their home communities. The importance of students' worlds—their backgrounds and family identities, their interests and experiences—is a relatively new emphasis in educational spaces. We applaud and encourage bringing students' lives into the classroom. Oddly enough, however, students are often expected to leave their home *language* behind when they come to school. "Standardized English only" is the norm in many classrooms. But here's the complication with this norm: the Standardized English[12] of formal writing and speech only lives in grammar and usage books. No one comes into or leaves your classroom (not even you) speaking it,

---

12. Although we've already included our rationale for *Standardized English* earlier in the book, we think it is worth repeating here. And to do so, we will quote from the same sentence: we use the term "Standardized English rather than Standard English to emphasize that standardization is a process enacted on language rather than an inherent property of a particular dialect of English" (Metz, 2019, p. 71).

because Standardized English is absolutely no one's native or home language. Obviously, becoming adept in controlling Standardized English is essential, but there's a friction here between school language and home language that needs some attention.

Let's take a look at some general language rules that linguists agree can help us negotiate the tension between Standardized English and the other ways that we speak, write, and communicate.

Rule 1: Standardized English Is a Dialect

Somewhere along the way, most of us were taught that Standardized English *is* the English language. Other kinds of English were *dialects*, with the corresponding implication that they mattered less. You can imagine Michelle's surprise in graduate school when she learned that Standardized English isn't as special as she had always been told. It's actually a dialect itself, just another variation of the language, though one with a lot of privilege, power, and prestige. We think that this fact is crucial when considering grammar instruction. When we teach Standardized English grammar, we aren't teaching the Holy Grail of language. We're teaching a standardized dialect that, when mastered, can be one piece of the puzzle to provide students with mainstream access and advantages in the United States and beyond.

Rule 2: All Variations of English Are Rule-Governed

All dialects of English have a rule-governed grammar—this makes sense if you think about it. Without unspoken rules and patterns, speakers of any dialect would not be able to understand one another. Call to mind a novel that includes characters speaking in a certain dialect—say the African American English in works by Alice Walker, Zora Neale Hurston, and Toni Morrison—and we'll find dialect rules being followed. In Table 3.5, for example, we see that all three authors follow a rule called "zero copula," meaning that the *to be* verb isn't needed in this particular construction.

Table 3.5 Standardized Rule of Nonstandard Dialects

Author and Book	Example
Toni Morrison, *Beloved*	You lucky (n.p.).
Zora Neale Hurston, *Their Eyes Were Watching God*	She dead too (n.p.).
Alice Walker, *The Color Purple*	Who that? I say (n.p.).

What's happening here is a rule of grammar, not a random mistake. Here's the rule, explained by linguists:

> Where contracted forms of *is* or *are* may occur in general American English, these same forms may be absent in some vernacular varieties. Thus, we get structures such as *You ugly* or *She taking the dog out* corresponding to the general American English structures *You're ugly* and *She's taking the dog out*, respectively. It is important to note that this absence takes place only on "contractible" forms;

thus, it does not affect *they are* in a construction such as *That's where **they are***, since *they are* cannot be contracted to *they're* in this instance. Furthermore, the absence of *be* does not usually apply to *am*, so that sentences such as *I ugly* do not occur. The deletion of *are* is typical of both Southern European American and African American varieties, although the absence of is not very extensive in most European American vernaculars.

(Wolfram & Schillings, 2015, n.p.)

As you can see from this discussion from Wolfram and Schilling, all varieties of English follow rules that are as sensible as those for Standardized English.[13]

Our point here is that when we encounter students using their home languages in their formal writing, we should remember that they may be following the rules of a dialect rather than making sloppy mistakes (Wheeler, 2019). Embracing the rule-governed nature of other dialects allows for more equitable conversations with students about language. It may well be the case that forms of English other than Standardized English *may not* fit all kinds of formal writing, but that's a different kind of discussion than traditional assumptions about an inherent, unquestionable, and absolute value of Standardized English.

Rule 3: We All Have Implicit Beliefs About Language Variation

A person's language use can be a defining aspect of one's identity. This commonsense idea, however, can be distorted through the power of stereotype. Examples of superficial judgments of a person's worth and intelligence based on language use abound. For example, the Southern accent automatically equals "dumb" or uneducated for many listeners. When these stereotypes are taken up in TV shows and films and other media forms, as they often are, what's clearly a false assumption often gets affirmed through repetition: simplistic, exaggerated, and inaccurate depictions taking the place of experiences with actual people and how they use language.

These media-crafted "truths" can shape our implicit beliefs about language variation and affect how we interact with others. We all have latent biases about how other people speak. That's an uncomfortable reality. But as teachers, we all should be working toward an awareness of and a grappling with these language beliefs. We know this is difficult. And while these implicit beliefs are not our primary focus here, we couldn't write a book about language study without bringing these issues to light.

We think that your students' home language and language variations would make for some pretty interesting forays into language study. You don't have to be an expert in relevant dialects—your students will be the ones taking the lead here. But you do have to open a space in the classroom that embraces how your students use language in the ways that really matter to them.

You can do this any number of ways. We know one teacher who does a March Madness–style unit, using student-selected lyrics as texts to analyze and argue for (Ratti, 2019). Another teacher creates space for language inquiry in the classroom, engaging

---

13. See Devereaux and Palmer (2019) for a discussion of "ain't."

with questions such as, *Are emojis language?* and, *How is language used during elections?* (Damaso, 2019). Language variation in movies and TV shows are another avenue to discuss how people view and respond to language difference (Plackowski, 2019). You don't have to start from scratch. There's a galaxy of resources—books, articles, websites, and podcasts—that can help you teach how modern English, in its many diverse forms, actually works in our world. We've included an annotated bibliography of some of these resources in the **Appendix**.

Some General Advice

Hopefully these examples have sparked some ideas as to how you might begin a focused exploration of reality-based grammar in context in your own classroom and curriculum. Interesting, compelling, and distinctive language surrounds us, and you can certainly take your cues from what your students find fascinating. Here are some general recommendations for getting started.

Get Curious, Observe, Take Notes

Can you teach curiosity? Or at least nurture it? We believe you can. Most teachers value a classroom of curious and creative souls, and it sure helps if we model this stance. In your daily activities, be on the lookout for words at work. That doesn't mean carrying around a notebook and intentionally conducting research.[14] It means simply being open to the world: noticing the patterns of what people say in certain situations, realizing that a piece of mundane onscreen text contains its own conventions, taking an open stance toward language use that we might find initially strange, confusing, or uncomfortable.

This last piece is especially important. Whatever our relationship to Standardized English might be, let's keep in mind that no one is a native user of that artificial dialect. In those moments, episodes, and encounters with language that don't quite square with our own set of expectations, we might practice extending grace—to others and ourselves—rather than reacting with judgment. It's not easy most of the time. We humans seem to have a knack for seeing difference as a possible threat, to "otherize" that which is (or sounds) unfamiliar.

As your capacity for acknowledging and valuing the peculiar and the intriguing grows, channel that curiosity into the classroom. A mentor once told us that "it's a good thing if students think you're a little weird."[15] Show them what an adult who's open to wonder, speculation, oddity, and alternative thought looks like. Yeah, it's a risk, and we still have to remain true to ourselves. Maybe you're more the dry humor type (like Darren) or maybe you're more of a joy-embracing soul (like Michelle). Whatever your axis, find a way to be a divergent force for possibility in the classroom.

---

14. Though if that works for you, fantastic.

15. Or offbeat, or idiosyncratic, or just different. Embrace your oddball adjective.

Reciprocate and Be a Student

Most of us remember what it's like to be a teenager. Kind of.

In reality, most of us are locked into our adult headspaces with all the choices, responsibilities, and considerations that come with maturity: family, career, life goals, and all the rest. That's the thing about adulting. The years bring wisdom (hopefully) as we slowly get better at anticipating problems, making good decisions, learning to help others more consciously, and coming to know ourselves. But for all that we gain, there's much that we inevitably lose. We may work with young people every day and do our best to know and respect them as individuals. But their emotional and social dramas, the daily ups and downs of adolescence, all now hypercharged by social media–influenced pressures? That interior world and its concerns is probably inaccessible to most of us. We're not living their experiences. But we can commit to staying attuned to their well-being and needs.

In their own ways, all students must also deal with the challenges of institutional learning. Some of them have mastered the process; they know the system and use it to prosper. Many haven't, however, and their daily school lives are a purgatory, something suffered through without much meaning. And a few are not far from giving up on the whole prospect. This is the irony of education. Humans are naturally learning creatures—we're really good at it. But in dealing with the many mandates of a modern bureaucracy, schools can paradoxically deaden what they should be nurturing: a genuine curiosity for learning, doing, experimenting, growing.

As teachers, we're constantly dealing with institutional forces that trivialize learning. So part of our mission might amount to resisting this phenomenon. That can involve grounding your teaching in real-world relevance, anchored in students' own lives.

Students are learners. Can you be the same? What might that look like? Even if you're not literally a student, what does it look like to be a constant learner? To be someone dedicated to evolving through life? There are a million ways that this can happen. Sharing your interests. Modeling curiosity. Being a novice with enthusiasm. Willingly struggling with newness just as they might be struggling, and sharing what that feels and looks like.

What can your students *teach you*? What do they know a lot about? And how can you show them what it looks like to be open to learning? Music might be the easiest pathway for this reciprocity. Ask your students for a recommendation of an artist or band that they find important—and realize that this may be the first time that any adult has ever posed that question to them. Spotify, YouTube, Soundcloud, and assorted similar resources make listening to anything amazingly easy. Sure, you might not be into country/rap/grindcore/EDM. But that's not the point. It takes minimal effort to listen to a series of tracks, and now you have a point of reference and a foundation for building a deeper relationship. And, you'll have demonstrated what it looks like when a person doesn't let stereotype, prejudgment, or assumption get in the way of new experiences. You're modeling openness to the world and showing that you care enough to treat a kid's personal interests as worth your time. That's beyond value.

Can you model a curious, engaged stance on the world rather than something more limited? "I don't do math—I'm an English teacher." We've probably heard this lighthearted apology uttered a thousand times over the years. We understand this perspective, but can we push back just a little? Even if we're not so great with numbers, we don't have to suggest to young people that it's okay to close off entire areas of knowledge and meaning-making. Much better, we think, to express something like the opposite. "I'm an English teacher—and I'm interested in just about everything the world has to offer. And I'm always trying to learn more."

Bottom line, you don't need to be some kind of Renaissance human. But we can all try to model the honest pose of a curious mind.

Reward Extended Analyses of Unorthodox and Contextual Language Use

Conventional school assignments fit neatly within a small, orderly box. There's safety in the familiar essay assignment and comfort in standard forms applicable to everyone. But safety and standardization may not be what students always need. We want to encourage you to remain open to alternatives with your students. There are many ways for them to demonstrate their understandings and skills, and if their work meets the spirit rather than the letter of an assignment, might that sometimes be acceptable, and valued?

For instance, annotation is a common skill taught in ELA courses, with the intent that students use this tactic as an aid in constructing meaning from particular assigned texts: poems, dramatic passages, articles, and so on. This conventional and fairly straightforward exercise is complicated a bit, however, when we ask larger questions. What's the broader goal here? Are we hoping that students will use this tool to unlock the correct interpretation of a canonical text? Or is it the general usefulness of the skill itself—on exams, or in college and beyond—that is more important? Is there a way for students to both practice a skill *and* contribute new knowledge (rather than simply affirming settled meanings)?

With this example, we wonder about the applications of crowd-sourced annotation sites such as Genius.com. Music plays such a central role in most young people's identities, and Genius invites annotative insight about lyrics along with peritextual analysis of artists, albums, and songs, all within a community operating through specific processes, criteria, and group assessment.[16] If your goal is to build students' abilities to think critically about texts and share meaning that stands up to scrutiny, it makes sense to consider *actual opportunities to do this work meaningfully* beyond the relatively artificial walls of a classroom.

The English language is endlessly evolving. That's a challenge in the instructional space, which tends to value order and certainty over creativity and variance (which we sometimes tag with a vaguely pejorative term like *slang* and dismiss). If you can stay attuned to how language works in situations beyond traditional school spaces, you may open more routes for student achievement. Yes, that will mean more effort on your part along with some risk. But maybe the returns in student engagement through language-in-action are worth these costs.

---

16. Wikipedia and wiki-based pop culture encyclopedias such as Wookieepedia (Star Wars) and Minecraft Wiki (devoted to the video game) operate under the same principles.

Creating Authentic Scenarios

Throughout Chapter 4 in this book (and throughout our first book), we use scenarios as a way for students to engage with grammar. These scenarios present an engaging and relevant situation where using particular grammar moves can help students navigate different youth-relevant situations. And while we offer many scenarios in this book, every classroom is different. That means you must be able to diagnose your students' needs and create your own scenarios accordingly. Here are some guidelines to get started.

General Principles of Scenario-Creation

If you're wondering about the central challenge in making grammar instruction relevant, look no further than that age-old student complaint: "Why are we doing this?" Why indeed? The typical teacherly answers to this question (*It's on the test*; *It's in the standards*; *The state/district says we should*; *It's just what we do in English class*) are woefully inadequate. Rather than fumbling through some rationale entirely unconvincing to a teenager, consider creating a scenario that makes the immediate, practical, and relevant use of a grammar concept abundantly clear.

Pushing Beyond Conventional Framing

Very few people are fired up by the prospect of learning about *gerunds* or *dependent clauses* or *conjunctive adverbs*. But you know what people do care about? Negotiating their way through various encounters with other people and using language to accomplish specific goals. And we do these things every day. Our task, then, is to (a) figure out how we actually use grammar in real communication situations and (b) build this awareness into our lessons in such a way that the question "Why are we doing this?" is unnecessary. Here are the general steps for doing this work.

1. **Dig into actual use.** This takes some thinking. When do we use gerunds spontaneously in our speech or writing? What's a complex sentence good for doing out there in the world? Paying attention to language around us and thinking through applied use is the first step. If this seems like a daunting place to begin, use the **Grammar Shortcut Sheet** in the **Appendix** to help you begin thinking about what grammar *does*.
2. **Determine a real situation, purpose, and outcome.** You've considered how the concept is actually used in real life. Now it's time to increase the stakes by imagining a situation in which the concept might play a pivotal role in solving a problem or addressing a situation. That's what language is for: finding common ground through shared meaning.
3. **Create an in-the-moment, teen-focused conflict, problem, or need.** Here's where some imagine is helpful—and make no mistake, we see teaching as imaginative and creative work. Can you invoke a scenario in which the grammar concept under study might matter in the life of a teenager? Where knowledge and ability will help a young person solve a problem, right a wrong, preserve a friendship, advance an

interest? Make a move, voice a dissent, argue a point, influence the undecided? The ability to at least imagine what kids care about and build a scenario from these imperatives is what we're after.

Experiment. Then Adjust and Try Again

As teachers ourselves, we find the concept of "frame experiments" very useful (Smagorinsky, 2008, pp. 65–66). The basic idea is simple. You create an experience for students designed to emphasis a certain applied skill or demonstration of knowledge, and after moving students through the experience, you reflect on the results in order to adjust. It's a more structured form of trial-and-error, with a built-in recursive element to make initial ideas progressively better.

We're not going to get it exactly right the first time. But asking students to engage with dilemmas, scenarios, and situations—and then using their implicit and explicit feedback to improve the exercise—can help fine tune this process.

REFERENCES

Albert, V. (2019, January 20). New video, details emerge of Kentucky high school students' viral encounter in D.C. *The Daily Beast.* Retrieved from www.thedailybeast.com/new-video-details-emerge-of-kentucky-high-school-students-viral-encounter-in-dc

Aniston, J., Hahn, K., Costigan, M., Hofmann, T., AlRafi, M. (Producers), & Fletcher, A. (Director). (2018). *Dumplin'* [Video file]. Retrieved from www.netflix.com

Barclay, M. (Producer), & Bonfiglio, M. (Director). (2018). *My next guest needs no introduction (with David Letterman)* [Video file]. Retrieved from www.netflix.com

Berman, G., Kondo, M. (Producers), & Sandberg Wallis, J. (Director). (2019). *Tidying up with Marie Kondo* [Video file]. Retrieved from www.netflix.com

Chamberlin, S. (2018, October 9). Missing journalist Jamal Khashoggi believed killed, dismembered at Saudi consulate in Istanbul, report says. *Fox News.* Retrieved from www.foxnews.com/world/missing-journalist-jamal-khashoggi-believed-killed-dismembered-at-saudi-consulate-in-istanbul-report-says

Chamberlin, S. (2019, January 20). Kentucky student seen in viral confrontation with Native American speaks out. *Fox News.* Retrieved from www.foxnews.com/us/kentucky-student-seen-in-viral-confrontation-with-native-american-speaks-out

Coen, J., Coen, E., Ellison, M., Naegle, S., Graf, R. (Producers), Coen, J., & Coen, E. (Directors). (2018). *The ballad of Buster Scruggs* [Video file]. Retrieved from www.netflix.com

Damaso, J. (2019). "Mr. D, is this, like, a real word?" Stories of a linguist in a high school English classroom. In M. D. Devereaux & C. C. Palmer (Eds.), *Teaching language variations in the classroom: Strategies and models from teachers and linguists* (pp. 32–37). New York, NY: Routledge.

Devereaux, M. D., & Palmer, C. C. (2019). *Teaching language variations in the classroom: Strategies and models from teachers and linguists.* New York, NY: Routledge.

Duffer, M., Duffer, R., Levy, S., Cohen, D. (Producers), Duffer, M., & Duffer, R. (Directors). (2019). *Stranger things (season 3)* [Video file]. Retrieved from www.netflix.com

Fantis, M. (2019, January 19). Trump offers DACA protections in exchange for border security funding. *ABC74.* Retrieved from https://upnorthlive.com/news/nation-world/trump-offers-daca-extensions-in-exchange-for-border-security-fundingFeige, K. (Producer), & Coogler, R. (Director). (2018). *Black panther* [Video file]. Retrieved from www.netflix.com

Feige, K. (Producer), Russo, A., & Russo, J. (Directors). (2018). *Avengers: Infinity war* [Video file]. Retrieved from www.netflix.com

Holland, S., & Wolfe, J. (2019, January 20). Trump proposes wall-for-DACA in bid to end shutdown. *Reuters.* Retrieved from www.reuters.com/article/us-usa-shutdown-trump/trump-proposes-wall-for-daca-in-bid-to-end-shutdown-idUSKCN1PD0KF

Hurston, Z. N. (2009). *Their eyes were watching God.* New York, NY: HarperCollins. Retrieved from https://teachers.phillipscollection.org/sites/default/files/Excerpts%20from%20'Their%20Eyes%20Were%20Watching%20God'%20by%20Zora%20Neale%20Hurston.pdf

Krevoy, B., Krell, A., Miller, L. (Producers), & Rohl, M. (Director). (2018). *The princess switch* [Video file]. Retrieved from www.netflix.com

Mack, E. (2018, October 24). U.S. island "destroyed" by super typhoon Yutu, the most powerful storm of the year. *Forbes.* Retrieved from www.forbes.com/sites/ericmack/2018/10/24/the-most-powerful-storm-of-the-year-typhoon-yutu-is-now-slamming-into-u-s-territory/#404d2e469a14

Metz, M. (2019). Principles to navigate the challenges of teaching English language variation: A guide for nonlinguists. In M. D. Devereaux & C. C. Palmer (Eds.), *Teaching language variation in the classroom: Strategies and models from teachers and linguists* (pp. 69–75). New York, NY: Routledge.

Morgan, C., Clark, D., Townsend, C. (Producers), & Bier, S. (Director). (2018). *Bird box* [Video file]. Retrieved from www.netflix.com

Morrison, T. (2007). *Beloved*. New York, NY: Vintage. Retrieved from www.bookbrowse.com/excerpts/index.cfm/book_number/1908/page_number/3/beloved#excerpt

Orwell, G. (2013). *1984*. Boston, MA: Houghton Mifflin Harcourt.

Pennington, M. (2009, August 29). *Why daily oral language (D.O.L.) doesn't work* [Blog post]. Retrieved from https://blog.penningtonpublishing.com/grammar_mechanics/why-daily-oral-language-d-o-l-doesnt-work/

Plackowski, A. (2019). "Word crimes" and linguistic ideology: Examining student ideas about language in the English language arts classroom. In M. D. Devereaux & C. C. Palmer (Eds.), *Teaching language variations in the classroom: Strategies and models from teachers and linguists* (pp. 3–10). New York, NY: Routledge.

Ratti, J. (2019). Using music to bridge language diversity. In M. D. Devereaux & C. C. Palmer (Eds.), *Teaching language variations in the classroom: Strategies and models from teachers and linguists* (pp. 47–53). New York, NY: Routledge.

Rosser, E. (2019, January 20). We have a long history of disrespecting Native Americans and denying their humanity. *The Hill*. Retrieved from https://thehill.com/opinion/civil-rights/426257-a-long-history-of-disrespecting-native-americans-and-denying-their

Rowling, J. K. (2015). *Harry Potter and the Sorcerer's stone*. London, UK: Pottermore Publishing.

Smagorinsky, P. (2008). *Teaching English by design: How to create and carry out instructional units*. Portsmouth, NH: Heinemann.

Smiley, D., & Flechas, J. (2018, October 24). A Florida governor's debate so intense a racial slur was spelled out on live TV. *Bradenton Herald*. Retrieved from www.bradenton.com/news/politics-government/state-politics/article220478140.html

Smith, A. (2019, January 20). Trump warns Nancy Pelosi to "be careful" after democrats signal they won't accept his shutdown offer. *NBC News*. Retrieved from www.nbcnews.com/politics/donald-trump/trump-warns-nancy-pelosi-be-careful-after-democrats-signal-they-n960686

Sullivan, E., & Kennedy, M. (2018, October 19). Jamal Khashoggi died in consulate in Istanbul, Saudi state TV reports. *National Public Radio*. Retrieved from www.npr.org/2018/10/19/658732039/turkey-questions-employees-of-saudi-consulate-over-journalists-disappearance

Thomas, A. (2017). *The hate u give*. New York, NY: HarperCollins.

Visser, N. (2019, January 21). New video complicates uproar over incident between student and Native American man. *Huffington Post*. Retrieved from www.huffingtonpost.com/entry/native-american-make-america-great-again-student_us_5c455270e4b0bfa693d4d1e1

Walker, A. (2011). *The color purple*. New York, NY: Open Road Media. Retrieved from www.thesunmagazine.org/issues/455/from-the-color-purple

Wheeler, R. (2019). Attitude change is not enough: Changing teacher practice to disrupt dialect prejudice in the classroom. In M. D. Devereaux & C. C. Palmer (Eds.), *Teaching language variations in the classroom: Strategies and models from teachers and linguists* (pp. 109–119). New York, NY: Routledge.

Wiesel, E. (2012). *Night*. London, UK: Macmillan.

Wolfram, W., & Schillings, N. (2015). *American English: Dialects and variations* (3rd ed.). Hoboken, NJ: John Wiley & Sons, Inc. Retrieved from www.americanenglishwiley.com/appendix.html#

Yousafzai, M. (2013). *I am Malala: The girl who stood up for education and was shot by the Taliban*. Boston, MA: Little, Brown and Company.

CHAPTER 4

Daily Lessons for Ten Grammar Concepts

Congratulations! You've made it to the how-to portion of this program. Of course, we have a few more caveats. There's no getting around the fact that teaching grammar is hard no matter your approach, so here's our last round of tips to help you teach these slippery concepts.

NEW WAYS OF TEACHING, NEW VOCABULARY

Through the rest of this book, you'll see some vocabulary that may be new to you. Let's take a look.

The lessons in this book are based in **rhetorical grammar**. But what does it mean to teach "rhetorical" grammar versus "traditional" grammar? Traditional grammar instruction is probably clear to you, with its emphasis on definitions, right/wrong answers, identification, drills, and worksheets. As we mentioned earlier, research suggests that this approach doesn't help students use language any better (Hillocks, 1986).

Rhetorical grammar, meanwhile, widens the language lens, starting with questions such as, "What's happening here?" and, "What is this tool good for?" and, "Why does this matter?" Let's illustrate rhetorical grammar at work with an example.

Jax finally has a date on Friday night, and he really wants to borrow his older brother Connor's car. Problem is, his bro is super-protective of his baby—a 1968 Ford Mustang Shelby GT500KR that he spends all his money restoring. It's a big ask. But Jax has a bargaining chip: a couple of concert tickets for a country band Connor loves, plus backstage passes.

So, we've got a situation here. Somebody wants something from someone else. This happens to us all the time, right? We need a favor, or we need someone's attention, or we need someone's permission, or we need someone's understanding. And we get these favors, attention, permissions, and understandings through the language that we use. Being aware of how we're using language to get these things done is part of the rhetorical grammar parcel.

Let's get back to Jax. He wants to borrow the car. He has a bargaining chip. He can use language to get done what he needs. He can honor how his brother feels about his car and then pivot to make his request with conjunctive adverbs or dependent clauses:

> *Connor, I know you're not crazy about me borrowing your ride; however, I'm thinking that I may be able to make a good trade for one night.*

> *Because I know how much you care about your ride, Connor, I want to make a fair offer for borrowing it for one night.*

He can paint a picture of what Connor will get from the trade with participial phrases and absolutes phrases:

> *Imagine what Saturday can be, Connor—getting up close at the show, hearing those songs live, maybe even partying with the band.*

Or he can soften his request and emphasize the benefit of the switch with modals:

> *Could I borrow your car on Friday? I know you would have a great time at the show on Saturday.*

This is rhetorical grammar at work: a focus on language options that fit our needs, which is more important than asking whether a verb is transitive or intransitive.

Our lives are defined by situations in which effective language use is critical to happiness and success. How cool would it be to teach your students to use language in ways that matter? To teach them that a dependent clause is way more than a conjunctive adverb, a subject, and a verb; it's a tool that shows that you understand another's point of view. This is a far more useful and interesting way of teaching grammar. In the lessons that follow, you'll see that we use *rhetorical* quite a bit to emphasize this point.

LABELING WHAT THEY DO

At the risk of frustrating some purists, we change some traditional grammar labels in this book. Again, we do this to align with a rhetorical grammar emphasis—we're after what grammar actually does in real use. *Participial phrase* doesn't describe what a participial phrase *does*. Sure, we have a definition for this concept (a phrase that includes a participle and modifies a noun), but the definition doesn't get us any closer to what it *does*.

Rather than the same old terms, we experiment with new names to emphasize use. We discuss participial phrases and absolutes together (because they basically do the same thing), and we rename them *illuminators*.[1] When we discuss conjunctive adverbs, we don't start with the term *conjunctive adverbs*—please, no—we split conjunctive adverbs

---

1. Check out **Absolutes and Participial Phrases** for our justification.

into two groups based on what they're doing, *accelerating* or *shifting* meaning. When we teach students what these tools can do, how they can get things done, students will be far more powerful users of language than if they memorized terms and definitions. Trust us. We've tried.

THIS IS NOT A SCRIPTED CURRICULUM AND HERE'S WHY

We are staunchly against scripted curricula. Teachers are professionals, and they should have the freedom to adjust curriculum based on the strengths and needs of their students. *Then why offer scripts for these lessons?* The answer is easy: teaching grammar is hard. We've worked with preservice teachers for years and taught grammar classes for years, and the central question is always there: *but how exactly do I do it?* New teachers tend to be petrified of grammar, and when a rhetorical lens on language is a new concept, they tend to fall back into traditional grammar instruction because that feels safe. Our "teacher talk" in these lessons is much more like a safety net than marching orders.

Let's return to that teachers-as-professional idea. Teachers know their students and their curriculum and will need to alter these lessons according to the needs of both. We have ten days of lessons for each concept. But two weeks is an arbitrary amount of time for a deep, engaged dive with a grammar tool. Maybe you spend two days with a scenario instead of one. Perhaps your students really get that known-new contract[2] quickly, and you only need to spend one day on it instead of three. You are the professionals. Change these lessons to best meet the needs of your students and your context. Each lesson is way more of a might-do rather than a must-do.

You've Been Talking a Lot About Grammar in Context—This Doesn't Seem Like Grammar in Context to Me!

You're right. While we think our discussion of the concepts is certainly *rhetorical*, it isn't *in context*. Yet another reason that this isn't a scripted curriculum. You have to add the context. We've provided the rhetorical framework; it's your job to contextualize it within a unit that makes sense. For more discussion on how to do this, check out Chapter 3.

Why We Chose What We Did in the Order We Did . . .

You'll probably notice that we didn't include several grand old grammar concepts, notably adjectives, prepositions, and common adverbs (to name a few). Perhaps you love teaching adjectives for descriptive writing, or maybe you think prepositions are a lot of fun to teach because you get to talk about what an airplane can do in relation to a cloud (go in it, under it, over it, through it, etc.). We're pretty confident that by the time your students walk into a middle school classroom, they've learned about these concepts countless times. By middle school, students are ready to move on to more nuanced ideas about language, and while adjectives, adverbs, and prepositions can certainly be used in

---

2. See the **Glossary** in the **Appendix** for more on this concept.

subtle ways (see our other book for a discussion of how), there is a range of other tools that can help students become better writers, better readers, and better thinkers.

The order of the topics in this chapter is purposeful, a suggestion for how you might approach these concepts. Starting with the nature of the sentence is usually a good idea, as "sentence sense" is the basis for understanding other concepts. Teaching phrases or dependent clauses is way more difficult when students struggle with the nature of sentences. Similarly, before considering hyphenated nouns, it's probably a good idea to explore the dimensions of nominalization. Ultimately, however, you're the professional. Make these decisions based on the needs of your students, your curriculum, and your teaching context.

Our suggested order, detailed and explained below, is just that—a suggestion.

What is a sentence, and how do sentences, sentence parts, and clauses work together?

1. Sentences and Nonsentences
2. Dependent Clauses and Complex Sentences
3. Coordinating Conjunctions
4. Conjunctive Adverbs

How can we use words and phrases to help readers understand our goals and intentions?

5. Noun Phrases, Appositives, and Nominalization
6. Absolutes and Participial Phrases
7. Active and Passive Voice

How does punctuation help us nuance meaning and clarify purpose?

8. Semicolons and Colons
9. Hyphenated Adjectives and Nouns
10. Dashes

Checking Student Understanding Without Demoralizing

Michelle remembers vividly the first time she taught a grammar class. She'd write a sentence on the board, ready to talk about some grammar concept at work in that sentence. She'd ask a question of the students. And then, the inevitable response: silence. Dead silence, and no eye contact. And the all-too-common fear reverberating around the room, unspoken, but familiar to any veteran teacher: *don't call on me, don't call on me, oh, please, don't call on me.*

Michelle knew that no grammar class (indeed, no class in general) would ever be successful with so much fear in the room, so she learned some tricks to get students to talk about grammar while still feeling safe.

Trick 1: Many students are hesitant to answer a class-posed question if they're unsure about their answer. Makes sense—no one wants to look "less than" in front of peers. Try this. Ask a typical question ("Where's the noun phrase in this sentence?"). But rather than waiting for someone to answer the question, follow with a direction such as, "Put your finger on your nose if you *know* the answer, finger on your cheek if you *think* you know the answer, and your finger on your chin if you have *no idea*." Make sure you don't move on until everyone in class has a finger somewhere on their face (lots of students will try to be the student who doesn't participate). You can then call on students who have their fingers on their noses.

This is a useful informal assessment. Gauging how many students understand, kinda understand, and totally don't understand can guide your instruction and reteaching. And don't be totally disappointed when no one puts a finger to the nose—that will absolutely let you know it's time for more teaching.

Trick 2: Quick comprehension checks are good with new concepts. A simple thumbs up if they're good with the concept (or down if they aren't) can work. Michelle also lets her students indicate 25%, 50%, and 75% understanding, an adaptation students asked for. Again, this is a quick check to let you know if you can move on from the topic at hand.

Trick 3: Sometimes Michelle just asks students whether they understand what she's talking about and to shake their heads yes or no. You have to be on the watch for this one because a lot of students won't want to do this, but if you keep making the whole class shake their heads until everyone does it, those holdouts will finally shake yes or no too.

Trick 4: We all know the power of walking around the room while students do work. When teaching grammar, this can be particularly powerful because it gives you an opportunity to see what students are doing. During your walk, you can identify really good examples, and ask students, before you come back together as a class, if they will share their magnificent, fabulous, and just downright genius grammar example. This works for several reasons: (1) students know their answer is right and teacher-approved, so sharing isn't such a terrifying idea, and (2) when you ask who will share their answer, you've already identified some students who will so you don't have that deafening silence in return.

Trick 5: Snowball. Many teachers already know this activity, but we think it is particularly good for grammar. Students write something on a piece of paper (a couple of sentences, a scenario, etc.)—make sure they don't write their names on it—and then they ball up their paper and throw it across the room. Everyone picks up a paper ball responds to what was written on it, and then throws it once more. Students pick up paper balls again and decide whether or not to share what is written with the class. There are several layers of anonymity here, so the labels of right and wrong are anonymous as well. It is safe. Often, the examples that are shared were written by those students who never think they're right. How awesome for their confidence when they, safely and anonymously, get their peers' approval. This is powerful.

What Do I Do with the Scenarios?

We provide some suggestions about carrying out the scenarios in this chapter. Here are a few general ideas for how you might ask students to work through these applied activities.

First, be flexible with grouping. With some of these concepts, students can work on their own, but with others, they'll need the safety of a partner. You may need to do a few scenarios as a class first. Be flexible in how you let students complete these scenarios, and keep in mind that a lot of responses can be scripted as a skit. In our experience, students tend to respond to any activity that gets them out of their seats.

Michelle sometimes takes up all scenario responses and gives students a quick five-minute task while she finds useful examples and non-examples.[3] These are good for sharing what's done well and where misunderstandings tend to originate.

You can also ask students to write a scenario and then work in groups to check for understanding and rhetorical effectiveness. For example, have students work in a group of three. They should pass their paper to the right, and that person should check for understanding of the concept. They then pass their paper to the right again, and the next group member analyzes the rhetorical effectiveness of the grammar move. If you want this process to be anonymous, ask students to write (for example) a vegetable name on their scenarios, then take them all up, and randomly distribute scenarios to students. At the end of class, students can pick up their scenarios to see how others analyzed their work.

Just One Answer . . .

Our take on these grammar concepts is certainly not the only one possible. In this chapter, we discuss how dependent clauses and conjunctive adverbs can help students "make a turn" in their writing; however, these grammar moves can do many other things too (did you see how we made a turn in this sentence with our conjunctive adverb?). If you see that a grammar move does something beyond what we have in this book, do some experimenting, find some examples, and teach it with confidence. We all use a variety of language moves for a variety of purposes. What you find in the rest of this chapter is such a very small slice of the huge and sometimes confusing language pie.

WELCOME TO THE MESSY WORLD OF GRAMMAR!

It can be daunting to teach grammar without an answer key. You're going to run into multiple situations in which you and your students simply aren't sure of an answer. But if you're really teaching in ways that matter, this is going to happen anyway—regardless of the subject. So, do what you do: praise students for their efforts and turn these moments into more opportunities to talk about language, together.

---

3. Non-examples are pretty useful for learning anything. Choose wisely, looking for common misconceptions while protecting student anonymity.

CONCEPT #1: SENTENCES AND NONSENTENCES

Reasons for Teaching This Concept

A sentence has a subject and a verb!

Seems easy enough, right? Sure. A subject and a verb. But what about this one?

> Trey: When are you going to the movies?
> Carlos: Tonight.

Is "tonight" a sentence? It contains a complete thought, which is a popular definition for a sentence. But there's certainly no verb in "tonight."[4]

A sentence has a subject and a verb! Okay. What about this one?

> Because she knew the game.

Hmmm. We know that's not a sentence; that's a dependent clause (which, like all dependent clauses, contains a subordinating word, a subject, and a verb).

Let's stick with this traditional definition of a sentence for one more point: *a sentence contains a subject and a verb*. If we use this definition, we should probably teach verbs. But we take issue with the idea of teaching *all* verbs[5] and their many, many labels. Here's why: there are *verbs* and then there are lexical categories that look, smell, and taste like verbs but aren't, and that's where things get messy.
   As an example, let's look at this sentence.

> Traveling to the airport can be tiring because security lines have been known to be excessively long.

Now, we feel pretty confident in saying that a sentence like the one above isn't going to pop up in any Daily Oral Language book or worksheet you pull from the Internet. But it may be the kind of sentence that one of your students creates. Let's look at the real issues surrounding a sentence like this when teaching verbs.

- *Traveling to the airport*: gerund phrase (a verbal)[6]
- *Can be*: verb phrase of the sentence[7]

---

4. Linguists would argue that "tonight" is an elliptical sentence. In the same way we use ellipses to note removed material in quotations, an elliptical sentence doesn't have all parts of a complete sentence written because these parts are already understood: here, "I am going" is implied but not present.

5. Notice we said "all verbs" here—we have a caveat below.

6. Verbals may look like verbs, taste like verbs, and smell like verbs, but they aren't verbs.

7. Just to keep any linguist who might be reading this happy, we have to note here that in the linguistics world, the predicate—typically everything that follows the subject—is considered a verb phase. So in this case, a linguist would say that the verb phrase is "can be tiring because security lines have been known to be excessively long." However, in the context of ELA, most would consider "can be" the verb phrase.

- *Tiring*: Participle (a verbal)[8]
- *Because security lines have been known to be excessively long*: a dependent clause, which in this case contains a verb phrase (*have been known*) and an infinitive, which is also a verbal (*to be*)

Yeah. That's pretty confusing, especially if you read that long footnote for the participle.

Many students would look at those verbals (the gerund, the participle, the infinitive) and go, "There's the verb!" Or they may look at the verb phrase in the dependent clause and go, "There's the verb!" And while they would be "wrong" by Standardized English definitions, their conclusions make sense.

We also don't advocate teaching verbs to students because, when it comes to naming verbs in verb phrases, it's a messy, messy world. Just look at this:

- She **was eating** a piece of cake.

  - *Was* is a helping verb; *eating* is a main verb
  - *Was* is an auxiliary verb; *eating* is a participle
  - *Was* is a *to be* verb; *eating* is an action verb

- She **might eat** a piece of cake.

  - *Might* is a helping verb; *eat* is a main verb
  - *Might* is an auxiliary verb; *eat* is an infinitive
  - *Might* is a modal; *eat* is an action verb

- She **eats** a piece of cake.

  - *Eats* is an action verb
  - *Eats* is a transitive verb

- She **eats** through the cake.

  - *Eats* is an action verb
  - *Eats* in an intransitive verb[9]

All of those terms are considered Standardized English labels. And your students' teachers over the years have probably used different labels at different points in your students' lives. Whew! That's a head spinner.

---

8. However, we can complicate this even further. Our supersmart linguist friend explains "tiring" like this: "I think you could interpret 'tiring' in this case as either a present participle acting as a predicate adjective (the 'equals' test works) or as the present participle acting as part of the main verb following two auxiliary verbs (the test question is, can the subject 'traveling' tire? Since the answer is yes, then it's a possibility). Note that this means that 'be' is getting interpreted in two different ways here: for a predicate adjective, 'be' would be a linking verb (with 'can' as an auxiliary for 'be'). In the second interpretation, 'be' is an auxiliary for 'tiring' (as is 'can')." (Palmer, personal communication)

9. From *Grammar to Get Things Done: A Practical Guide for Teachers Anchored in Real-World Usage* by Darren Crovitz and Michelle D. Devereaux

When we step into the wild world of verbs, students are probably going to get more frustrated than anything else. It's a tangle of alienating terms not easily simplified.[10]

Okay, we hear you: if the subject/verb definition for a sentence doesn't work, then what does?

The answer is actually simple—truly, when Michelle finally realized this solution after working for years with teachers and students, she almost cried. Sometimes the easiest solution is the best one.

Key
Bold: Teacher talk
Italics: Teacher notes

DAY 1: WHAT'S YOUR HISTORY WITH THE SENTENCE?

Okay, today we're going to start working with sentences—what they are and how you know. First, tell me what you know about a sentence. How have you been taught sentences in the past? What do you remember? There's no wrong answer here. I just want to hear your experiences.
We recommend that you write students' answers on the board so you can note patterns in their previous instruction. This will help you better shape your instruction over the next few days.

Fantastic. Thanks for sharing!

DAY 2: "IT'S CERTAINLY TRUE THAT"

All right, let's begin with how to identify complete sentences. I want to start like this: talk to your neighbor and come up with a sentence—it can be a complete sentence or an incomplete sentence. It doesn't matter. Then, one of you come and write it up here on the board when you're done.
Depending on your class size and board space, you may have to change this a little (e.g., groups of three, several phases of sentences on the board, etc.). Also, this is certainly going to be impromptu grammar instruction. If you aren't comfortable working with student-created sentences (because, let's be honest, when you're learning how to teach grammar, a key in the back of the book can be a great relief), then you can create your own sentences for this portion.

So, I am going to show you the easiest, most awesome way to identify a sentence. Are you ready for this? Your mind's going to be blown. I'm going to add "It is certainly true that" to these and that's going to tell us whether or not they are sentences. Let's check it out.

---

10. We do want to clarify that we aren't totally against teaching all verbs—we think a focus on action verbs can help students' writing, and a focus on modals can help students control tone. But getting into the archaic language of verbs with a class of 15-year-olds? That's just not doing anyone much good.

Try this with several student-created sentences. Make sure you play up how incredibly easy it is to identify sentences this way. Repeat the phrase "It is certainly true that" several times as you go through their sentences on the board.

We are sure that your students will write a multitude of different sentences and nonsentences. In the beginning stick with simpler examples. If students have written complete sentences that begin with verbal phrases (e.g., gerunds, participles, and infinitives), prepositional phrases, or dependent clauses, skip those right now. Tell the students, "Whew! These are just way too advanced right now. Excellent sentences, but we'll come back to these later. We're going to deal with the simple stuff right now."

Also, make sure that somewhere on the board you have freestanding dependent clauses and freestanding phrases with a verbal (if students didn't create these constructions, here are a few you can write on the board):

Dependent clauses
Because the basketball was flat.
Since the dance was last night.
When he gets home from school.

Phrases with a verbal
Making cookies with my mom.
To be the first one to do it.
To the camping store.

Students should begin to notice that actual sentences sound sensible with "It is certainly true that" added while nonsentences sound off. As you are having this discussion, make sure you define a sentence and a nonsentence this way. (A sentence works with "It's certainly true that" and a nonsentence doesn't.)

At this point, students may do something we call "internal justification." Sometimes when we're looking at a nonsentence, we may add the context to justify it being a sentence in our heads.

We've worked with students who will take "Because the basketball was flat" and add, in their minds, "he couldn't play," turning it into "Because the basketball was flat, he couldn't play." (Students' minds are really quite amazing.)

You may have to have an explicit conversation with them about internal justification; the challenge here is to get them just to think about what's on the page in front of them. When we've had these conversations with adolescents, it goes something like this.

Ah, yes. I absolutely see what you're doing here with this nonsentence: "Because the basketball was flat." In your mind, you see the rest of the context, right? You see that the girl can't play because the ball was flat. Right on. That makes total sense and that's super smart of you to imagine the situation where this fits.

With the "It is certainly true that" trick though, we can't add any other words. It is amazing that you can do that, that you can add the context. For right now, though, let's just look at the words we have. Okay?

Let's look at just what's written on the board:

Because the basketball was flat.

Now let's add, "It is certainly true that" to the beginning:

It is certainly true that because the basketball was flat.

Does that make sense on its own? No. Not really. We'd need to add more words— like you did—for it to make sense.
We have found that after a conversation like this—in which you explicitly recognize the fluency in the student's context-building while also explaining the parameters for using a trick effectively—can help students.

Students will need to practice with this, which is why we'll do it again on Day 3.

DAY 3: MORE PRACTICE WITH "IT IS CERTAINLY TRUE THAT"

Okay, who remembers our sentence trick from yesterday? Yes, "It is certainly true that." Nice. So remember we can put that little phrase in front of a might-be-a-sentence and figure out whether or not it actually is a sentence, right? Excellent.

   Today we're going to play around with some more sentences, nonsentences, and our fancy new sentence trick.
Students can do the activity described below individually or with partners. It depends on where your students are in understanding this idea.

I want you to take out a sheet of paper and write three sentences or nonsentences on it (some of one, some of the other). Try to keep the sentences and nonsentences simple at this point. Don't write your name on the paper. That's not important.

   Okay, now that you've done that, I want you to ball up your paper and throw it across the room. Next, pick up a balled piece of paper that's landed near you.[11]

   Now that you have someone else's sentences and nonsentences, write "It is certainly true that" in front of each sentence or nonsentence. Put a big check mark next to the sentences and a big X next to the nonsentences. Okay, now we're going to ball up the paper one more time and throw it. Pick up a piece of paper near you and read what's on the paper.

   Who has a really good example of a sentence or nonsentence that they want to write up here on the board?
You can either have students talk through why the example is a sentence or a nonsentence (you can help them), or you can talk through the sentences yourself.

Okay. Excellent job today, folks.

---

11. This is the "snowball" activity described in the introduction to Chapter 4.

DAY 4: SCENARIO

Welcome! Let's see how you handle a real-life situation. Ready?

You can't believe it. Theresa, your best friend from like forever, just got her first boyfriend. The problem? It is your ex-boyfriend! You're only a little upset. I mean, JayJay was nice and everything, but the two of you together just didn't work. And now your best friend is dating your ex-boyfriend. You're not really sure what you should feel. Are you happy that Theresa has found a nice guy (because JayJay was really nice to you)? Are you upset because, at the end of the day, your best friend is dating your ex-boyfriend, and that's weird?

In cases like this, you've always found it best to write yourself a letter, to figure out how you feel about all this crazy before you talk to Theresa or JayJay.

Put pen to paper to figure all of this out. (You're going to use sentences and nonsentences, because this is one hot mess.)

Tell students not to write their names on the papers because they will snowball them tomorrow.

DAY 5: SCENARIO CHECK

Okay, folks, today we are going to play with the scenarios you wrote yesterday. *Here are the instructions.*

Step One:

- Ball up your scenario
- Launch it across the room
- Pick up someone else's scenario
- Go through it with the "It's certainly true that" trick and find the nonsentences
- Underline the nonsentences

Step Two:

- Ball up the paper again
- Toss it back across the room somewhere
- Pick up a piece of paper and check the nonsentences—did the first person get them all? Do you see one that was missed?

Step Three:

- Everyone will choose a sentence or nonsentence from the scenario in hand
- Write just the sentence or the nonsentence on the board

Step Four:

- As a class, do the "It's certainly true that" trick with the sentences on the
  board

Excellent work today.

DAY 6: THE UTILITY OF NONSENTENCES

Okay, let's refresh.

Discuss what students have learned to this point: the "It's certainly true that" trick can help them identify sentences and nonsentences. You'll want to move this discussion further, though, considering the rhetorical effects of both sentences and nonsentences. Here are some guiding questions:

- Should we always write with only sentences?
- What audience might expect us to write with only sentences?
- Do authors use nonsentences? What might be some benefits of using both sentences and nonsentences in your writing?
- Do you think both sentences and nonsentences have a place if your writing? Why do you say this?

The goal here is to help students consider rhetorical purposes: Who is your audience? What's the situation? And, what is your purpose? You want students to understand that authors use nonsentences all the time, both in formal and informal spaces; however, they make these choices with a rhetorical justification. Tell them that they're going to start exploring sentences, nonsentences, and rhetorical purpose.
  Here is an example of how you might have this conversation with students.

Okay, so I'm going to start with a question—how many of you have ever felt angry? Sad? Confused? Excited? All of you? Right, most of us have felt these emotions, maybe every day. Well, authors often need to show these emotions. It would be boring if an author said, "Now the character is sad." Or, "Hey, my character, Joe, is now angry." That would be one heck of a boring read, right? So authors use sentence structure to help us, as readers, understand what's going on, and nonsentences are one way they do this.
  Take a look at these two paragraphs.

He'd looked everywhere. Everywhere. He knows she took it. Her and her greedy little fingers. He slumped in the corner of the room. The room undone. Drawers pulled out. Bookcases toppled. She had it. He knew she did. He had to get back what was his.

He'd looked everywhere. He knows she took it with her greedy little fingers. He slumped in the corner of the room. The room was undone. The drawers were pulled out. The bookcases were toppled. She had done it. He knew she did. He had to get back what was his.

Okay, in our first paragraph here, where are our nonsentences?
Students may be confused by "The room undone" and "Drawers pulled out. Bookcases toppled." The word undone *isn't a word you look at and go, "Hey! That's an adjective!" And since the other two nonsentences don't have verbs either,* pulled out *and* toppled *may seem like verbs to them (because they are verbals, participles, actually, meaning they are functioning as adjectives describing the nouns, but you don't need to explain all of that to students). Have them try the "It is certainly true that" trick and none of those sentences make sense. (You may have to remind them to clear their minds—make sure they aren't internally justifying.)*
Here are the nonsentences in that first paragraph:

> Everywhere.
> Her and her greedy little fingers.
> The room undone.
> Drawers pulled out.
> Bookcases toppled.

Are there any nonsentences in that second paragraph? No? All of those are sentences, right? But let's talk about tone. Which one sounds more frustrated and desperate?
Some students may say the second one and they may have really good justifications for why it sounds more frustrated and desperate. Listen to all responses. When it comes to rhetorically analyzing grammar, we need to be flexible.

So, in the first paragraph, the nonsentences help us sense the protagonist's desperation, right? And we also get a quick view of what the room looks like. With all of the words added in the second paragraph, our reading slows down a little, right? When we're frustrated and desperate, we're really not thinking in complete sentences, are we? Then why would an author use complete sentences?

Just food for thought. Today, I wanted to convince you that nonsentences aren't evil. Tomorrow, we're going to look at some more nonsentences, and you'll get a chance to play around with them as well.

DAY 7: SCENARIO

Here we go! Another challenge!

You got it! You can't believe it! You sent in your application six weeks ago, and it was starting to feel like you would never get into the Gamers Association of the Greater Northwest. But you just got the email and you're in!

Shoot a quick (and passionate) email off to your friend Joseph, who's been waiting to hear whether or not you got in too! Joseph's been in the association for a while. It is amazing that you are now both in!

Take up these scenario responses and glance through them quickly, finding the funniest ones to share with class tomorrow. (It shouldn't take long. You are just glancing at them for the ones that the class would most enjoy.)

DAY 8: LOOKING AT SCENARIOS

Okay, so today we're going to look at some of your scenarios that you wrote yesterday.

Based on your classroom community, you can keep these anonymous, ask students for permission to share, or otherwise proceed based on shared values and routines. Talk through three to five examples. You can ask questions such as the following:

- *Where are our nonsentences? How do you know?*
- *Do the nonsentences help or hurt the "story" Why do you say that?*
- *Would you change anything in this response? Do you think it is effective? Why do you say that?*

DAY 9: SCENARIO (IF STUDENTS NEED MORE PRACTICE)

Guess what? We have another real-life situation that needs your expertise!

The local newspaper is having a Halloween writing contest—the scariest story wins $250! That money would be a good start to finally buying that skateboard you've been eyeing. You've been working on the climax of the story for a while—you know, the scariest part. In English class, though, you just learned about nonsentences. Give that terrifying part of your story one more revision using nonsentences to really scare the reader!

Take up these responses and glance through them quickly, finding effective examples to share with class tomorrow. (It shouldn't take long. You are just glancing at them for the ones that the class would most enjoy.)

DAY 10: LOOKING AT SCENARIOS (IF STUDENTS NEED MORE PRACTICE)

Okay, so today we're going to look at some of your scenarios that you wrote yesterday.

Again, follow the form and routine you've established for sharing student work in your classroom. Talk through three to five examples. You can ask questions such as the following:

- *Where are our nonsentences? How do you know?*
- *Do the nonsentences help or hurt the story? Why do you say that?*
- *Would you change anything in this response? Do you think it is effective? Why do you say that?*

CONCEPT #2: DEPENDENT CLAUSES AND COMPLEX SENTENCES

Reasons for Teaching This Concept

Many teachers are familiar with a particular kind of basic writing from students: they are able to produce a paragraph or two in response to a particular topic, but the sentences seem rudimentary. Students may lean heavily on simple and compound structures, and the line of thought moves haltingly, without much rhythm and pacing. The writing may convey thoughts and stay focused on the subject, but it somehow seems to lack dimension and energy.[12]

What to do in these situations? One solution might be helping students master the complex sentence, which means mastering the relationship between independent and dependent clauses.

As teachers, we can build on what students can already do in order to help them deepen their ideas. *Complex sentences* (which are independent clauses combined with one or more dependent clauses) are telling markers of writing fluency. They allow students to concisely articulate a whole variety of relationships—chronological, conditional, cause and effect, comparison and contrast—that in turn allow them better control of meaning and thus, better control of how their readers and listeners see their worlds.

In short, complex sentences help students express complex thoughts. We don't delve into all the purposes of complex sentences in this set of lessons, but we hope we chart a path for how you might come to this work constructively.

Key

Bold: Teacher talk

Italics: Teacher notes

DAY 1: NOTICING THE FEATURES OF COMPLEX SENTENCES (WHEN AND WHY)

Good morning, everyone. Let's get started. What do you notice about these sentences? What's happening in them?

- Juli started on her science project after she finished her math homework.
- I always throw up before we have a big football game.
- We usually have a snack when we get home from school.

Students will likely focus on the content of the sentences first—what they're saying. You may need to prompt them to consider other aspects ("Okay, yes, these sentences all relate to school. What else? What's happening at school? When are these things happening? What words let you know this?")

---

12. Interestingly, we've had high school students tell us that they stick with easy sentence forms intentionally. They know they won't lose any points on their grammar grade if they stick with simple sentences. Kinda makes you want to shed a tear, doesn't it? (And maybe even commend these students for learning how to survive within the system.)

Students will probably notice that there's a when *connection between the two sentence parts (clued in by the words* after *and* before*). That is, there's a sequence established by the sentence organization. They'll also likely notice the frequency words (*always, usually*), which is normal given that these words describe how often the* when *happens.*

At this point, it's not necessary to get into any specific terminology with students (e.g., complex sentence, dependent clause, etc.). Instead, it's probably good enough to just do some low-risk observation.

Great. We see that there are *two things happening* in each of these sentences. And the words you noticed—*after, before, when*—are separating these two things.

These words are pretty important. They're sort of acting like a turning point, or a hinge, or a sign giving us direction. For right now, let's call these words *turning words* because they indicate some kind of turn in our sentences.[13]

In this discussion, make sure you clarify that these turning words indicate when *something happened.*

Okay, what do you notice in these sentences? What's happening here?[14]

- The soccer team quit playing because it started to rain.
- I got grounded for the weekend since I never did my chores.
- Rob can't come over to play video games because he's going to see the doctor.

As with the first set of examples, students will probably see that there's a why *something happened connection going on here (but they may need some prompting): the second part of the sentence provides a reason or explanation for the situation in the first part of the sentence.*

You might ask students to consider the questions that these sentences answer, such as, "Why did the soccer team quit playing?" and "Why did I get grounded?" There's a turn happening in the response—we want students to focus on the word that makes that turn. You want to help them see that the because *and* since *give answers to questions.*

Seeing this connection between sentence parts might take a little prompting—for example, "How does the second half of the sentence relate to the first?"

Good. Each sentence has two things happening, with a word in between, and this word is also acting as a turning word. What's the word doing this time? What's the connection?

---

13. As we said earlier, we change some grammar terms so that they reflect what the grammar move actually does. In this section, *subordinating conjunctions* become *turning words*. Yes, yes, we do know that *subordination* deals with relationships between clauses and that, of course, *conjunctions* combine. You could spend two days explaining all of that to students, or you could just call them *turning words*. We vote for the latter.

14. Days 1 and 2 can easily be broken down into four days: two days of *when* complex sentences and two days of *why* complex sentences. That's up to you, your students, and your curriculum.

You're looking for students to recognize the cause-and-effect, event-reason relationship: this happened (and as a result) this other thing happened. Make sure students boil down this understanding to why: *"Why did something happen?" Because* and since *answer that question for us.*

Before ending the lesson, take a quick look again at all six sentences. Point out the turning words *again (after, before, when, because, since) and emphasize to students that these turning words indicate a turn in the sentence—this is happening, [turning word], then this is happening. Some turning words tell us* when *something happened (before, after, when) and others tell us* why *something happened (because, since).*

DAY 2: MORE ON WHEN AND WHY

Start with yesterday's sentences on the board.

So, yesterday, we talked about these sentences. Anyone remember what we noticed?

- Juli started on her science project after she finished her math homework.
- I always throw up before we have a big football game.
- We usually have a snack when we get home from school.

Likely responses: relationship between parts of the sentence; the word that connects them and what it does; the term turning word *and why we call it that.*

After a short discussion, remind students of the importance of those turning words and what they're doing (i.e., when), then introduce the following scenario.

Scenario #1
Your friends are all planning to hang out this Saturday night. Sounds like it will be a fun time, and they want you to be there.

But guess what: your family has other plans for you.

Your parents want you to help wash the car, the lawn needs to be mowed, and then you're expected to take your kid sister to the playground. Plus, you have the draft of an essay to write before Monday.

Task: In a written note, explain to your family how you plan to meet all your obligations, either *before* or *after* your big Saturday evening plans (think about the sentences we looked at yesterday and today).

You can spice up such scenarios in any number of ways. You could have students write in pairs and make it a dialogue to be performed in front of the class; you could have students read their responses aloud and when the class hears a turning word, they snap their fingers (or hit their desks once); or you could have them write in groups on poster paper, place the responses around the room, and have students identify the turning words in each other's responses.

We also talked about these other sentences. What did we see going on here? What did we decide about them?

- The soccer team quit playing because it started to rain.
- I got grounded for the weekend since I never did my chores.
- Rob can't come over to play video games because he's going to see the doctor.

After a short discussion reminding students of the importance of those turning words and what they're doing (i.e., why), introduce the following scenario.

Scenario #2

You're inviting a few friends over for a movie marathon. One of your pals, Andrei, is crazy about filmmaker Stanley Kubrick and is pushing hard for another viewing of *2001: A Space Odyssey*. Thing is, your crew has seen that film . . . like, numerous times. No one but Andrei is all that interested in another viewing right now.

Task: Write a note to Andrei that thanks him for his suggestion but also explains why it's not a good idea. Use *because* or *since* to break the news gently to him. Think about the sentence examples above if you need some help.

These student writing examples will provide some information about how your students are understanding complex sentences. This gives you information about what to do next. Do they need to revisit the first two lessons, or are they ready to move on?

DAY 3: REINFORCING THE FIRST FEW LESSONS

So, the last couple of days we've been working on special kinds of sentences: ones that give us some information, use a turning word, and then continue with more detail based on what type of turning word was used.

Now let's try something new. In these sentences, you see the first part of a sentence, and then a question in parentheses. How can you finish the sentence using a turning word?

You could certainly list some turning words on the board for students to reference.

1. It's not really a good idea to be texting in class (why?) . . .
   It's not really a good idea to be texting in class because Ms. Melon might take your phone.
2. I was finally able to relax (when/why?) . . .
3. We had a rough bus ride home (when/why?) . . .
4. Classical music seems appropriate (when/why?) . . .
5. The party went from mild to wild (when/why?) . . .
6. Jalyssa deleted her Facebook account (why?) . . .

Note: Using the word when *can lead to different grammatical constructions. For example, students may create sentences with prepositional phrases instead of dependent clauses* (after *and* before *can be both subordinate words and prepositions, depending on whether or not a verb follows the word). Remember, if the added sentence part contains a verb* (e.g., "after the game ended"), *it's a dependent clause; if the added part doesn't include a verb,* (e.g., "after the game"), *it's a prepositional phrase.*

It's normal for students to create prepositional phrases in this work, and at this point, that's okay. The goal of this exercise is to gauge how students are doing.

In a few days, we'll get into the fact that dependent clauses can move around within a sentence. Then you can tell students that when *dependent clauses are often more useful or common at the beginning of a sentence, as they immediately establish time and sequence:*

After I passed the test, I was finally able to relax.

DAY 4: DIGGING DEEPER

You all have been creating some great sentences so far this week! Here are just a few. *Choose a few sentences from student responses for this part of the lesson. You might also use the sentences and discussion below as a model or guide.*

- I will meet all my family obligations before I go out.
- Jamie half-listened to her dad while she fired up the PlayStation.
- They'll start to leave because they won't like the music.
- I don't want to flake on my friends since I don't want to be seen as unreliable.
- Andrei wasn't happy because no one wanted to watch Kubrick again.

What are some of the turning words in these sentences? What are they doing? Let's look closely at the first sentence. Here's the first part.

I will meet all my family obligations.

That's an understandable statement, right? But the author then makes that turn. That word *before* lets us know when we might expect those family chores to be completed.
   Let's look at the second sentence.

Jamie half-listened to her dad while she fired up the PlayStation.

Here, we have several actions happening at once. The word *while* complicates the scene, suggesting something about Jamie's attention.
   What about the next one?

I don't want to flake on my friends since I don't want to be seen as unreliable.

There's some reasoning going on here, right? This author is using *since* to make a turn in her sentence. There's a deeper explanation in this turn—I can't *not* go since (the turn) I don't want to be seen a certain way.

What about the last two sentences? Where are our turns in these? What work are they doing?

Let students talk these through. In the activity that follows, you'll need to create ten simple sentences to go with a group of turning words.

Okay, we're going to work more with these turning words today. You're going to work in pairs; each pair will get an envelope. Inside are five turning words along with ten sentences. Your job is to combine two sentences with one of the turning words. Do this at your desk. Talk to your partner and decide which sentence you like the best and then come up and write it on the board. You may need to help me talk through it, explaining where the turn is, so be ready!

Okay, who can help me talk through these sentences on the board? Where is the turning word? What change happens in the sentence because of the turning word?

Discussion.

Great job! Tomorrow we're going to look at how we can change up these types of sentences even more!

Note: Save these sentences for the next day, either by taking a picture of the board or by having a student type them out and send them to you electronically.

DAY 5: MOVING SENTENCE PARTS AROUND

Use the sentences that students created yesterday as the examples today. If you aren't comfortable doing this, you can use our examples below instead.

Okay, you guys did a good job building new sentences using a turning word. Now we're gonna play around a little bit with the sentences that you made.

Here's something kind of cool about these sentences: you can change the order of information by *starting* with the turning word. Take a look.

a. Alex was late to class because he was causing trouble in the hallway.
b. Because he was causing trouble in the hallway, Alex was late to class.

What do you notice about these two sentences? I mean, obviously they're in a different order, but what else?

Students will likely notice the comma.

Great! There's a comma. That's because if you start a sentence with a turning word, you're gonna need a comma between the sentence parts.

Is there anything else you notice?

You may get silence. That's okay!

Let me ask you this: do these sentences say the same thing?
If you get a "no," follow up by asking for an explanation. As noted below, we're looking for an awareness of differing emphasis.

Okay. If you think the sentences mean the same thing, let me ask you another question. Let's look at sentence a.

a.   Alex was late to class because he was causing trouble in the hallway.

If someone was telling you the story of what happened to Alex, what do you think they would say after this sentence? What would be talked about next?
Answers will vary, but you may get a student saying that the next sentence will deal with what Alex was doing in the hallway. If not, you can delay suggesting this to go on to sentence b.

b.   Because he was causing trouble in the hallway, Alex was late to class.

Okay, what about sentence b? If someone was telling you about Alex, and they said sentence b, what do you think they would talk about next?
You're more likely to get an answer here about the consequences of being late, or what happened next in the classroom.
    Even if students don't provide these responses, you can point out that what comes at the end of the sentence is often the most important piece of information, which means we're likely to get more detail in the next sentence about that information.[15]

Okay, great. Let me ask you a trick question. Which version of the sentence is *better*? Which should you use?
You may get a variety of responses, but the ideal might be something like, "It depends."

It depends. It depends on what?
See what students think.

Great. It depends on what you want to talk about next. You get to decide. Do I want to talk about what happened in the hallway, or do I want to focus on what happened after, in the classroom? It depends on what you want to emphasize.
    Now, remember, what comes at the end of the sentence is the most important, right? So, that means you can control the information that you want to focus on.

Because he was causing trouble in the hallway, **Alex was late to class.** →
His teacher gave a pop quiz, and Alex got a zero.

The important part of this version is that Alex's lateness resulted in something negative: he got a zero, right? Okay, let's look at another version.

---

15. See the **Known-New Contract** in the **Glossary**.

Alex was late to class because **he was causing trouble in the hallway.** →
He'd brought "Kick Me" stickers to school and was using a friendly pat
on the back to prank other students.

**Okay, how is the focus here different from the other version? Right—this one
focuses on Alex's troublemaking and what that looked like.**

*Emphasize and reemphasize with students that what comes at the end often gives
us information about what's happening in the next sentence—and that's how we
decide whether the dependent clause comes at the beginning or end of the sentence.*

Practice: Based on what comes at the end of the sentences below, write out a possible second sentence for each.

1. The mixing pot is always carefully covered because anything that falls in it is hard to get out. →
2. Since the training isn't open to viewers, the referees announce a score for each player. →
3. Anthony was not particularly attached to the treasure he found, even though it had made him famous.[16] →

DAY 6: COMPLEX SENTENCES WITH "UNDER WHAT CONDITIONS" RELATIONSHIPS

You all have done awesome with turning-word sentences. Let's check out a few more kinds and see what you think.

1. Tomas stepped on to the court **even though** he was exhausted.
2. Kelly is the lead singer in our band although he only has an average voice.
3. My dog won't fetch sticks even though he went to pet-training school.
4. I drink grapefruit juice every morning **although** I don't really like the taste.

What kind of connection does the turning word make in these sentences?
*This might be challenging for students. These turning words (subordinating conjunctions) show nuance by adding important detail to the independent clause.
Basically, they add complexity by telling us more of the story.*

*Tomas didn't just step on the court, he did so in spite of (even though) the challenges he was facing, which might suggest something about him: bravery, courage,
etc. This creates interest. Why did he do this? Why didn't he want to? It makes the
situation more interesting by generating drama and curiosity. If students can notice
this move, that's good!*

---

16. These same sentences are used on Day 8 to demonstrate that important information comes at the end of sentences.

The although *in sentence 2 conveys some dissatisfaction with the situation. The* even though *in sentence 3 is similar. It suggests a little bit of tension and frustration between the two ideas. That makes the situation more interesting—a reader wants to know more! Why don't they do something about Kelly? Why is your dog so dumb? Same with sentence 4. Why the heck would you drink it if you don't like it?!?*

Are *even though* and *although* doing the same thing? *(Yes, basically.)* So, what's the difference?

Even though *sounds more casual, and students may use this construction in their own speech, if not their writing.* Although *has a more formal register. If students can use* even though *confidently, they can be encouraged to stretch with* although, *especially in their writing, as it conveys more sophistication.*

See if you can connect the sentences below using turning words.

even though   although

- Jozy went to the club meeting. He wanted to go to the movies instead.
- I'm getting good grades this semester. I have a heavy course schedule.
- I'll eat this pizza. I'm not crazy about pepperoni.

Nice work! Now see if you can start your sentence with the turning word that you used.

1. I'm getting good grades this semester **even though** I have a heavy course schedule.
2. **Even though** I have a heavy course schedule, I'm getting good grades this semester.

See if students can tell you the difference here in terms of what might come next. For 1, we might expect the next sentence to tell us more about that tough schedule. For 2, we'd expect to hear details about those good grades. Also talk to them about the comma placement in these variations.

DAY 7: COMPLEX SENTENCES WITH "UNDER WHAT CONDITIONS" RELATIONSHIPS

For Scenario 1 below, try to use the turning words *even though* in your response.

1. Puppies are Cute . . . But No Thanks

Your friend's dog had puppies, and they're so cute! But then comes the hard ask: will you please adopt one of these puffballs? Your friend's family can't take care of them all, and they really need good homes. Trouble is, you already have a pet, and you know your family won't be keen on toilet training a new animal.

You need to write a note to your friend and explain the situation. You can't take a puppy. Be as understanding as possible in passing on the bad news, and try to use the turning words *even though* in your writing.

For Scenario 2 below, try to use the turning word *although* in your response.

2. **"Scholar Fridays"**

"Spirit Fridays" are a popular thing at school: pep rallies, free pizza, student rock bands and hip-hop groups playing in the quad, and themed dress-up days. But now the principal is considering a proposal that this day be changed to "Scholar Fridays," with an emphasis on student projects, academic teams, and raising test scores. He wants to speak with you because he knows that other students respect your opinion. Should this change be made?

Write out what you'll say to your principal. Make sure that you consider the benefits and drawbacks of your position. And try to use the turning word *although* in your writing.

DAY 8: THINKING ABOUT TURNING WORDS IN PASSAGES

Let's go over the turning words we've talked about.
Students should list the turning words they know—this list should go on the board.

Okay. Great. Let's look at how professional writers used these same turning words.

Notes:

- *Each excerpt below can go on its own PowerPoint slide.*
- *Students form small groups. Each group gets an excerpt.*
- *Ask students to look at the turning word—where is it in the sentence? Is it at the beginning or the middle of the sentence? Why does it make sense there? How does it set up what comes next?*
- *Have the groups explain their excerpt to the class.*

Excerpts

1. The kimchee is scooped out with a huge wooden ladle. The pot is always carefully covered because anything that falls in it is hard to get out. Strands of hair—it would have been impossible to get them all out (Park, 2012, p. 104).
2. Before that though, they'll give me a score so low, no one in their right mind would sponsor me. That's what will happen tonight. Since the training isn't open to viewers, the Gamemakers announce a score for each player. It gives the audience a starting place for betting that will continue throughout the Games (Collins, 2008, p. 184).

3. So Anthony got the golden statue. It was his now. But he was not particularly attached to it, even though he and his statue had become famous. He had appeared on a TV show with it, and an article had been written that appeared in the *Reader's Digest*. It was entitled "Pie in the Sky: A Plucky Lad's Struggle for a Millionaire's Gold." Anthony got a little money out of this, but not much. As people sometimes find out, much to their sorrow, you can't eat fame (Bellairs, 1997, p. 175).

DAY 9: EXPERIMENTING WITH THE TURNING WORD *WHILE*

While *is a good word for moving from one viewpoint to an opposing or contrasting viewpoint. It allows writers to detail something that a lot of people may think or believe, and then pivot to something more accurate or true. This makes it a pretty good tool for students to tackle clichés, stereotypes, or misconceptions and provide their own alternative insight.*

Okay, you guys are killing it with all of these turning words. Let's try another one. Take a look at these sentences.

- People sometimes think Charles is a country music fan while he's actually deep into the Atlanta trap scene.
- While some people think Keonna is a criminal or a thug, she's actually the best student at our school.

What's happening in these sentences? What's the word *while* doing?
Students may notice that while *is contrasting two different viewpoints; it's comparing something false (or something that's an assumption) with something true.*

Could we replace *while* with other turning words that you've practiced?
Although, though, *or* even though *could work.*

Awesome. Now take a look at those sentences again. Do you see another word that appears in both of them?

- People sometimes think Charles is a country music fan while he's actually deep into the Atlanta trap scene.
- While some people think Keonna is a criminal or a thug, she's actually the best student at our school.

The word, of course, is actually*.*

What does that word do in both sentences?
*Ideally, students will be able to articulate that it emphasizes the difference between an assumption or false belief and the truth. Basically, **it emphasizes the difference between two views.***

Scenario

Think about some of the stereotypes people have about you. What are some of things people believe about you that aren't true?

Write a paragraph that starts with the stereotypes people might have about you. Then, hit them with the actual truth about your identity. Try to use a turning word or phrase (like *while, though, although,* or *even though*). Also, see if you can use the word *actually* to emphasize the truth.

Example from Michelle:

I've had to deal with stereotypes all my life. A lot of people assume things because of how I talk. I've had others who have literally tried to silence me because they didn't like my accent. It can be really frustrating to fight against these stereotypes. People often think I'm dumb because I have a Southern accent even though I'm actually a professor—who writes grammar books.

DAY 10: EXTENDED APPLIED PRACTICE

Scenario #1

Ever notice that some people love judging others, especially when they don't really know them?

Think about your neighborhood, or where you grew up. In a paragraph, tell about some of the stereotypes or negative beliefs that people might have about this place. After this, explain the truth about this place. What's real and good about where you're from?

In your writing, try to use turning words (like *while, although, though,* or *even though*) along with the word *actually* to show the difference between stereotype and reality.

Scenario #2

Chickasaw High School is considering a new policy: no cell phones allowed in classrooms during school hours. The idea has many students in an uproar.

See if you can summarize what people are talking about using the structure below.

First paragraph
Explain why some people might think that a cell phone ban would be a good thing.
Second paragraph: Start with the phrase below:
"Although banning phones in class seems like a good idea, it actually . . ."
Then write a few more sentences explaining this different view.

Scenario #3

One of your friends, Von, is in some trouble at school. A harmless prank turned into a giant mess, with trash in the hallway and water flowing out of the restrooms.

Now you need to write a note of support so that Von isn't suspended (or even expelled) from school. Use the format below for your letter.

You need a salutation, since this is a letter. Something like this:
Dear Principal Hardcastle,

First paragraph

In two to three sentences, explain that you understand the situation and why the school leadership is upset. Von did a dumb thing, right? Admit that. (You can make up whatever details you like about the prank.)

Second paragraph

Write two to three more sentences explaining why your friend is actually a good person and not a vandal. Provide some positive info about Von.
See if you can use a sentence with the structure below:
"Even though what Von did was . . ., my friend is actually . . ."

Final paragraph

Just a couple more sentences asking the principal to go easy on Von.

The real evidence of learning is spontaneous use of knowledge or skills in novel, applied situations. As you consider ways to reinforce what students have learned about dependent clauses and complex sentences, consider the following opportunities.

Arguments and Thesis Statements

Complex sentences come in quite handy in conventional argument writing. Part of making a case typically involves consideration of other views; the complex sentence structure allows us to recognize a differing viewpoint while pivoting toward our own position:

Example: Although environmental concerns are worth considering, the economic benefits of the new factory outweigh the drawbacks.

Students can usually state a belief or position without too much trouble. Can they use a complex sentence to also acknowledge disagreement?

Defending Artistic Decisions

Good art often questions, provokes, and unsettles. Students engaged in artistic creation and inquiry—as a stand-alone assignment or as a piece of a larger, more conventional work[17]—can use complex sentences structures to justify their aesthetic choices in order to help audiences understand their intentions. Cause-and-effect and assertion-reason are two relationship purposes that fit especially well in this domain.

---

17. Tom Romano's (2000) concept of the multigenre research project, for instance, invites students to represent understanding in multiple modes, often with a reflective component.

Delicate Negotiations: The Art of Compromise

There may be no more important skill in a democracy than finding solutions when people disagree. The American legislative process, for instance, has traditionally been anchored on compromise, which seeks to find a middle pathway between competing interests. The language we use through compromise is crucial. Again, complex sentences suggest the complex nature of real-world solutions. When we use words carefully to recognize the validity of differing viewpoints—even knowing that no single position gets a complete "win"—we are acting to preserve relationships through linguistic tools.

Try invoking a scenario[18] in which parties are at odds over some intractable issue, in which students must take on the role of bridging differences. Doing so requires tact, diplomacy, and careful use of language. This work also reflects real-world challenges. Businesses and professional organizations commonly seek out specialists (such as arbitrators and ombuds) to handle challenging circumstances and reach fair and just decisions.

---

18. See Chapter 3 for guidelines for developing authentic applied scenarios, or use the examples in our books as inspiration.

CONCEPT #3: COORDINATING CONJUNCTIONS

Reasons for Teaching This Concept

Why bother with conjunctions, you might be thinking. *Of all the grammatical concepts students might struggle with, this one is pretty low on the list.*

It's true that most students have at least a rudimentary handle on how to use *and, but, or,* and *so.* But when we talk about building students' confidence and rhetorical fluency, we might consider spending some time on topics that students feel pretty good about instead of just hammering away on more confusing subjects. We agree that struggling through difficulty is a part of learning, yes, but so is noticing our existing fluency and building from there. In the series of lessons below, we consider how to both expand a functional use of conjunctions while also building students' ability to use these tools for potentially powerful stylistic and rhetorical ends.

To some extent, we're trying to increase *sophistication*[19] in student writing, and one way to do this is through intentional language decisions. Because conjunctions are fairly easy to grasp on a literal level, we can set up situations in which students can feel confident while taking reasonable risks experimenting with other uses. There's a payoff here in a number of contexts. For one, scorers of standardized writing exams note the markers of higher-level language use, and well-chosen rhetorical moves are one such indicator.[20] Another payoff is that in professional and social situations, the ability to muster arguments that are not simply logical and credible *but also emotionally resonant* can't be understated.

We're not trying to create cynical manipulators of language. But we do want to help students see how the building blocks of communication can also function stylistically to move others. A little bit of focused work with conjunctions can help.

Key
Bold: Teacher talk
Italics: Teacher notes

DAY 1: THINKING ABOUT THE CONCEPT OF "JOINING THINGS": METAPHORS AND MEANING

Good morning! We're going to start with a question. When you hear the words *junction* and *conjunction*, what do you think about?
You may get a variety of responses to this (including silence). Railroads, highways, and electrical connections might be some associations with junction, *and the old* Schoolhouse Rock! *episode of "Conjunction Junction" (easily available online) is still a cultural touchstone for some. List any ideas on the board (perhaps providing*

---

19. We acknowledge that this word has connotative issues—namely, a class-based bias (i.e., an association with exclusivity in education, wealth, and culture) and an etymological connection to argument unencumbered by particular principles (as in "sophistry"). Nevertheless, we hope its denotative use here—roughly, "demonstrating careful language choices for particular purposes and audiences"—has merit.

20. See **Semicolons and Colons** for a similar discussion.

your own as well). If students aren't volunteering anything, you might prompt them a bit by pointing out that the word join *has the same meaning as the* junc *syllable in each of these words.*

Okay. Next question. Is there a common idea that connects all of these things?
Students will likely arrive at the idea of joining: *a railroad junction is where different tracks meet; a spaghetti junction is a confusing meeting of highways and roads; a junction box is the central place for all wiring in a building. Depending on your students, this might also be a good place to point out English/Spanish connections. Junction is* unión *in Spanish, which is clearly similar to the synonym* union *in English.*[21]

Okay, great. You guys know a lot about these words. A *junction* is a place where two or more things are united or joined (such as railroad tracks). A *conjunction* is pretty similar: it's something that joins or brings together two other things. Over the next few weeks, we're going to be playing around with *joining words* to see how they can help us do specific things with language. Exciting!

Day 1 Bonus (optional): Etymological connections
   Vocabulary is still often taught with weekly sets of disconnected words that students memorize and then forget. Consider asking student to explore how the words below all have a meaning connection to join. *These are almost all words that students will encounter again out in the world, and the fact that they're related in meaning makes them easier to process and remember.*

Let's take a look at some words. Some of these you may know, and some you might not. Each of these words is connected somehow to the idea of *joining* something. Let's see if you can figure out how each one has a *join*-type meaning. You can work with a partner and use whatever resources you like. Be sure to write down a clear explanation for how each word connects to the concept of *joining*.
   Word list: junction, conjunction, join, conjoined, juncture, yoke (for joining a pair of pulling animals), yoga (which literally means unity), conjugal, jostle, joust, juxtapose, joint, subjugate, zygote

---

DAY 2: HEARD ABOUT FANBOYS? HELPING STUDENTS RECOGNIZE WHAT THEY KNOW

Okay. Nice work yesterday thinking about the words *junction* and *conjunction*. Some of you probably remember that there's a grammar connection here too. Anyone know what that is?
Students may volunteer examples of conjunctions, the FANBOYS acronym, or even a linguistic definition of conjunction. *They also might not respond at all, in which case . . .*

---

21. In fact, *union* is hidden right there in *junction*. See it? j**UN**nct**ION**. The phonological connection is a little clearer if we remember that "j" is usually voiced as an "h" or "y" sound in Spanish.

Okay, let's see if any of you recognize this. *(Write FANBOYS on the board.)* Anyone know what this means?

If students know some or all of the conjunctions, great. If not, you can help out.

Okay, great. So, what do we have here? Conjunctions! FOR, AND, NOR, BUT, OR, YET, and SO. These are words that join things together. Let's try some of these out. With a partner, I'd like you to write four sentences, and each sentence should include one of the conjunctions below.

and but or so

When students are finished, ask pairs to write their sentences on the board (or projector). Start with and *and proceed through the others. You're looking for variations of conjunction use: joining two nouns or verbs, joining two independent clauses, etc. Depending on your students, this may be well within their comfort zones, and that's fine. At this stage, the goal is emphasizing student knowledge, facility, and confidence with conjunctions.*

You're after functional, literal examples of these conjunctions created by students. These sentences might look something like the following:

- Today I took a math test and ate pizza for lunch.
- We went to Miami, Orlando, and Tampa.
- Migos and Drake are his favorite hip-hop artists.
- I like Skyrim, but I don't like Fortnite.
- We can go to the football game this Friday, or we could just hang out.
- She got grounded yesterday, so she can't go to the party.
- Nia got mad at Lev, so she went home.

Notably, some of what students create will contain irregular forms, particularly when it comes to commas. At this point, we're after general competence rather than punctuation precision, so it's probably a good idea to ignore such issues for now.

*For each conjunction, ask students to articulate what each one **does** in a sentence (that is, what function it fulfills). See if they can articulate something like the following:*

- *And*: signals that something is being added, extended, or emphasized
- *But*: signals that a contrast, obstacle, or limitation is coming
- *Or*: signals that options, choices, or different outcomes are next
- *So*: signals cause-and-effect or a reason for something

Rather than reading these functions to students, it's probably better that they think through the possibilities. A partial understanding of function is fine for now.

Great job. Thanks for working on this stuff!

DAY 3: WOW. YOU GUYS ARE SOLID WITH THOSE CONJUNCTIONS. WHAT'S NEXT? COMMAS

Okay, you all did really well with those conjunctions yesterday. Do you all remember which ones you worked on? You demonstrated that you're pretty confident with using *and, but, or,* and *so*. Today we're going to dial in a little closer on the sentences you created. Here are some of them.

If you are comfortable using the student-created sentences from yesterday, please do so. If you're not quite there yet, no problem. Use our examples below.

- Today I took a math test and ate pizza for lunch.
- We went to Miami, Orlando, and Tampa.
- Migos and Drake are his favorite hip-hop artists.
- I like Skyrim, but I don't like Fortnite.
- We can go to the football game this Friday, or we could just hang out.
- She got grounded yesterday, so she can't go to the party.
- Nia got mad at Lev, so she went home.

All right. Let's talk about commas. Most of the time when you use a conjunction, you won't need a comma at all. That's pretty easy to remember.

   Sometimes, though, you *do* need a comma. Take a look at the examples above. Anybody got a guess about when you might need a comma with that conjunction?

You will likely get students who recognize that a comma is called for when separating items in a list. Option: If you think your students might be interested, you might engage them in a discussion of the Oxford comma. Should it be used? Why or why not? Google a few amusing examples to help the discussion.

   If you're lucky, you might have a student who recognizes that when a conjunction connects two independent clauses (or, in language more familiar to students, two sentences), a comma is needed.

Check out this example. Can you see the parts that could stand alone as separate sentences without the conjunction?

   I like Skyrim, but I don't like Fortnite.
   I like Skyrim. I don't like Fortnite.

If you have two sentences,[22] you can often join them with a conjunction plus a comma. A conjunction alone isn't strong enough for the job.

   Ready to try this out? Grab a partner, and working together, come up with two sentences. Then, use a conjunction to join them . . . and don't forget the comma!

Ask for volunteers to put examples on the board or the screen and discuss.

---

22. Of course, this presumes that students can identify sentences (i.e., independent clauses) reliably. If they need some practice, check out **Sentences and Nonsentences**.

DAY 4: GETTING RHETORICAL WITH BOAS: MOVING BEYOND FUNCTIONAL USE

All right, you all are killing it with these conjunctions. It looks like you feel pretty confident in using *and, but, or,* and *so.* Is that accurate?

And, yesterday, we learned a little bit about when conjunctions need commas. Anybody remember what we practiced?

Okay, great. Now let's do some stretch work with these four conjunctions. We'll start by looking at a new acronym. You all know FANBOYS already. How about BOAS? What do you think BOAS stands for?

Good. You all know how these conjunctions work in sentences. Now let's talk about how you can make these conjunctions work to influence other people.

First. Anyone remember hearing this rule when you were younger? Does this sound familiar?

You cannot begin a sentence with a conjunction.

What do you think about this rule?
Some students might argue that people can begin sentences with conjunctions; follow up by asking about situations or examples.

Interesting. What do you think of the following sentences?

- And that's why you should never try to pet an alligator.
- But today would be different.
- So we decided to ask a very simple question: where did the money come from?
- Or we could just stay home where it's warm and dry.

Some students may land on an important realization here—that these sentences may be appropriate. It depends, of course, on the situation, which often means that it depends on the wider communicative context.

So, it looks like some of you think these sentences are okay, and some of you don't. I like the comment that "it depends." It depends on what came before this sentence, and maybe, what comes after it.

Now, a challenge. With a partner, here's your task. Choose one of these sentences, and see if you can create a paragraph that ends with this sentence.

DAY 5: MORE RHETORICAL BOAS: MOVING TOWARD RHETORICAL FLUENCY

Welcome back. Thanks for working on your paragraphs. Let's take a look at some of these and see what we think.

Reasonable expectations are called for here. Mastering stylistic and rhetorical moves takes a lot of time and practice. More successful attempts will demonstrate an audience-focused awareness. That is, the passage is designed to increase suspense, provoke a humorous reaction, convey a writer's ironic or sarcastic stance, and so on. In such cases, the conjunction is not just joining words, phrases, or clauses—it's now joining sections of a larger passage to create an intentional experience that can be dramatic, amusing, or otherwise interesting for others.

You might consider using the example below along with those students have produced.

Take a look at this example. Talk me through what you see happening here.

> Monday started out just like any other day. I got dressed, ate breakfast, and rode the bus to school without incident. My first couple of classes were pretty routine: going over homework, working on papers, prepping for a test. At lunch, I got my usual slice of pizza and sat at my usual spot in the cafeteria.
>   But today would be different.

What kind of feeling does that conjunction-led sentence create? What's it trying to do? How does it make you feel?

Short discussion. It might help to compare this passage to another version.

Here's another way this passage could be written. How does this change the effect?

> Monday turned out to be pretty crazy. It started out just like any other day. I got dressed, ate breakfast, and rode the bus to school without incident. My first couple of classes were pretty routine: going over homework, working on papers, prepping for a test. At lunch, I got my usual slice of pizza and sat at my usual spot in the cafeteria.

It's important here to make the point that one version is not necessarily "better" than the other. It really depends on a writer's particular goals. If storytelling drama is the point, the rhetorical use of a conjunction might be a good play. If clarity of explanation is in order, then other options might be better.

DAY 6: WHAT ABOUT NYF? AN INTRODUCTION TO FUNCTIONALITY

Okay! Wow. We got into some deep material the last few lessons. How do you feel about using BOAS for dramatic effect? Do you think it's useful? Have you noticed anyone using conjunctions in this way?

A few examples culled from social media and pop culture might help, such as, "Or not." "But that's none of my business." "So there's that." "And . . . curtain."

Solid. Keep your eyes open for BOAS leading off sentences in these ways; we'll keep a list of examples that you notice. Meanwhile, we're gonna take it a little bit further. It's time for NYF. You know what that means, right?

Okay, first thing. Let's see how you do coming up with sentences using *nor*, *yet*, and *for*. Partner time again. Try to write three sentences, each one using a NYF. Work together to see what you can come up with, and then we'll talk about it. It's okay if you're not sure about how to use these words. Just try your best. Sound good?

Results here will vary. These conjunctions are far less common than BOAS, and as the next several lessons investigate, they have both particular uses and connotations. Of the three, students will almost certainly be familiar with yet *and* for, *though for different lexical uses (i.e., as an adverb and a preposition respectively).*

When you review student attempts, we recommend celebrating any thoughtful uses for the time being—and acknowledging efforts that might be less successful.

Okay, good work. It's clear that you're somewhat familiar with how these words will sometimes appear in sentences. Over the next couple of days, we're going to take a look at each of these words when they function as conjunctions. They're a little weirder than BOAS but nothing to be afraid of.

DAY 7: TAKING UP *NOR*. WHAT YOU KNOW, AND HOW TO USE IT

Last time, we talked a little about *nor*, *yet*, and *for* as conjunctions. Let's take a closer look at *nor*. Does anyone want to take another shot at using *nor* in a sentence? Let's hear some examples.

Show student examples on the board or projector.

Okay, that's pretty good. *Nor* is kind of a weird conjunction. What kind of patterns can you notice in its use?

See if students recognize any of the following patterns.

- *Nor* pairs with a previous statement or situation to emphasize a negative position

   We don't need a ride to the dance nor do we need a chaperone.

- *Nor* sometimes pairs with *neither* for the same purpose (and "not" can usually substitute for "neither")

   I'm neither interested in your test prep coursework nor do I want a free trial.
   I'm not interested in your test prep coursework nor do I want a free trial.

Did you notice that both of these sentences have a *not* or *neither* before *nor*? That's a pretty important rule when we're using *nor*. There must be a negative word somewhere before *nor* to use this fancy little word.

Great. Now let's see if you can come up with a solid NOR statement to finish these sentences . . .

1. I'm not what you'd call a good dancer . . .
2. She's neither convinced by your argument . . .
3. Kima won't be going to the talent show . . .
4. Our team didn't surrender a single goal in last week's match . . .
5. With your unreasonable position on environmental issues, we can't support your candidacy . . .

Pretty good. Okay, let's get real. Is *nor* (or *neither*) a word that you use often in your life?

Ask students responding in the affirmative to elaborate with an example or two. Other students may not be as familiar, however.

Does *nor* seem a little formal to you? A little fancy or elevated in tone? If *nor* feels unfamiliar or formal, does it at least have some kind of use for us? When might we use it, and for what reason?

These questions get at the formal register of nor *and its uses. As some of the examples above may suggest,* nor *is pretty useful when negative emphasis is needed. When we hear* nor *after a negative comment (or* neither *before one), we know what's coming: another negative reason, example, consequence, or decision. This combo of two negative statements gives* nor *some rhetorical power, which is useful for when we want to drive home a cumulative stance on some topic.*

All right. So, we've figured out that when we really want to emphasize several negative elements, *nor* might be a good choice. We also talked about *nor* having kind of a formal, academic quality. That means it's an option that you might use in only specific situations.

In short, we might help students understand the use of nor *for two purposes.*

- Emphasizing multiple negative circumstances or positions
- Raising the formal register of one's communication slightly

Let's see if you can come up with a passage that addresses one of the following situations. In the passage you create, use *nor* to emphasize your negative perspective or position. You can work with a partner if you like.

- At a public meeting, you step to the mic to argue against a plan to build an All-Mart on pasture land near your home.

- After a very bad experience at a restaurant, the waiter offers you a coupon. Now you're emailing the manager.
- You need to give a speech as a candidate for class president. You're not as rich or as popular as the others interested in the job. But you want real change at the school.
- People love to stereotype your neighborhood. Now you are going to tell the truth about where you live.

DAY 8: *YET* AND THE POWER OF IRONY AND EMPHASIS

Okay, let's continue our exploration of these weirder conjunctions. *Yet* is up next. Can anyone use the word *yet* in a sentence? Let's hear a few examples.
Students will likely have little problem doing so, as yet *is familiar in everyday communication as an adverb, as in the following.*

- I can't play basketball because I haven't finished my homework yet.
- We have yet to make plans for the weekend.

Yet *as a conjunction, however, is less common.*

- We're running out of supplies, yet we still have hope of rescue.
- The game is over, yet the band plays on.

We recommend writing out several student examples on the board or projector for everyone to see. If students only produce examples of yet *as an adverb, that's fine. It's helpful for students to feel comfortable with this common function before you introduce something new. If students spontaneously create conjunctive* yet *examples, all the better.*

Okay, solid work. Looks like you're all pretty familiar with *yet*, at least with how it's used to show that something hasn't been completed. Does that sound right?
   All right, let's take a look at *yet* when it's used as a conjunction. Remember, it's part of FANBOYS, so that means it's used to join two things. Check out these examples. What do you notice?

- We're running out of supplies, yet we still have hope of rescue.
- The game is over, yet the band plays on.
- Brandon had every priviledge in life, yet he did not take advantage of his opportunities.
- We're working hard on the project, yet problems continue to slow us down.

Students may note how yet *acts as a pivot in these sentences, transitioning the sentence from a positive to a negative statement (or vice versa). In that sense,* yet *acts much like* but, *a much more familiar conjunction. Students may also remark that* yet *carries a slightly more formal tone than* but.

Those are all good observations. Let me ask you a question: can we replace *yet* in these sentences with *but* and still get pretty much the same meaning?
Students will likely agree that we can, though some may point out a subtle difference.

Okay. If *but* does the same kind of work, why the heck would we need to use *yet* at all? Can somebody make a case for *yet* having a slightly different function here? Does it make a difference?
By this time, some students may recognize the difference in register between but *and* yet. *As with* nor *and* for, yet *operates on a higher valence than more common conjunctions. That makes* yet *a specialized tool, one for use in specific situations and for specific purposes, including rhetorical emphasis through contrast, irony, and sarcasm.*

Nice work. You've figured out that *yet* is better for more formal situations than *but*. And, you also noticed that *yet* can be used to make a point in how it contrasts two different elements. Take a look at these examples. What's going on here?

- Derrell is a dedicated C student, yet he outscored everyone in the school on the SAT.
- Senator Francis calls himself the "law and order" candidate, yet his own campaign is the subject of several investigations.
- Dio is always talking about his mad flow, yet actual examples of his freestyling ability are rare.

While students may not use the term ironic, *they may sense the tension between expectation and actual outcome that underlies the concept. And since young people tend to have a fine sense of sarcasm, they may also key in on this possible use of* yet: *to subtly note hypocrisy, false boasting, or other bogus behavior.*

We've noticed that *yet* is helpful when we're pointing out something surprising or ironic or when we want to communicate our own sarcastic perspective. Now let's see some examples from your own lives. With a partner, use *yet* as a conjunction in a couple of sentences to (a) show a surprising outcome, and (b) convey sarcasm.

DAY 9: *FOR*—AN EVEN MORE SPECIALIZED TOOL.

All right. This week we've been looking at *nor* and *yet* and figuring out when we might use these peculiar conjunctions. We have one more to talk about. Remember how *yet* is a pretty common word in general but not-so-common when used as a conjunction? Well, this final conjunction is similar.

Let's do this. Write two sentences that both use the word *for*. I'm pretty sure that you won't need a partner, but go ahead and find a friend if you'd like.

Students will almost certainly write examples such as the following. As with yet, *it's worth making some of these examples public in order to emphasize students' solid grounding in using* for *as a preposition.*

- We ordered a pepperoni pizza for Jackson and a Hawaiian pizza for Kyle.
- I didn't bring any candy for you—sorry!
- For breakfast I had cereal.
- For once it would be nice to eat lunch outside.

Well, it's clear that you all have a pretty solid understanding of *for* **as it's commonly used. Now check this out. In these next sentences,** *for* **will be used as a conjunction. With a partner, read through these and write down several observations that you think might be worth talking about.**

- You must kneel in her presence, for you are speaking to the queen.
- We are without hope, for there can be no victory without the One True Ring.
- I turn my face to the wind and take the road out of town, for this place is no longer my home.
- Abandon all hope, for this is a realm of dark magic and wild beasts.

It will be interesting to hear about what students notice in these sentences. Used as a conjunction, for *can convey an archaic, elevated, or erudite tone that is quite rare in modern, everyday interactions.*

So, I appreciate your thoughts on these sentences and how *for* **is being used. I agree with most of your comments. Let me ask you this: is there another more familiar word that could take the place of** *for* **in these sentences while still maintaining a very similar meaning?**
Students may notice that the word because *can substitute in the examples above.*

Yes, *because* **works pretty well. That's helpful in remembering how the** *for* **conjunction acts—it's kind of like an old-fashioned** *because***. For our next practice, let's see if you can come up with some good** *for* **conjunction sentences that the following characters might utter.**

1. A king proclaims a new national holiday.
2. An evil wizard casts a spell on a young woman.
3. A preacher gives instructions during a ceremony.
4. A Halloween haunted house attraction needs a scary statement over the entranceway.
5. An ancient poem tells about the fertility of the landscape.
6. A hero gives a speech before facing long odds.
7. A detective reveals a criminal perpetrator at an elegant dinner.
8. An old woman offers her blessing to her granddaughter.

DAY 10: SOME APPLIED CONJUNCTION PROJECTS

All right! We have come a long way on conjunctions! I'm impressed by the work you've done. Now we're gonna level-up by using these tools in creative ways to get things done.

Remember that this work is anchored in building students' comfort and stretching their ability with conjunction options. It takes time and applied practice. The ideas below aim to embed this work in broader contexts of use and situation.

Controlling Audience Experiences: Judicious Use of BOAS for Style and Voice

1. Something crazy happened to you over the weekend. Rumors are flying—and there's a story there, all right. Get dramatic and tell it, and use a BOAS in a standalone sentence to raise the suspense.

2. The plan to replace the old Peace Park by selling the property to a dog food company is the worst. The town leaders justify this change by saying, "Jobs." But you disagree. Say so in a statement, and use a BOAS in a stylistic way to make your points pop.

Shifting Register Intentionally: Comfort with Nor and Yet in Specific Situations

1. Out of the blue, you get an email from your ex about maybe getting back together. That ain't happening, especially after the way you were treated. But you're not gonna get too salty about it. Instead, your ex will get a response that is polite but direct in shutting down that nonsense. Now go write it, and be sure to get *yet* or *nor* in there.

2. It was supposed to be the blockbuster movie of the summer. You were excited and happy to drop $12—only to be very disappointed. Now make your critique clear in a review that employs *yet* or *nor*.

The Archaic For: It Has a Purpose

1. A eulogy might be one of the most meaningful ways that we can use words. Capturing the essence of someone we care about, someone unique and special who is now gone—the situation calls for careful language that speaks to a person's full life, character, and influence. It might be time to use a special language tool: the *for* conjunction. See if you can make it happen.

CONCEPT #4: CONJUNCTIVE ADVERBS

Reasons for Teaching This Concept

There are just some grammar moves that sound *fancy*. Think about when authors use *for* instead of *because*, as in, "I must go to the shop now, for I must buy bread!" Doesn't that sound posh and formal—or at least a little out-of-the-ordinary, like something uttered by a time-traveling knight?

We think that conjunctive adverbs can be put into that formal language category— probably because it's pretty rare for most people to say words like *consequently* or *therefore* or *nonetheless*. We find these words more commonly in certain kinds of writing rather than everyday speech. Like most language moves, conjunctive adverbs imply something about the communication context. Often, the implication is about status: you're reading a serious document of some kind, a piece of writing that calls for elevated language.

Conjunctive adverbs can be powerful tools that bring academic and professional weight to one's writing. Fortunately, they're relatively easy for students to learn. Simple to teach and powerful in use. That's quite the combination.

While we think the order in which you teach grammatical concepts will obviously depend on your curricular needs, it might be a good idea to begin a conversation about conjunctive adverbs following a discussion about coordinating conjunctions. Doing so offers an opportunity to reinforce the concept of *connection* through discussing the meaning of *conjunction* and *conjunctive* and what this looks like in action.

Key
Bold: Teacher talk
Italics: Teacher notes

DAY 1: IT ISN'T WHAT THEY ARE; IT'S WHAT THEY DO

Start by writing the words accelerating *and* shifting *on the board.*

Okay. I've got two words here on the board. Let's talk about what these words mean. What do you think about when you hear these words?
Since these words are fairly accessible, students should be able to give you some clear ideas about them. They might connect these words to driving, for instance. If so, that's great. The point of this first lesson is for students to grapple with these words and to understand their basic meanings. You'll want to guide students toward understanding that accelerating *means speeding up on the path you're already on, and* shifting *means changing directions.*[23]

---

23. We'll be using *accelerating* and *shifting* as metaphors for different kinds of conjunctive adverbs. You might find them useful, but feel free to develop your own comparisons. We thank Michelle's students Amber Steele and Faith Cowley for allowing her and Darren to use these terms, which they created for a presentation in Michelle's writing class.

Excellent job, everyone. Tomorrow, we're going to learn about some language moves that can either help you accelerate your point or help you shift the direction of where you're going. As you go through your day, you might want to consider what these language moves can do—why would we want to accelerate our point? When might we want to shift our point? Just food for thought for today.

DAY 2: EXPLORING WHAT THEY DO—*ACCELERATING* AND *SHIFTING*

Okay. Who remembers the two words we talked about yesterday? Yes, *accelerating* and *shifting*. Good. Let's go back to the question I left you with yesterday—when might we want to accelerate our point, and when might we want to shift our point? *Brief discussion here.*

Alright. I'd like you now to think about a subject or topic that you care about. A topic that you've thought about for a while, that you have an opinion about, and that gets you fired up. This should also be a topic that other people feel differently about. To get you thinking, here's a list.

- The most influential hip-hop artist of the last few years
- The best all-around basketball player in the NBA
- The worst fast food restaurant
- The most fascinating social media influencer
- The most boring (or exciting) hobby you've ever experienced
- The best new app for teenagers

Okay. Once you have chosen a topic, go ahead and write down how you feel. I'll do one too.
You can ask student volunteers to read their statements out loud or write them on the board. You're looking for statements that express a clear stance on a subject. You can use a student example for the next step or use the one below (or your own).

Great. Okay, let's see where we might go next with one of these statements. Here's mine.

Geocaching is a really cool hobby.

If I was going to keep on talking about geocaching, what do you think I might need to talk about next?
Answers will vary, but "why you think it's cool" or "what exactly geocaching is" might be typical responses. You're trying to get at the notion that an assertion or claim is often followed by an explanation, details, and reasons for that claim.

Thank you. Let's see what we can do here.

Geocaching is a really cool hobby. Basically, you use a map app to hunt for "caches," which are tiny containers that are hidden all over the place: in neighborhoods, cities, and forests. Geocaching combines hiking and map-reading skills. Plus, it's kind of like a treasure hunt, which makes it exciting!

Okay. I told you a little bit about geocaching with these sentences, right? I'd like you to look closely at that last sentence.

Plus, it's kind of like a treasure hunt, which makes it exciting!

Are there any other words or phrases I could use instead of *plus*? What do you think?

Students responses will vary. Give them some time to think about it, and offer suggestions before considering the options below.

- **Plus,** it's kind of like a treasure hunt, which makes it exciting!
- **Also,** it's kind of like a treasure hunt, which makes it exciting!
- **Additionally,** it's kind of like a treasure hunt, which makes it exciting!
- **Furthermore,** it's kind of like a treasure hunt, which makes it exciting!
- **Indeed,** it's kind of like a treasure hunt, which makes it exciting!

We can think of these words as *accelerators*. When you're driving a car, what happens when you accelerate? That's right—you go faster. You go forward in the same direction you were heading in.
Help students make the connection between accelerating and providing more detail, support, or evidence.

Now you try it. You all have an opinion statement, something that you feel strongly about. Write a couple more sentences that provide more details. And, use one of the accelerator words that are listed above.
Have students report out or otherwise make their work public, and discuss. Part of this discussion might include the levels of formality of the accelerator words.

Great. You all used accelerator words to amplify your opinion. Nice work. Let's go back to that first example and keep talking. I told you a little about geocaching. Now that you know something about it, I want you to brainstorm some reasons why people *might not like that hobby*. Got it?
As students brainstorm aloud, write their responses on the board.

That's a solid list. Let's see how one of these might look.

- It's kind of like a treasure hunt, which makes it exciting! **However,** if you don't like the outdoors, this is not the hobby for you.
- It's kind of like a treasure hunt, which makes it exciting! **On the other hand,** if you don't like the outdoors, this is not the hobby for you.

- It's kind of like a treasure hunt, which makes it exciting! **Nevertheless,** it does require some exercise, and if you hate the outdoors, you might want to pick another hobby.

Do you notice how these words kind of switch the focus? We go from positive elements to a different outlook. We might think of these as *shifting* words, because they shift the reader from one view to another.

　　Okay, now you try it out with your own topic. See if you can use one of these *shifting* words or phrases to change the focus.

Again, take some time to review and discuss student examples.

Excellent! You all really seem to understand these *shifting* words. There are lots of uses for these—take a look.

- *Comparing your topic to one that is similar but not the same*

  Geocaching involves finding specific objects. Orienteering, **meanwhile,** deals with finding a series of spots on a map to reach a goal.

- *Explaining common misconceptions*

  You don't keep the item you find when geocaching; **rather,** you add something to the container or write your name and date on the slip of paper inside.

- *Anticipating questions that an audience might have*

  Geocaching is supposed to be a hobby open to everyone; **for example,** you wouldn't hide a cache on private property. **Instead,** the container should be placed publicly, where anyone can access it.

- *Explaining challenges involved*

  In populated areas, geocachers can seem a little strange to bystanders; **therefore,** you should be prepared for someone asking you, "What the heck are you looking for?"

Ready to try these out with your own topics? Go for it.
More discussion and review of student efforts.

Whew. Okay. You all did a great job of thinking about how accelerating and shifting can help us explain ourselves better.

　　Let's look at some accelerating and shifting sentences and see what they're doing.

1. The guitar is a popular instrument; however, I think the banjo takes more skill. *(shifting)*
2. Jana volunteers at the local animal shelter; furthermore, she spends two Saturdays each month training service dogs. *(accelerating)*
3. Rhonda, who runs cross country, says her sport requires endurance; conversely, Shanice, who throws the javelin, says her sport takes more raw skill. *(shifting)*

4. Multiplayer video games are popular with lots of people; nevertheless, analog role-playing games such as Dungeons & Dragons still have a large following. *(shifting)*
5. My sister plays in several basketball leagues; moreover, she volunteers at an elementary school teaching students the basics of the sport. *(accelerating)*

Okay, we've got five sentences up here. Some of these sentences are accelerating the information in the first part of the sentence, while others are shifting directions. Talk with a partner and see if you can figure out which sentence is doing what. Make sure you can explain why you think one is accelerating and another is shifting.
Once students have had some time to think about it, open up a class discussion. At this point, you shouldn't be worried about students getting everything correct. The point here is to gauge their thinking, which means focusing on the "why they think this" portion of the conversation. Understanding the thought processes behind why they claim accelerating or shifting *tells you how much more scaffolding your students will need in order to understand and use this concept. You do want to make sure students know which examples are which; however, your explanations should be based on expanding their understanding rather than on solely ensuring that they have the right answer.*

Excellent job, everyone. As you can see, the sentences that are accelerating stick with the same subject, giving us more information about or support for that subject.
At this point you can draw a straight arrow on the board.

We are moving in one direction, and we continue forward in that same direction with more information.

But when we look at the shifting sentences, we notice that the topic has changed in the second part of the sentence. That second part of the sentence still relates to the first part. If we imagine an arrow, this one would be bent.
Here you might draw an arrow on the board that turns: ↱.

Wonderful job today with this. Great thinking.

DAY 3: TO BE OR NOT TO BE FORMAL: CONJUNCTIVE ADVERBS AND CONTEXT

Let's start today by looking at the sentences from yesterday.

1. The guitar is a popular instrument; however, I think the banjo takes more skill. *(shifting)*
2. Jana volunteers at the local animal shelter; furthermore, she spends two Saturdays each month training service dogs. *(accelerating)*

3. Rhonda, who runs cross country, says her sport requires endurance; conversely, Shanice, who throws the javelin, says her sport takes more raw skill. *(shifting)*

4. Multiplayer video games are popular with lots of people; nevertheless, analog role-playing games such as Dungeons & Dragons still have a large following. *(shifting)*

5. My sister plays in several basketball leagues; moreover, she volunteers at an elementary school teaching students the basics of the sport. *(accelerating)*

Remember that we decided which sentences were accelerating and which ones were shifting? Can you all remind me which sentences are which? Excellent.

Now, let's look at these sentences again. There's one word that is doing the accelerating or shifting. Can you identify the one word in each sentence that's doing that work?

Students may need a moment to work with partners to identify the word in each sentence. Or, they may zero in on them quickly.

Excellent. So, our words that are doing the work of accelerating are the following *(write these down on the board)*:

however, furthermore, conversely, nevertheless, moreover

Use prompts such as the following to open a conversation.

- Have you all ever seen these words before? Maybe some of them? If so, where have you seen them?
- Do you hear people saying these words more often than you see them in writing?
- What about *however*? Is that word more common? Do you use it? (To varying degrees, students may be familiar with this word.)
- What about *conversely*? Have you ever heard anyone say that one? What about *moreover*? How do these words sound to you?

While students may use a variety of descriptors, you're after the formal quality of these words.

Of course, the range of descriptions here is pretty wide. Try to honor whatever sense students bring to these words, even if it's only partially articulated.

- Can you think of some situations in which a person might use these words? Or, to put it another way, what are situations in which someone *wouldn't* use these words?

Since these words are unlikely to be a regular part of students' vocabulary, this question might be helpful to get them thinking about appropriate use in context.

Maybe you would never say these sentences that we've been looking at. If you're really trying to explain your sister's basketball activities, would you actually say "moreover, she volunteers at an elementary school"? Maybe, if you're talking to someone in college admissions. But you're probably not going to explain your sister's involvement in this way to your aunt or your friend, right? You might use such a sentence in a speech, but not when your DMing with someone.

So, what we're talking about here is context, right?

Some words and phrases are more common in formal contexts than others, and these are some of those words. We might not use these words when talking to our family members or friends. But when might we use them?

You want to get students to understand that these words are appropriate for formal writing contexts—school papers, college application essays, AP tests, professional writing situations, etc. They would also be appropriate in formal speaking contexts like a prepared speech or debate.

Excellent. So, we've decided these are formal words for formal contexts. These can be pretty impressive words to use. Such words communicate that (a) you understand their function, and (b) you're confident in using these tools. We need to be careful, however, since using these words too often or in inappropriate situations can backfire. You can come across as pompous or snobby instead of thoughtful. Tomorrow, we're going to look at how to use these words in a formal context effectively.

DAY 4: ACCELERATING YOUR POINT

Okay, so far, what have we learned about these words we're studying?
You want to help students remember that they are typically used in formal contexts and can either accelerate or shift your point.

Today, we're going to focus on the accelerating words. Remember, they are the words that help move your point along.
Make sure that you place the word list below somewhere in the room. On the board for today's lesson is good, but students will need to see this list for quite some time before they can pull these words out of the word bank in their heads. Make sure they are on a poster somewhere around the room and that they are labeled as accelerating words.[24]

accordingly, additionally, also, certainly, consequently, finally, furthermore, hence, indeed, likewise, moreover, similarly, still, therefore, thus

Remember, these words help move along—they help accelerate—the points you are trying to make in your writing. Let's look at some more sentences with these words.
Here are guiding questions to help students consider these sentences.

---

24. Note: the list of words here and the list of words we include in the *shifting* list tomorrow do not include all of the words known as conjunctive adverbs. The point of these lessons is rhetorical competence. Students can use all of the conjunctive adverbs when, and if, they move on to become copy editors or authors or English teachers.

1. Sarah sold two hundred boxes of candy for the band fundraiser; consequently, she'll be able to travel to the regional championship for free.
2. Horatio has the highest GPA in our school; therefore, he'll be giving the valedictorian speech at graduation.
3. The lunchroom was wrecked during a food fight; accordingly, everyone involved had to stay late to clean up the mess.

Here are guiding questions to help students consider these sentences.

- First of all, where are our accelerating words?
- How are these words helping accelerate the point being made in the first part of the sentence?

You want to help students understand that there's one point in the beginning of the sentence, then we have this accelerating word, and we get more information in the second part of the sentence.

At this point, you'll want to remind students about contextual appropriateness. Ask them where they might see sentences like these. Are they written or spoken? Do they occur in a formal or informal context?

Excellent thinking everyone. Let's play around with these words a little.

Here's a scenario:

You see some big issues around your school, and you've decided to do something about it! You're going to run for class president! But the debates are next week, and you have to organize your speech. Here are the big issues you see at your school that you would change as class president. Write a short introduction speech and use accelerating words to inform your audience of the issues at your school.

1. The food in the lunchroom is always cold and unhealthy
2. There should be seven minutes between class changes rather than five (there isn't enough time to get to class)
3. The school needs more extracurricular activities

Note that at this point, we haven't discussed punctuation with students. Some may have picked up on it intuitively. When asking them to do this scenario, have the other sentences visible so students can see how to use punctuation. If they ask what they are supposed to do, tell them to imitate the sentences used earlier in the lesson (which, again, should be visible).

DAY 5: SHIFTING YOUR POINT

Okay, what did we learn yesterday?
You'll want to guide students to remember that they played around with accelerating words. You also want to remind students that accelerating words accelerate the information—moving the point found in the first part of the sentence further along.

Great job, everyone! Today we'll work with shifting words.
Make sure the word list below is somewhere they can clearly see. On the board for today's lesson is good, but students will need to see this list for quite some time before they can pull these words out of the word bank in their heads. Make sure they are on a poster somewhere around the room and that they are labeled as shifting words.

anyway, besides, however, instead, still, nevertheless, otherwise

Let's look at some of these words in sentences.

1. Terry should have broken up with Katherine; instead, he asked her to prom.
2. She was always talking about trying out for the softball team; however, she surprised everyone and auditioned for the spring drama production instead.
3. Dante is going to have to get a job; otherwise, he's never going to get the car he wants.

Use questions such as the following to open a discussion.

- Where are our shifting words?
- How are these words shifting the focus of the sentence?

You want students to see that the sentences are heading in one direction—Terry should have done this, but shift *he did something else. She always wanted to play softball, but* shift *she did something else. Dante has to get a job or* shift *he's not going to get that car. These shifting words help us easily move the reader or listener in a different direction without it seeming too abrupt.*

Let's play with some of these in a scenario.

Your friend Cash is starting to drive you crazy. He says he's going to do one thing and then he does a completely different thing. He's a great guy, really, but his flip-flopping just isn't working for you anymore.

Draft an email to Cash giving him specific examples of how he isn't being consistent. Make sure to use shifting words to help explain these examples.

Note that at this point, we haven't discussed punctuation with students. Some may have picked up on it intuitively. When asking them to do this scenario, have the other sentences visible so students can see how to use punctuation. If they ask what they are supposed to do, tell them to imitate the sentences used earlier in the lesson (which, again, should be visible).

DAY 6: PUNCTUATION: CONJUNCTIVE ADVERBS THAT COMBINE TWO SENTENCES

Okay, so we've been working with these accelerating and shifting words these past few days. Tell me one more time, for good measure, what these words do. *Brief discussion here.*

We've talked about the shifting; we've talked about the accelerating. Now, let's talk about the punctuation! Let's go back to some of our previous sentences.

1. The guitar is a popular instrument; however, I think the banjo takes more skill.
2. Jana volunteers at the local animal shelter; furthermore, she spends two Saturdays each month training service dogs.
3. Rhonda, who runs cross country, says her sport requires endurance; conversely, Shanice, who throws the javelin, says her sport takes more raw skill.
4. Multiplayer video games are popular with lots of people; nevertheless, analog role-playing games such as Dungeons & Dragons still have a large following.
5. My sister plays in several basketball leagues; moreover, she volunteers at an elementary school teaching students the basics of the sport.

You want students to notice certain things at this point in the lesson. For example, you want them to notice the punctuation surrounding the accelerating *and* shifting *words— the fact that there is a semicolon before the word and a comma after the word. You also want students to notice that there are complete sentences on each side of the accelerating or shifting word. Here are some questions that can help guide students thinking.*

- What do you notice about the punctuation in these sentences? Is the punctuation the same?
- What's happening before and after each of our extending or shifting words? (Follow-up question if needed: are they complete sentences or incomplete sentences?)
- So what can we gather are the punctuation rules when using these accelerating and shifting words?
  - ○ You want students to notice the following:
    - There is a semicolon before and a comma after these words
    - This punctuation can be used when these words combine (i.e., join)[25] two sentences

      Write these rules somewhere in the classroom so they are visible (perhaps on a poster on the wall). Tell them that there is another way to use these words, which they will learn over the next couple of days.

Have students go back to the scenarios they completed the past two days and see if they followed the rules of sentence structure and punctuation. Students can work in partners to look at one another's papers.

---

25. See **Coordinating Conjunctions** for how to guide a discussion on the word *conjunction*.

DAY 7: NAMING THE GRAMMAR MOVE

So, we've been working with these accelerating and shifting words for a few days and everyone has done an amazing job with them. Now, I want to give you the super fancy, official term for this grammar move that you've been mastering: they are called *conjunctive adverbs*. **Why am I even telling you this? Well, because their name can help us understand (as well as confuse us a little about) what they do.**

Remind them (or teach them by using the **Coordinating Conjunction** *lesson plan) that* conjunction *means to join two things. Help them see how they have been using the accelerating and shifting words that are connecting two sentences.*

Here you may want to clarify two points for them:

What it is: conjunctive adverb
What it does: accelerate or shift

Does this make sense? Tomorrow we're going to look at another way that conjunctive adverbs can join two sentences; today I just wanted to let you in on the official grammar name of the words you've been working with.

DAY 8: MORE JOINING UP: USING SHIFTING AND ACCELERATING WORDS AT THE BEGINNING OF SENTENCES

Okay, so for the past few days we've been looking at shifting and accelerating words that look like this, right?

1. The guitar is a popular instrument; however, I think the banjo takes more skill.
2. Jana volunteers at the local animal shelter; furthermore, she spends two Saturdays each month training service dogs.
3. Rhonda, who runs cross country, says her sport requires endurance; conversely, Shanice, who throws the javelin, says her sport takes more raw skill.
4. Multiplayer video games are popular with lots of people; nevertheless, analog role-playing games such as Dungeons & Dragons still have a large following.
5. My sister plays in several basketball leagues; moreover, she volunteers at an elementary school teaching students the basics of the sport.

These words can combine two sentences, with a semicolon before it, a comma after it. Yes. Good. However, I want to show you another way you might see these words, these conjunctive adverbs, join sentences.

1. The guitar is a popular instrument. However, I think the banjo takes more skill.
2. Jana volunteers at the local animal shelter. Furthermore, she spends two Saturdays each month training service dogs.

3. Rhonda, who runs cross country, says her sport requires endurance. Conversely, Shanice, who throws the javelin, says her sport takes more raw skill.
4. Multiplayer video games are popular with lots of people. Nevertheless, analog role-playing games such as Dungeons & Dragons still have a large following.
5. My sister plays in several basketball leagues. Moreover, she volunteers at an elementary school teaching students the basics of the sport.

What's different in these sentences?
You want students to notice that the semicolon is gone and is replaced with a period, but the comma is still there.

Excellent job noticing these differences. Now, let's think about why a person might want to use a period and begin another sentence as opposed to using a semicolon.
Questions that might guide the discussion:

• What punctuation mark is stronger? A semicolon or a period?
• Why would you use one instead of the other?
• If we can just use a period, why bother with a semicolon at all?

A period is stronger because it marks the end of the sentence. A semicolon tells the reader that what follows is closely connected to the previous statement. One is a full stop (period) the other is a caution light (semicolon).

These are some pretty mature rhetorical understandings. If your students aren't there, or aren't getting there, it's okay. At this point, it is important that they know that conjunctive adverbs can begin sentences or connect sentences with a semicolon.

Excellent discussion! Just for practice, let's go back to your previous scenarios. Can you change one of your shifting or accelerating sentences to match the punctuation here? After you've made the change, think about which punctuation is better for your scenario—with the sentences combined (semicolon) or separated (period). Partner up with someone to discuss the difference between the two sentences and check your punctuation.

DAY 9: MORE THAN JOINING—INTERRUPTING AND ENDING

Okay, we've learned a lot about conjunctive adverbs—today we're going to learn the last little bit that will help you use these fancy words powerfully in your own writing. Conjunctive adverbs can join two sentences, yes, but did you also know

that they can interrupt or end a sentence? Yup. These words don't really have to "join" anything. They can act almost like an exclamation in the middle of a sentence.

Let's take a look.

1. Marlene may have applied; however, she will never get the job.
2. Marlene may have applied. However, she will never get the job.
3. Marlene may have applied. She will, however, never get the job.
4. Marlene may have applied. She will never get the job, however.

1. John woke up late; therefore, he missed the bus.
2. John woke up late. Therefore, he missed the bus.
3. John woke up late. He, therefore, missed the bus.
4. John woke up late. He missed the bus, therefore.

What's happening in these sentences? What looks familiar? What looks new?
Students may realize that options 1 and 2 look like what you've been studying in class and that 3 and 4 are new constructions.

You want them to realize that in option 3, the conjunctive adverb is interrupting the sentence and is set off by commas, and that in option 4, it ends the sentence and is also set off by commas. Explain that these are the other two ways that they can use conjunctive adverbs. Discuss the rhetorical implications of all four ways.

Recap a discussion of options 1 and 2 based on the previous day's discussion (a period is more of a final statement, while a semicolon notes a stronger connection between the two statements).

Option 3 feels like a more final statement, almost like the villain in a movie announcing his sinister plan:

She will, however, never get the job! Mwhahahah!

Or noting the success of a scheme:

He, therefore, missed the bus! My plan worked!

While option 4 is grammatical, these sentences have a clunky quality. This is a good discussion to have with students—just because something is Standardized English doesn't mean it is effective English. You can also bring in conversations about the known-new contract (see "Illuminators" in **Absolutes and Participial Phrases** *and the* **Glossary***).*

Okay. We've learned four ways that you can use conjunctive adverbs. Tomorrow we'll play around with these a little more. Excellent job today.

DAY 10: REVIEW

Okay, we've learned a lot about conjunctive adverbs. Let's see what we can remember.

We recommend writing these major points on the board as students share them. You want to help them remember the following:

- What they are (conjunctive adverbs) and what they do (shift or accelerate)
- When they combine two sentences, they have a semicolon before them and a comma after them *or* a period and a comma
- When we're deciding how to connect the sentences (with a period or a semicolon) we have to consider how related the sentences are—the more related they are, the more appropriate a semicolon is
- Conjunctive adverbs can also interrupt or end a sentence. If they do this, we need commas around the conjunctive adverb.

Okay. Very well done!
  Now that you know all of this amazing stuff about conjunctive adverbs—you know what they do, you know how they can be used, and you know how to punctuate them—let's play around with them a little.
Have students complete a scenario (below).

> Your best friend is applying for a job, and it requires a letter of recommendation from a peer. Your friend has asked you to write that letter! Write the best letter you can using conjunctive adverbs to emphasize how your friend is different from typical people (*shifting*) and in his or her own way, a remarkable individual (*accelerating*).

Have students exchange papers and analyze each other's use of conjunctive adverbs. Possible questions for this analysis include the following:

1. Which conjunctive adverbs are accelerating? Which ones are shifting? How do you know this?
2. Did the author use the conjunctive adverbs to combine two sentences? Did the author use a period and comma or a semicolon and comma? Do you think that is a good rhetorical choice? Why?
3. Did the author use the conjunctive adverb to interrupt or end a sentence? Did the author use commas? Do you think it is an effective use of an interruption or ending? Why?

CONCEPT #5:   NOUN PHRASES, APPOSITIVES, AND NOMINALIZATION

Reasons for Teaching This Concept

As "parts of speech" go, nouns are pretty easy to grasp at a basic level. Still, we think some sustained attention to "how we noun" (and "how we verb," for that matter) can yield some interesting and useful conversations with students, especially about how language actually works in the world beyond classroom walls.

Here's the deal. Nouns are a common subject in early grades—and then they're rarely discussed in detail again. That's unfortunate because traditional definitions of what makes a noun ("a person, place, thing, or idea" or "the subject of a sentence") don't account for the richness and creativity of nouns as they're actually used. In the lesson sequence below, we base the concept of "noun-ness" on the linguistic idea of *lexical categories* instead of *parts of speech*. This latter term implies a static view of language (i.e., that words tend to be only "one thing": verbs, adjectives, adverbs, or whatever). *Lexical categories*, meanwhile, suggests that words can take on different functions according to context (i.e., they can take on "noun-ness" or "verb-ness" as needed).[26]

We also include a discussion of *appositives*—a really helpful language tool despite the technical name. Appositive phrases rename nouns (or noun phrases) in sentences and provide additional detail. Importantly, they also can shape how other people understand certain subjects. By way of quick example, we could follow the proper noun *Kim Kardashian* with any number of appositive phrases describing this person. Some are neutral (e.g., "a reality TV celebrity and spokesperson"), some could be positive (e.g., "a media-savvy star, trendsetter, and multimillionaire"), and we'll leave it to your imagination for examples that offer a more negative version. In essence, the appositive phrases we choose help shape a vision of reality for others.

In this section, we also take up *nominalization* as a higher-order thinking skill—one that has some important connections to expository and argumentative writing. When students master nominalization, they can imagine, contextualize, and manipulate generalized concepts that capture a range of specific items or actions (e.g., *Amazon basin deforestation, virtual reality gaming, social media manipulation*). At the same time, using nominalization comes with added rhetorical responsibilities, including credibly defining these terms, articulating their validity as concepts, and choosing specific examples for a communicative context.

Essentially, the nouns we choose are one way of creating a lens on reality and meaning. And when we help students grapple with this lens, we help them understand how ideas are socially vetted and ultimately used as the basis for policies and decisions by those in power.

Key
Bold: Teacher talk
Italics: Teacher notes

---

26. Do you need to introduce that phrase—*lexical categories*—to students? Maybe not. It's certainly more important for students to *understand* this concept rather than trying to remember another technical label.

DAY 1: EVERYBODY KNOWS WHAT A NOUN IS—RIGHT??

Let's start off today with something you might be a little familiar with. Let's pretend you have a friend who's not sure about *nouns*. How would you explain the concept of a noun? Go ahead and write down a couple of ways you might explain that idea.

When students report out, you're quite likely to get the following kinds of responses:

- A noun is a person, place, or thing (plus perhaps an idea, feeling, or some other abstract concept)
- A noun is something you can touch, hold, or see (i.e., it's something that can be sensed)
- A noun is the subject of a sentence

It's important to acknowledge these kinds of responses as valid (because they are!). However, we'll soon see that they are somewhat limited too (although there's no need to say that to students right now).

All right, great. Are these explanations familiar to you? Have you heard some or all of them before? *(Perhaps a short discussion here.)* Yeah, they're familiar to me too. When I think of common kinds of nouns, I think about *things*: rocks, buildings, chickens, pencils. What about things you can't see or touch or sense but that are still nouns? Like certain ideas? What about the word *idea* itself? Got any examples?

You may get more abstract concepts such as freedom, happiness, or teamwork. If you don't, go ahead and supply these examples.

Are these nouns? Do they fit with the explanations you gave above?

Time for discussion here. Students may decide that abstract nouns do fit with common definitions with a little bit of creative license.

Okay, let's see what you think about these sentences. See if you can find the nouns. Anything seem a little strange?

- My post got 600 likes!
- The package had a message on the outside: "This box contains awesome!"
- My cousin is a carpenter specializing in beach builds.
- Her phone has categories for Contacts and Recents.
- The sticker from the grocery store reads "I love Krogering!"

Aside from routine nouns (post, carpenter, sticker, etc.), students will probably notice the more unorthodox noun use here—namely, likes, awesome, builds, recents, and Krogering. Ask students to identify how these words are usually used: what kind of function do they typically serve in a sentence? A list like the following is worth building:

Typical Uses:

- *like*: verb, as in, "I like pizza."
- *awesome*: adjective, as in, "She has an awesome voice."
- *builds*: verb, as in, "That company builds houses."
- *recent*: adjective, as in, "Our puppy is a recent addition to the family."
- *Krogering*: a new form of a proper noun, as in, "I shop at Kroger."

So are these words also nouns? What do you think?
You may get a variety of responses here. Some students may feel that this new usage is slang and, therefore, not appropriate. Others may decide they are nouns as used above, but, generally, they are not.

For tomorrow, I'd like you to just pay attention to the words you hear and see. Try to come to class with an example of a word being used as a noun, even though it usually works as something else in a sentence.

DAY 2: WHAT MAKES A NOUN?

Welcome back. Let's hear about some unusual nouns that you noticed since our last class.
As students respond, create a list on the board (compile a list of your own and add your examples as well). Take a few minutes to talk about how these words have been used and whether or not students have encountered such uses.

Okay, great job. It looks like *lots* of words can act like nouns, even words that typically do some other job in a sentence.

Now, let's flip it around. Just like some words can do noun work, there are words that seem like obvious nouns but might be doing something else in a sentence. Take a look at this list.

- pencil
- rock
- helicopter
- ketchup
- swamp
- adult
- Facebook

Would you agree that these words all count as nouns? Now let's try this: see if you can use each of these words in some other way—as a verb, or an adjective, or something else. I'll give you a few minutes to work on this.
Students may need an example to get them started: "I penciled in my vacation on the calendar." You can ask students to work with a partner; follow this activity with a short discussion of their examples.

So, all of these words are usually nouns, but we can put them to other uses in a sentence. Interesting. Turns out there are a lot of words like that. Check out this list. Are these words nouns or verbs?

- pass
- dream
- race
- drink
- walk
- talk
- visit
- show
- catch

Students will quickly notice that these words—and many others—can act as both nouns and verbs. We want students to realize that the function of many words isn't set in stone—rather, it depends on context.

Great. So how do we know if *dream* or *walk* is a noun or a verb in a sentence?
Ideally, you're looking for responses such as, "You have to look at the sentence and figure out what the word is doing" or "It depends on the situation."

All right. Excellent. We've figured out that many words aren't locked in to a single role. Instead, we can use them in lots of different ways, and people still understand the meaning. If I say, "I Instagrammed my new haircut," you know what that means, right? Even though *Instagram* is also a noun. If I'm selling T-shirts and say, "We have two larges and a small available," you know what I mean, even though *large* and *small* are usually adjectives, not *things*, right?

It might seem confusing that words can change their function like this. But we do it all the time; it's part of the flexibility of language. We probably need to rethink those old definitions of nouns, though, since "person, place, thing, or idea" might not be enough.

Here's a simple test you can use to figure out if a word is acting as a noun:

- Can you put an *a, an,* or *the* in front of the word?
- Can you make the word plural?

Check it out:

- "I got a like within five seconds on my post."
- "I got 300 likes on my waterfall photo."

In these situations, *like* and *likes* are acting as nouns. We can put an *a* in front of *like*, and we can make it plural.

This conversation gets at an idea mentioned in the introduction to this concept: that it's more useful to think of words shifting roles for our everyday uses than to try to teach words as "locked in" to a part of speech such as nouns, verbs, or whatever.

DAY 3: PLAYING AROUND WITH NOUNING AND VERBING

Okay, we've been having some pretty good discussions about how words can do different things in sentences. Sometimes words that are usually adjectives can act as nouns, and sometimes typical nouns can act like verbs. This raises an interesting question.

Can *any* word act as a noun?

Remember the test for "noun-ness" from yesterday.

- Can you put an *a, an*, or *the* in front of the word?
- Can you make the word plural?

Let's see if you can make the following words function as nouns and still make sense. You can work with a partner. Don't change the words—just see if you can make them work as nouns by writing a sentence for each one.

Some will be easy; some will be challenging. Try putting *a, an*, or *the* in front of them, and try making them plural.

- think
- reveal
- eat
- purple
- yucky
- quickly
- better
- regular
- very
- wow
- the

Depending on your students, this may take a bit of puzzling through. Some may figure out a clever metalinguistic hack, coming up with sentences such as, "You use too many 'verys' in your writing." If you notice this bailout, challenge them to create a sentence with more literal noun functions:

- *We preferred the purple over the orange when shopping for paint.*
- *She got a bunch of wows for her performance.*

No doubt, some of these words are tough to move into a noun slot![27] See if students notice any patterns (exclamations and adjectives are easier than adverbs; some verbs already have close noun forms such as think/thought, etc.).

---

27. Music buffs might find the name of the post-punk band "The The" worth considering.

Okay. That was interesting! Nice work. Now let's do something similar, but this time, we're looking to "verb" words that usually do something else in a sentence. You're already used to doing this! Check it out.

- He Snapchatted all the way through math class.
- No need to worry about the recipe—I'll just Google it.
- Jeremy Ubered to the concert.
- She beast-moded the exam.

See if you can make the words below function as verbs. You can do it!

- wow
- carpet
- Christmas tree
- ghost
- Picasso
- Starbucks
- skyscraper
- 'Merica
- Alabama
- Fyre Festival
- shark
- Kanye
- Bigfoot
- your own name

Follow this activity with a discussion. Do students notice any patterns? Are there certain kinds of words that are easier to "verb" than others? Why might that be?

Finally, you might see what students make of this tweet. (See Figure 4.1) What might it mean "to Alabama"?

Nicholas Grossman
@NGrossman81

How hard will Alabama
Alabama?
Might be one of the
Alabamist Alabamings
Alabama ever Alabamas.
Or not.

8:20 PM · 11 Dec 17 from Urbana, IL

Figure 4.1 Lexical Varieties of Alabama

(NGrossman81, Dec 11, 2017).

DAY 4: NOUN PHRASES, APPOSITIVES, AND CONTROLLING MEANING

We've been talking about the flexibility of language, how words that are usually verbs or adjectives can also act as nouns, and so on.

Now let's take a look at what you can *do* with nouns. That means we're gonna talk about power—the power you have to control how other people see the world.

Seriously!

Okay, by now, you all have a solid grasp on what nouns look like. There are all the common nouns you're familiar with, plus words acting as nouns because they can be made plural and can take an *a*, *an*, or *the* in front of them.

You all are becoming noun experts. Now let's talk about one related term: the *noun phrase*.

Here's a noun.

* dog

A *noun phrase* includes the noun and all the words that we might park in front of that noun.

* a dog
* the tiny dog
* my neighbor's dog
* the world's smelliest dog
* an extremely large, hungry, growling dog

You're all familiar with these kinds of phrases for describing something. But just dumping a bunch of descriptive words in front of a noun sometimes doesn't sound that great.

* an extremely large, brown, dirty, hungry, growling, smelly, one-eyed junkyard dog

Sure, that's descriptive, but the list of words in front of *dog* starts to sound excessive. Fortunately, one of the cool things about noun phrases is that you can use them in different ways to provide detail while also creating rhythm. Check this out.

* The junkyard dog, an extremely large Rottweiler, stood growling at me.

Do you all see what we did there?

We have a noun phrase (*the junkyard dog*) followed by another noun phrase (*an extremely large Rottweiler*) that acts like a synonym, giving us more detail about the dog.[28] And doesn't that sound better than the other version, with an endless bunch of adjectives in a long line?

---

28. Technically, this second noun phrase is an *appositive phrase*. Being an English teacher, you should probably be familiar with this term and its function. Do students need to know this label? Maybe not . . . unless you feel like exploring its inherent meaning: *apposition* literally means "positioned next to," and so *appositive phrases* are literally *positioned next to* the nouns that they elaborate upon.

Let's give this a try. Using the sentence starters below, come up with another noun phrase that provides more detail about the first noun phrase.

- My dog, Skippy, a _____, is my best friend.
- Taylor Swift, the _____, . . .
- Seashell Beach, my _____, . . .
- The sports car, a _____, . . .
- The new player, _____, . . .
- We went to Pizza Palace, the _____, . . .

Nice work! Think about this: when you wrote that second noun phrase, you *made us see something specific* in our minds! You got to decide which details were important and what you wanted us to notice. Wow. That is powerful!

Now, check out this picture of a dog. (See Figure 4.2)

Maybe you love Boston terriers and think this dog is cute. Or maybe you're not a dog person, or you don't like Boston terriers, in which case you might have a less positive description.

The point is, you have the power now to control what others "see" when they read your words. For example,

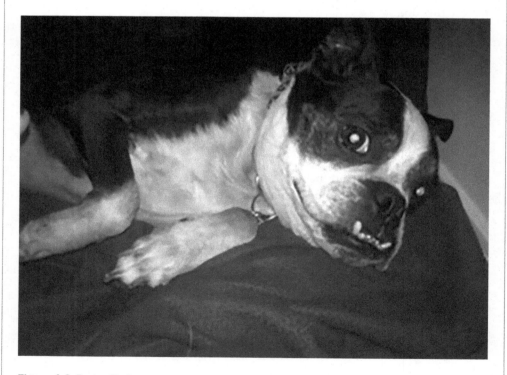

Figure 4.2 Boston Terrier

(anneheathen, 2010).

- I took a pic of their dog, the cutest little Boston terrier.
- I took a pic of their dog, a snaggletoothed beast with bad breath.

Which of these descriptions is correct?
You may get some howls here from dog lovers. At some point, however, we want students to realize that both of these characterizations—and many others—can be factually accurate. This leads logically to a follow-up question.

If both of these sentences can be true, then which one should you use?
Students will likely have a variety of responses. Some will struggle with the idea of multiple "true" interpretations of a subject or event. Others will already have a grasp on how subjectivity plays a role in how we use language to depict reality.

DAY 5: APPOSITIVES AS MIND CONTROL

Welcome back. We got into some deep territory last time. Turns out that when we use language, we're sometimes *defining what is real*. Whoa. Is that dog cute or ugly? Depends partly on the words we use to describe it—especially if we don't have a picture in front of us, and we're just relying on words.

Let's take it to another level. Check out this photograph (See Figure 4.3): How would you describe this scene? Turns out that you have a lot of different options, and the words you choose can influence how others understand what's happening here.[29]

Try adding a noun phrase to the sentence starter below to give a *positive interpretation* of this scene.

- The crowd, _____, . . .

Discuss the examples student create. You might come up with a few as well.

Now, we're going to do it again, but your goal is a *negative interpretation* of the scene. Then, try seeing if you can come up with a *neutral* example. Remember, you have to be accurate. You shouldn't describe something that isn't evident from what we can see.
Discuss again as students grapple with rendering the scene in different ways.

Okay. I think we're doing a good job at noticing how words can shape—or even distort—how we see people and events.[30]

---

29. See **Absolutes and Participial Phrases** for another grammatical move that does something similar.

30. See Chapter 3 for more examples of how appositives and noun phrases can shape people's understanding of an event.

Figure 4.3 Crowd with Signs

(Do, 2011).

DAY 6: EXPERIMENTING WITH APPOSITIVES FOR PASSAGE CONTROL

Last class, we talked about how we can use details to describe a noun and how that description can shape a reader's understanding of a situation.

Today, we're going to see how we can control the focus of a passage and do something similar. We'll start by imagining a friend named Arturo. Here are a few details about him.

Arturo is

- my best friend
- a math whiz
- the point guard on the varsity basketball team
- a US citizen whose parents are from Ecuador
- a Rubik's Cube expert
- a member of the jazz band (saxophone)
- a resident of Holly Springs
- a fan of manga

We could continue with this list for a while; we all have many qualities, experiences, and interests that make us unique.

Now, let's imagine that we're writing a short piece describing in detail some special aspect about Arturo. Rather than a giant list that tries to capture everything, our job is to introduce him, and then go into detail about one specific item that we think is interesting. Obviously, there are a lot of options here. Let's look at how we might use noun phrases to get started.

1. Arturo Arias, a math whiz and jazz band member, is also a fan of manga.
2. Arturo Arias, my best friend, is of Ecuadorian heritage.
3. A Rubik's Cube expert, Arturo is also the point guard on the basketball team.
4. Arturo, a math whiz, is also a really nice guy.

We have a lot of options—that's clear. The idea to remember here, however, is this: we can use this structure to set up our writing because in English *whatever topic ends a sentence tends to be the focus of the next sentence.*
That's probably important enough to say again.

Whatever topic ends a sentence tends to be the focus of the next sentence.[31]

If we know this, then we can use it to our advantage. Let's say we're starting off with the following sentence:

Arturo Arias, a math whiz and jazz band member, is also a fan of manga.

Given that, it's reasonable to assume that the series of sentences that follow will focus on his interest in Japanese comics rather than his mathematical or musical prowess. We might expect to learn how he got interested in Japanese comics, why he likes this genre, which titles are his favorites, and so on. In this case, we might think of the sentence as a formula:

Arturo = math whiz and band member = manga fan → specific focus of the passage

Notice too that if we rearranged the sentence, we'd expect a different focus for the following paragraph.
Arturo Arias, a manga fan, is also a math whiz.

In this case, we'd expect that we'd next get a detailed look at all his math skills.
Okay, let's give this a shot with someone you know well. It might be a friend or family member—your choice. Here's the process:

1. **Make a list of possible details using the same form as Arturo's list above.**
2. **Choose one of these as the focus of the passage/paragraph you're going to write.**
3. **Craft a sentence of noun phrases that concludes with your focus.**
4. **Write the paragraph of details that extends from your focus.**

---

31. See **Absolutes and Participial Phrases** and **Dependent Clauses and Complex Sentences** for a further discussion.

DAY 7: "NOMINALIZATION"—BALANCING THE CONCRETE AND THE ABSTRACT

You all have been doing some great work thinking about how the nouns we use can affect how others see the world. This is powerful stuff.

Let's take a look at a special kind of noun that you all already know a lot about. First, check out the common verbs and adjectives in the list below. Then, see if you can figure out a noun form for that word. If you want, you can work with a partner. There are a couple examples to get you started.

Adjective/verb form	Noun form
Happy	*Happiness*
Communicate	*Communication*
Sad	
Difficult	
Complex	
Decide	
Analyze	
Free	
Exist	
Consider	
Arrive	
Depart	
Transport	

Nice work. Now, one of the ways we were taught nouns is that they are often *things*. Do you notice anything special about the *things* in the noun column?
See if students notice that these noun concepts are all abstractions. Students may need some prompting here. That is, these nouns exist in a different category than nouns such as apple, desk, *or* bus, *which are tangible objects. Abstract nouns can be qualities or concepts, broad categories, conditions, events, or actions.*

Some students will probably notice that the nouns sound more formal, official, serious, or important, an astute observation that we'll return to later.

Okay, yes. These nouns are abstract ideas. That means they exist as concepts that we understand, even though they may not be actual things we can see or touch in the actual world. We might be able to see examples *of happiness*, but *happiness* itself isn't something we can put in box or a bottle, or sell in a store, or collect. Pretty weird, huh?

Even some nouns have a related abstract form that we can figure out. Take a look at this list and see if you can come up with the more abstract noun form.

Concrete Noun	Abstract Version
child	*childhood*
friend	*friendship*
musician	
mother	
owner	
boy	
fellow	
sister	
citizen	
father	
partner	
leader	

Okay. Tell me a little bit about what you notice about these abstract nouns. For instance, what sort of ideas are associated with *fatherhood*?

See how well your students can articulate these nouns as broad concepts. They may be able to recognize that the category suggested (fatherhood, *for instance*) *can be expressed as a set of typical details, conditions, or actions (e.g.,* caring for and raising children, providing for a family, *etc.).*

Okay. Great. Now it's activity time. With a partner, I'd like you to choose three abstract nouns from the list above. For each, see if you can list some concrete examples of specific actions, activities, or behaviors that would fall under that heading. Let's look at an example.

   For *fellowship*, I might list some specific examples like the following:

- Hanging out with friends telling stories
- Helping someone out with a difficult task (like moving or painting)
- Working together as a team on something you care about
- Acknowledging a group of friends for their great qualities
- Arranging a special event for people you care about

Make sense? Okay, go ahead and give it a shot, and we'll see what you can come up with. Extra bonus if you come up with an abstract concept that's not on the list and follow the same process.

DAY 8: CREATING NOUN CATEGORIES . . . AN IMPORTANT POWER

Let's keep going on our noun conversations.
   First, we'll go back to the abstract nouns we investigated last time. Here's a list of other words in the same category.

management	government	activism	statehood	organization	initiative
marketing	publicity	recreation	athletics	entertainment	business
tourism	academics	industry	development	manufacturing	outreach
fundraising	research	experimentation	service	scholarship	hospitality

We talked a little bit about how these kinds of words can have a serious, important, or formal quality to them. What do you think? How do you make sense of these words? What do they make you think of?

A variety of responses are possible here. From a cognitive development perspective, students may be at different levels. Most will be quite capable of thinking in a "concrete operational" fashion, and some will be comfortable with "formal operational" thinking, grappling with abstractions, deductive reasoning, and theoretical concepts. Such students may be able to explain how an amorphous concept like citizenship *is seen in practical and concrete ways.*

It might be worth considering both the concrete and abstract meanings of some of these words. For instance, experimentation *can be fairly concrete ("We practiced experimentation in the chemistry lab") or more abstract ("A spirit of curiosity and experimentation make this company unique").*

A lot of these words can have both a specific and a general meaning. For example, we can talk about a specific business, like the gas station down the street. Or we can talk about *business* in general. How are those different?

With a partner, choose several of these words (such as *service, scholarship, organization,* or *initiative*). Try to explain the difference between a literal example of this word and the more general use as a category of actions or ideas.

This will be a challenge for some students, and that's okay. Help them understand that a little bit of confusion or struggle is normal, that even a tentative attempt at figuring out meanings is worth the effort.

DAY 9: NOMINALIZATION—ONE WAY TO ORGANIZE YOUR THINKING

These noun category words are sometimes hard to figure out. But they're pretty important when it comes to communication in the professional and academic world.

Let's take a look at how you can use these concepts in your own life. To begin, make a list of things that annoy you or make you mad, some frustrating thing in your everyday life. Your list might look something like this:

- People drive too fast in my neighborhood—it's dangerous!
- The rule about no cell phones in class is too strict.
- The playground equipment at the local park is all busted, so my cousins can't play on it.

- There's nowhere to go with a skateboard in town without getting yelled at by some mean adult.
- The food in the cafeteria is bad.
- I hate getting up at 5:30 am for school every day.
- It costs way too much for an Uber around here.

One of the key features of argumentative writing is the ability to envision specific events or situations as instances of a larger trend, concept, or idea. See if you can figure out the broad category that matches each frustration. Here are a few examples:

People drive too fast in my neighborhood—it's dangerous! → speed restrictions
The rule about no cell phones in class is too strict. → cell phone policies
The playground equipment at the local park is all busted. → park funding and maintenance
I hate getting up at 5:30 am for school every day. → school start times

How did you do? Let's hear some examples.

Okay, good work. Now, next step. That category you identified? That can be the broad statement that you can use to organize your writing. You already have some of the personal details—and that makes writing come alive. Now you have the more general topic too. For instance.

Park funding and maintenance in my town is a serious problem. Just last week I took my cousins to a local playground, and every piece of equipment was busted! The slide was cracked, half the swings were hanging by one chain, and the basketball rim was bent. Kids can't play safely in these conditions—it's dangerous!

What do you notice happening here?
We want students to be aware of the movement between general statements and specific examples. Nominalization allows them to conceive of the former as a way to organize the latter.

All right. You know what's next, right? It's your turn. See if you can write a passage that uses a broader category along with the specific details of your annoyance.
Subsequent discussion of student-created examples might consider the various ways to organize this kind of writing. For instance, students might take an inductive, anecdotal approach—telling the story of their annoyance first as a way to lead into the broader issue.

DAY 10: SCENARIO

Specific to General: Some Survey Research

Survey your classmates with the following question:

What's something that bothers you in your day-to-day life?

Once you've gathered some written answers, please do the following:

1. Try to create categories (maybe three to five in number) that encompass various kinds of responses.

    a. For instance, studying for tests and doing homework might fall within the broader category of "Academic Pressures."

2. Write a summary of your research in which you explain both the general categories you noticed along with some of the specific examples.

3. Next, interview some adults you know. Gather responses and try to discern categories. How do your results from adults differ from results from your peers?

From General to Specific: Finding the Concrete Examples

Now let's flip this around. A recent study of issues relevant to young people determined that the following general categories are the most common concerns:

- Cyber Harassment and Bullying
- Environmental Issues, Including Climate Change and Pollution
- The Rising Costs of a College Education
- Coping with Stress and Anxiety

You have a couple of options here.

1. Choose an issue from this study that you find compelling, and make a list of specific examples, events, or experiences you know about that fit within this category. Then, craft a paragraph that notes the importance of this topic, and be sure to balance your focus between the general category and these details.

2. No connections with the broad concerns listed above? Focus on a different area that you know students care about. Follow the same process, constructing a series of specific examples that show how the broad issue is experienced in your own world. Then, craft a passage that helps others understand.

CONCEPT #6: ABSOLUTES AND PARTICIPIAL PHRASES

Reasons for Teaching These Concepts

Wait! Absolutes *and* participial phrases? Together? Can we do that? They're two different grammatical concepts, after all.

Well, yes. They *are* different. But if you've ever taught these constructions, we bet you already know what we know—students consistently produce absolutes when they're trying to write participial phrases (and vice versa). This "error" is understandable. The difference between absolutes and participial phrases is pretty small. And if we're going to teach use-based grammar—grammar that gets things done—we need to be more concerned with the *doing* and less concerned with memorizing terminology.

While we could get into the technical weeds with these two grammar concepts, at their most basic (and most commonly taught) level, the difference between an absolute phrase and a participial phrase is that an absolute has a noun in front of the participle. Check it out.

- *Shining with excitement*, the bride walked down the aisle. (participial phrase)
- *Eyes shining with excitement*, the bride walked down the aisle. (absolute phrase)

The first example is a participial phrase, but add the noun *eyes* and suddenly you have yourself an absolute phrase. Just for our grammar nerds out there, what participial phrases and absolute phrases modify technically differs. A participial phrase typically modifies a noun (in the example above, *bride*) and so behaves like an adjective, while an absolute phrase modifies the entire sentence and so behaves like an adjective or an adverb. Got that?

And, while we're in the technical weeds, we'll go ahead and show you all the forms absolutes can take. Here's the list from Christensen (1968, as cited in Noden, 2011, p. 79), which offers the absolute forms from his examination of classic and modern literature:

- Noun + -*ing*, -*ed*, or -*en* verb[32] (*lip quivering, fist knotted, heart broken*)
- Noun + adverb (*head down, hat off*)
- Noun + adjective (*head sweaty, shirt white and crisp*)
- Noun + preposition (*pen in hand*)
- Preposition + noun + any of the above variations (*with hair standing up on the back of her neck*)
- Possessive pronoun + noun + any of the above variations (*his knees drawn to his chest*)[33]

Are you confused yet? Let's be honest. All of this is a lot to think about, even for teachers. Why would we drop all these nuanced rules and uses on students and expect some kind of magical uptake?

---

32. This "-*ing*, -*ed*, or -*en* verb" is another way to say "participle forms."

33. From Crovitz and Devereaux, *Grammar to Get Things Done: A Practical Guide for Teachers Anchored in Real-World Usage* (2016).

We aren't sure.

These two modifiers, absolute phrases and participial phrases, are basically doing the same thing: they offer more detail about the sentence or some part of the sentence. This is a really useful grammar move (in ways we'll discuss below). But take our recommendation—if you want students to really use these tools, please don't hammer on the difference between participial phrases and absolute phrases. Your students, most of whom won't go on to be teachers or editors, don't need to know the nuances between the two. They'll never be asked to distinguish between these concepts. What they do need is the ability to employ these grammatical concepts so they know how to hone—or alter—a reader's perception of a subject. That is powerful grammar at work.

Key
Bold: Teacher talk
Italics: Teacher notes

DAY 1: WHAT ARE ILLUMINATORS? WHAT CAN THEY DO?

When students enter, have the following sentence on the board:

The teacher pauses in the front of the room.

Have ten modifiers (below) ready on separate strips of paper. Also, have a complete list of these ten modifiers hidden somewhere in the room—behind a poster on the board, covered with another sheet of paper on the document camera, etc. (so you can have a big reveal later!). Choose ten students and provide each of them with a sentence modifier on a strip of paper.

1. Grinning from ear to ear,
2. Tapping their[34] index finger on their temple and slightly smiling,
3. Laughing with the students,
4. Planting feet firmly, hands resting on hips,
5. Making a silly face at the students,
6. Hands clenching at their side,
7. Head turning to one side, eyebrow raising,
8. Twirling their keys around their fingers,
9. Loudly counting to five,
10. Clapping for students' marvelous answers,

---

34. We're using third-person singular pronouns here purposefully. Feel free to adjust.

You should stand in the front of the room next to the sentence on the board: "The teacher pauses in the front of the room." Then ask each student to read the sentence modifier aloud, one at a time. Act out whatever the modifier says you should do.[35]

Once all ten students have read their modifiers, display the full list, which you previously had hidden, and have a discussion with students.

So, if you haven't guessed already, we're going to start looking at another grammar move today. And guess what? These ten phrases are examples of that grammar move. Let's take a look at them. What do you notice about these ten phrases?
Students may notice that none of these phrases are complete sentences.[36] *They might also notice the large number of prepositional phrases or note that each phrase has an "-ing" verb (this "-ing" word is technically a* verbal, *but we don't need to muddy the waters with this information). They will also probably notice that each phrase has a comma at the end.*

In your discussion, see if students recognize that all of these phrases hone in on some aspect of the teacher's actions. Without these phrases, we just have someone standing still. With them, we create a more specific scene.

You might also point out that these phrases begin the sentence, and all of them are separated with a comma. These phrases can come elsewhere in the sentence, but they should be separated by a comma.[37]

Okay, it is clear that these phrases give movement to an otherwise boring image. Do each of these phrases also give you an idea of how I might be feeling at the given moment? For example, if I have my feet firmly planted, and my hands resting on my hips, what do you think my mood is? What if I combined some of these phrases? What if I still had my feet firmly planted and my hands resting on my hips, but what if I was also grinning from ear to ear? What do you think my mood is then?
You may want to mimic these moves as you discuss them so students can see what you mean. Experiment with combining several of these actions for what they might imply.

We are going to call these phrases *illuminators*. That's because they show—or illuminate—one part of the picture that wasn't emphasized before adding this phase. These phrases are like the shaft of light in the picture (see Figure 4.4), showing you something specific. Before this corner was illuminated, you wouldn't have been able to see the flowers. Think like this: these phrases illuminate a corner of a picture not seen before.

---

35. If you aren't comfortable playing actor in front of your students, have one of your more gregarious students stand in as the teacher.

36. Some students may think that phrases such as "hands clenching at their side" are sentences. At this point, you might commiserate while quickly reminding them of the "It's certainly true that" trick (see **Sentences and Non-sentences**). Don't dwell on this misunderstanding. The point is to have an open conversation about the things they notice.

37. Yes, we are fully aware that when participial phrases end sentences, there must be a consideration of whether or not those participial phrases are restrictive or nonrestrictive. However, ask the general population what restrictive and nonrestrictive mean in the world of grammar, and most folks will break out in hives. If you want to learn more about the restrictive and nonrestrictive worlds (because, as a teacher, it is important to know this distinction), check out our other book (Crovitz & Devereaux, 2017).

Figure 4.4 Illuminating

(Khatulistiwa, n.d.)

DAY 2: PAST TENSE ILLUMINATORS

You'll want a PowerPoint or other visual presentation prepared for today (see the figure below). On the first slide, list the ten phrases from yesterday's class.

Do we remember these phrases from yesterday? What do you remember about them? *Brief discussion here.*

Do you remember why we called these phrases *illuminators*? That's right—because they illuminate some part of a picture that was previously unseen.

 Writers might want to illuminate something that is happening right now. Other times, they may want to show what happened yesterday, or last year, or a couple millennia ago. Lucky for us, these little illuminators can be both present tense and past tense.

 Now, I know that when you hear present tense or past tense, you think verbs. But these little verb-like things in these phrases aren't verbs. Here are the verb-like things from our phrases that we worked with yesterday.

grinning	tapping	laughing	planting	making
clenching	turning	twirling	counting	clapping

Table 4.1 Sample PowerPoint Slide

	Energized by the first cup of coffee . . .	
Today		*Yesterday*
(Present)		(Past)
. . . the teacher **pauses**.		. . . the teacher **paused**.
in the front of the room.		in the front of the room.

These words look like verbs, but these verb-like things are part of a phrase, not part of the main sentence.[38] **Got that? Here, these verb-like things are not functioning as verbs, they are only verb-like. They can illuminate something that happened in the past or something that is happening right now.**

So today you're going to practice recognizing the difference between past and present illuminators. I've got some illuminators for you to consider. You're going to tell me where I should stand: next to the "today" sentence or next to the "yesterday" sentence. How are you going to know where to tell me to stand? You got it. The illuminator is either going to be present or past. But you gotta tell me where to go! Everyone understand? Okay. We're going to use the same sentence as we did yesterday, "The teacher pauses in the front of the room." Or maybe "The teacher paused in front of the room"—past tense, right? We'll have to figure it out together!

The other ten slides should include the illuminators listed below; design your slides to look like Table 4.1. Before you begin this activity, be sure students are clear about the directions (you may want to include the instructions on the board).

Here are the phrases for the slides (one phrase per slide).

1. Energized by the first cup of coffee,
2. Eating the apple,
3. Arms crossed across their chest,
4. Startled by the loud noise in the back of the room,
5. Arms waving frantically in the air,
6. Face shining with excitement,
7. Confused by the student's answer,
8. Looking puzzled,
9. Hands dropped by their side,
10. Thrilled by the students' incredible answers,

Ask students to tell you which side of the board to stand on and help them recognize the patterns in these examples. For example, "-ed" marks all of past tense illuminators, just as it marks past tense verbs.[39] *And yes, past participles also end*

---

38. We use *main sentence* to refer to the part of a sentence that remains when we strip away inessential phrases and clauses.

39. But remember, these are *not* verbs. You may need to remind students of this several times throughout these lessons—it's an easy point of confusion. There's always the "It's certainly true that" trick (see **Sentences and Nonsentences**), which can help them realize that these are not sentences.

in "-en," but we don't think you need to get into those irregular verb forms right now (or ever, even). Students will likely figure those out on their own with practice.

Students will also notice that each phrase, again, ends with a comma (and that each phrase comes at the beginning of sentences). Remind them that these illuminators don't need to come at the beginning of a sentence, but just for learning's sake right now, that's where we're putting them.

As students are noting these points, write them on the board. You'll have a list at the end of class about the traits of illuminators. Your list should look something like this:

- Illuminators have something that looks like a verb (but doesn't function as a verb)
- They illuminate something happening in the sentence
- They can illuminate something that is happening right now or something that has happened in the past
- They are separated by a comma

As you will note, some of these illuminators are participial phrases (numbers 1, 2, 4, 7, 8, and 10) and others are absolutes (numbers 3, 5, 6, and 9). You don't need to point this out to the students. This is just for your information.

Okay. Great job, everyone! Let's look at our list of illuminator facts.
It might be a good idea to print these out and have them posted for the rest of the time you work on illuminators.

How does this list look? Good? Does everyone understand everything we've written up here?
Address any remaining questions.

Tomorrow, we are going to do a little more practice putting these illuminators into sentences. But this time, you're going to be the one making the choices!

DAY 3: PUTTING ILLUMINATORS WITH SENTENCES TO CREATE COHERENT (AND INTERESTING!) STORIES

Today is devoted to a hands-on activity. You'll need to print out the illuminators and sentences listed below in large font and cut each into separate strips. With partners, students must decide which illuminators work best with which sentences. This activity assesses whether or not students are able to build plausible sentences from these elements.

While there are present and past tense sentences and illuminators, keep in mind that it sometimes makes sense for past tense illuminators to be with present tense sentences and vice versa. You'll have to explain this in the context of yesterday's lesson in which students explicitly put past tense with past tense and present tense with present tense. Make sure you highlight that this doesn't always have to be the case with illuminators (past with past and present with present). You may need to give some examples to clarify.

Sentences:

- Sharlota heard the sound in the other room.
- She was scared by the ear-piercing shriek.
- She wanted to see what it was but wasn't sure she should go.
- She decided to walk toward the door.
- She trips over her teacup poodle who lets out a yelp.
- She puts her hand on the door.
- She turns the knob.
- She opens the door.

Illuminators:

- Startled by the suddenness of it,
- Pausing to take a deep breath,
- Hands shaking,
- Making up her mind,
- Feet shuffling across the floor,
- Head spinning from fear,
- Breath shortening and speeding up,
- Screaming loudly,

If you want to make this assignment a little more difficult, don't capitalize anything in the sentences or illuminators (except Sharlota's name, of course) and provide students with separate comma strips.

Let students work to put illuminators and sentences together. Walk around the room to monitor progress. Guide them with questions such as these if they are having difficulties:

- **Let's use our sentence trick here. Is this a sentence or is it an illuminator?**
- **Can I put "It is certainly true that" in front of this and create a sentence?**[40]

Of course, make sure you are giving them plenty of praise on the unique story they're creating.

After you've checked that everyone has illuminators with sentences, ask them to tape or paste their stories together and then post them around the room.

Okay, everyone's sentences are up on the walls. Take a walk around and see how other people's stories differ from yours. What do you notice?
Students might notice that different illuminators with different sentences change how scary or suspenseful the story becomes.

---

40. See **Sentences and Nonsentences** to help students learn this sentence trick.

DAY 4: A FUNNY ENDING TO A SCARY STORY

Okay, does everyone remember the stories we put together yesterday? They are still around the room. Today, I want you to go find a story and write an ending for it. It can be any of the stories you see on the classroom walls, not just the one you created.

Here's the catch, though. The ending to this story is actually *funny*. So, get back with your partner from yesterday and see if you can write an amusing ending. Make sure you use illuminators to describe that funny ending a little bit better. *Have students exchange their work with one another. If someone thinks the other group's ending is particularly funny, have that group share the ending aloud.*

DAY 5: ILLUMINATOR SCENARIO

Yesterday's lesson should have served as a formative assessment. If you think your students still need more scaffolding, you might provide a story frame for this scenario and ask them to add illuminators to create more detail.

You just saw the funniest thing in the lunchroom! Ronnie, not just a class clown but the *school* clown, stood up on his chair and painted his face with mashed potatoes and chicken nuggets and started doing a dance. It was hilarious! Your friends weren't in the lunchroom though, and they didn't get to see Ronnie's A+ act.

Explain Ronnie's routine using illuminators to help your friends see the super funny details.

DAY 6: ILLUMINATORS AS OPINION

Begin today by reminding students of everything they've learned about illuminators. It's a lot!

Okay, folks. Let's recap what we know about illuminators:

1. They can tell us about something now or something that happened in the past
2. They are separated from the sentence by a comma
3. They illuminate some aspect of the sentence, giving readers a better idea of what they should see or focus on

Today, we're going to work with number 3 a bit here. Ready?

So far, we've talked about how illuminators can create a more vivid story by making us see specific things. Today, we're going to talk about how writers use illuminators to help *shape the truth* that you see and understand. Cool, right? This is going to help you understand when people are trying to make you think and

believe a certain way. But it's also going to help you in your arguments because you can also use illuminators to shape the reality that you want people to believe. Pretty powerful, huh? Okay, let's dig into what this looks like.

Let's look at these pairs of sentences.

1. Using their first amendment rights, the protestors gathered in the street.
2. Blocking traffic and walkways, the protestors gathered in the street.

1. Collaborating excitedly, the students worked on their project.
2. Yelling loudly across the room, the students worked on their project.

Okay, where are our illuminators in these sentences? Good. Now, what changes in these sentences?
Students should notice that the illuminator changes, but the main sentence stays the same.

Let's look at this first pair of sentences.

1. Using their first amendment rights, the protestors gathered in the street.
2. Blocking traffic and walkways, the protestors gathered in the street.

What's our main sentence here? Yes, "the protestors gathered in the street." Good. But that little illuminator—look at what it is doing. Remember that illuminators *shine a light* on what we want our reader to focus on, right? And we, as authors, get to decide what we want our readers to see, which can ultimately affect how readers *understand* things.
What is that first illuminator implying? Take a minute to write down your ideas. Is this light shining on something good or not-so-good?
Students may talk about how using the first amendment is a good thing, that this feels like a positive sentence. As readers, we might envision a gathering that celebrates our rights as democratic citizens. Try to help students see how this illuminator is altering our understanding of the main sentence.

Good. Now what is the second illuminator saying?
Students may talk here about how this illuminator paints a negative image, suggesting that the protestors are rowdy and making trouble. This version may imply that the protestors are doing something negative and disruptive. Again, try to help them see how this illuminator is altering our understanding of the main sentence.

The main sentence itself hasn't changed, but the author gets to decide how you, as the reader, are going to make sense of it.
Is it possible that both versions are true? Can the protestors be both exercising their first amendment rights but also simultaneously blocking traffic (perhaps not even on purpose)? Why might an author choose one illuminator over another?

You can discuss with students how writers have beliefs and perspectives, and sometimes they will use a statement of fact in the main sentence and then employ an illuminator to nuance how the reader perceives this fact.

Follow the same discussion format with the second set of sentences. Remind them that the main sentence is a fact, but the illuminator shows how the author is perceiving that fact.

Okay, good work today. Tomorrow we're going to look at more examples of how people use illuminators to affect the reader's perception of an event or fact.

DAY 7: ILLUMINATORS IN THE NEWS AND THE POWER OF PERCEPTION

Today we are going to look at how news sources use illuminators. Between today's and tomorrow's lesson, you'll see how journalists can be pretty clever about influencing how we understand facts using this little grammatical trick. Let's dig into some examples.

You can go to any news source and review any article, and chances are you'll find illuminators. They are common in news stories—where better to include a statement of fact and then illuminate what the writer or news source would like you, as the reader, to see and believe?

If you choose to locate your own examples, it's important to use sentences from a variety of sources with a variety of viewpoints (e.g., conservative, liberal, moderate, etc.). Check out www.allsides.com for a variety of stories from a variety of sources. Remember that our job as teachers isn't to get students to think the way we do, but to get them to think—through reading, writing, and talking about things that matter.

If you don't have time to find your own illuminators in news stories, Table 4.2 includes quotations pulled from various news sources.

Rather than showing this entire chart at once, show the Original Sentence column and discuss where the illuminators are in these sentences. Once students have identified them, ask them if they notice the pattern of what the writers are doing (there is a fact in the sentence and then the illuminator nuances that fact, just like we saw yesterday).

So what if we were to change these illuminators as we did yesterday. Would it change the tone of the sentence? *(Show students the Revised Sentence column.)* **Okay, do these illuminators change the story at all? How so?**

Give them some time to think on this, guiding the discussion carefully. Remember, again, the point here isn't to guide students to your ideological beliefs; the point is to encourage students to critically consider how the news uses illuminators to influence the reader's understanding of a topic. Our goal is to get students to think, *not to* think *like me.*

Table 4.2 Illuminators in the News

News Source	Original Sentence	Revised Sentence	What's the Difference?
Huffington Post	Republicans tried in 2014 to use Ebola as an issue against Democrats, *tying it to border security and blaming Obama for the spread of the virus* (Terkel, 2018).	Republicans tried in 2014 to use Ebola as an issue against Democrats, *questioning whether border security had an impact on its spread.*	Two major things changed between the original and the revision: "tying" was revised to "questioning," which may appear less accusatory. Additionally, Obama's connection has been deleted in the second version, removing blame for the president and keeping him from being painted in a negative light.
Fox News	Several analysts on CNN and social media immediately criticized Trump's remarks, *saying he has contributed to the declining civility in politics and should have shouldered more blame for the episode* (Re, 2018).	Several analysts on CNN and social media immediately criticized Trump's remarks, *considering whether he has negatively affected political discourse.*	The first sentence makes the analysts from CNN and social media seem as though they are attacking Trump through the specifics offered ("contributed to declining civility" and "shouldered more blame"). In the revised version, these interpretations are removed and the illuminator uses less inflammatory language: "considering" as opposed to "saying," and "political discourse" as opposed to "declining civility."
CNBC	Kemp rejects her call to resign in the name of election impartiality, *vowing to remain on the job even if the race ends up close enough for a recount* (Harwood, 2018).	Kemp rejects her call to resign in the name of election impartiality, *vowing to ensure a fair election process.*	While both versions use "vowing," what they are vowing differs greatly. The original paints Kemp in a light that seems as though he is self-serving (staying in the role of overseeing the election in which he is running), while the revision makes Kemp appear that he is dedicated to the democratic process.

Excellent. So here are some of the ideas I came up with *(show the What's the Difference? column).* **What do we think of this? How does changing the participial phrase change the message?**

So this is really neat, right? What if I were to tell you that journalists do this *all of the time*? **They regularly end their sentences with participial phrases to add interpretation to the main idea in the sentence.[41] This is one way that journalists help shape our beliefs about things that are happening. And journalists from all sources do it—liberal, conservative, moderate—they all use this tactic.**

---

41. It is also important to note here that journalists use illuminators (specifically, participial phrases) to build a bridge between sentences and include an additional fact. However, we want to make sure our students are critical readers; therefore, we think it is important to teach them to read illuminators thoughtfully through this lens.

What does this mean? How can knowing this about news sources help us read the news more carefully? How does it shift our understanding of facts and knowledge?

Short discussion here.

Excellent points. Now, very quickly, did anyone notice where journalists are using their illuminators? Are they at the beginning or end of a sentence? Yes, these are all at the end. You will find that journalists mostly use illuminators at the end of a sentence, and there is a reason for this that we'll talk about tomorrow.

DAY 8: THE KNOWN-NEW CONTRACT, ILLUMINATORS, AND WHY IT'S IMPORTANT

Let's go back to the news articles we looked at yesterday. At the end of the day, we talked about how the illuminators come at the end of these sentences, right?

1. Republicans tried in 2014 to use Ebola as an issue against Democrats, tying it to border security and blaming Obama for the spread of the virus.
2. Several analysts on CNN and social media immediately criticized Trump's remarks, saying he has contributed to the declining civility in politics and should have shouldered more blame for the episode.
3. Kemp rejects her call to resign in the name of election impartiality, vowing to remain on the job even if the race ends up close enough for a recount.

Here are some more, just for good measure, so you can see the pattern.

1. Still, it remains unclear whether Wednesday's attack will impact Trump's decision to pull US forces from Syria as top administration officials continue to qualify the terms and timing of a pullout—altering the President's December 19 assertion that forces would leave "now" (Cohen, Stracqualursi, & Liptak, 2019, n.p.).
2. With each day, this obstacle grows more imposing as Transportation Security Administration agents, unpaid for weeks, call in sick, creating ever lengthening lines (Shutdown is building a wall, 2019, n.p.).
3. "It is forbidden to block funding to cultural institutions because of the content they exhibit," Deputy Attorney General Dina Zilber wrote in a letter to Regev Tuesday, reminding the minister that the government could not interfere with the contents presented at cultural institutions because it provides financial support (Parke, 2019, n.p.).

You can see that all of these illuminators come at the end of sentences. Now, you might wonder, why would journalists want to put an illuminator at the end of the sentence? Remember, we've already discussed that these illuminators reveal a certain way the writer wants you to understand the sentence itself. Why put these illuminators at the end? What do you think?

Hold a short discussion here.

Well, it is a little-known rule of language called the known-new contract. Here's the gist of it:

> Known information comes at the beginning of a sentence; new information comes at the end of a sentence.

Seems pretty simple, right? But what's interesting is that this new information, at the end of the sentence, is also called the "stress" position. It's the place where we internally place more emphasis because as readers, we know that what comes at the end is usually the most important.

Let me say this again: our brains process writing better when authors use a known-new contract—putting known information at the beginning of the sentence and new information at the end of the sentence.

Now, think about this. What does it mean that journalists put illuminators—that is, interpretations of the facts—at the end of the sentence?

The rest of the time today should be a conversation about this known-new contract and the stress position. This conversation could go any number of ways, but here we want to reiterate our point above—the goal is that your students critically think about the information they encounter.

In this conversation, we recommend that you have several sample sentences in which the participial phrase is moved from the end of the sentence to the beginning of the sentence. You can then discuss with students what they might expect to follow each sentence.[42]

DAY 9: FINDING EXAMPLES OF ILLUMINATORS IN ARTICLES

If the class is tight on time, you can find examples of illuminators in news stories and have students analyze each illuminator's impact on the sentence's meaning.

Okay, folks, today we're going to find our own examples of illuminators in news stories. Here's a list of news sources.

Provide students with a list of news sources—make sure these sources represent all points of view. (Again, try www.allsides.com for a variety of stories and sources.)

I'd like you to go through some online articles and find examples of at least three illuminators.

Depending on your students, you may want them to work in partners or groups of three.

---

42. For a deeper discussion of the known-new contract and sentence construction, see **Dependent Clauses and Complex Sentences** and the **Glossary**.

Make sure you write down the entire sentence, underline the illuminator, and cite the source.

Once students are done with finding illuminators, ask them to exchange their work and discuss how the illuminator affects the reader's understanding of the main sentence. Here are some guiding questions:

1. What does the illuminator show about the main sentence?
2. Is it creating a positive or negative impression? Why do you say this?
3. Why might the writer choose to illuminate this fact or event in this particular way?

DAY 10: A CONCLUDING SCENARIO

The whole school has been talking about it—rewards for grades. It seems that a group of parents and administrators want to start giving treats to students for good grades, meaning that students who turn in all of their homework, pass every test, and do well on their essays will receive "goodies" from the school store.

Choice 1: You find this proposal unfair. Some students have access to tutors; some students have parents who do their homework for them; some students have more time for homework because they don't have to work after school. And of course, there are many students who have none of these advantages.

Write an opinion piece for the school newspaper explaining why you don't approve of the new school policy. Use some well-chosen illuminators to make your position on the facts clear. Remember that you're writing for fellow students, so make sure your work is engaging.

Choice 2: You think this is a great idea! A lot of kids you know don't seem to care much about their grades, and maybe rewards like these would motivate them. Plus, if students work hard to earn grades that get rewards, standardized test scores might also improve. You know that your district and state use these scores in their decisions to determine funding, and your school could definitely use more money. The football field is looking pretty rough, the band has secondhand equipment, and classrooms are drab and uninviting.

Write an opinion essay for the school newspaper explaining why you approve of the new school policy. Use some well-chosen illuminators to make your position on the facts clear, and make sure your writing appeals to your peers.

CONCEPT #7: ACTIVE AND PASSIVE VOICE

Reasons for Teaching This Concept

Language is such a constant part of our lives, woven into the fabric of just about every-thing that we do, that it often feels like a hardwired part of reality itself.

But language is not reality. Instead, language is a *means of interpreting or making sense of reality*. That means that the words we choose can actually define what is real, true, or even worth acknowledging at all. And even more mind-blowingly, this process is often unconscious. We're so used to language as a lens for defining what's real that we don't think twice about our assumptions.

If all this sounds totes deep, welcome to the immense world-shaping domain of words in action. Using language often means exerting power as we try to shape how others see or understand things. We *definitely* want students to both understand this power[43] and be able to use it ethically themselves.

There are many places for these conversations to start in an ELA classroom. Explo-rations of word choice options and how they shape understanding is perhaps the most obvious.[44] Likewise, some focused lessons on the uses of **active and passive voice** can also help.

We all know the conventional instruction for active voice and passive voice: students are told to use the former and avoid the latter. But this advice doesn't account for the numerous ways that these phrasings shape meaning for various intentions. In the lessons below, we explore these purposes in particular to help students build capacity with these tools. We start with everyday situations familiar to everyone and then delve into other areas:

1. Hiding or accepting blame or responsibility
2. De-emphasizing the "doer" in a sentence for field-specific reasons
3. Defining power and access to it

As with all of these lessons, you should adapt as your students' needs demand. No doubt you and your students will come across many new (and sometimes shocking) examples of these tools at work in day-to-day life, especially as those with power seek to maintain the status quo while those with less challenge what is considered right, normal, accept-able, or real.

Key
Bold: Teacher talk
Italics: Teacher notes

---

43. Author Neil Postman points out that we're not simply dealing with "**word** making" in the English classroom, but also with "**world** making" through our language use.

44. What's the difference in meaning between *The controversial singer was **slapped with** a lawsuit* and *The contro-versial singer was **targeted by*** a lawsuit?

DAY 1: ACTIVE AND PASSIVE IN EVERYDAY LIFE, PART 1

Good morning! I have a situation for you all to consider as a way to start us off today. Here it is.

> Five-year-old Brianna is playing in her bedroom when her parents hear a crash. Investigating, they find a broken lamp on the floor and Brianna with a worried look on her face.
> "What happened?" asks her mom.
> "The lamp got broke," Brianna says.

Who has a little brother or sister, or little cousins? Does this scene feel familiar to you? Here's what I want you to do. Think about what Brianna says to her parents. Is there anything interesting about her statement? I'll give you a minute to write down what you notice. Then, I'll have you talk it over with a neighbor.
   Okay, thank you. What do you all think? What's going on here?
The goal with this introductory activity is to get students thinking about how people use language to control how others perceive events. In thinking about Brianna's statement, students may come up with a variety of observations such as the following:

*   Lamps can't break by themselves.
*   Brianna makes it sound as if the lamp just magically fell and broke.
*   The reason the lamp broke is left out.

You might consider listing these observations on the board or screen.

Next step: with a partner, list three or four other options that someone could say in this situation when they're asked, "What happened?"
This prompt should be accessible to students. They may come up with possibilities like the following:

*   The lamp fell off the shelf and broke.
*   I bumped into the shelf, and the lamp fell off.
*   I knocked over the lamp and it broke.
*   I broke the lamp.

Again, it's a good idea to make this range of response options visible for the class.

Nicely done. So, next question. Why do you think Brianna said what she said instead of something else?
This will be pretty obvious to most students with the possibilities arrayed in front of them—and they've no doubt employed language like Brianna's in similar circumstances. If students can articulate that she's trying to minimize her culpability (in their own words, of course), great. It might be worth asking if students think Brianna is doing so intentionally or if her remark is more automatic.

Interesting. Even if she's not totally aware of the purpose of her words, Brianna's response sort of shields her from blame, right? She identifies that something not-so-good has happened but leaves off *how* it happened. Is this something people do often, do you think?

Here's what I'd like you to do for the next class. Think of a situation recently when you were to blame. Maybe you got into an accident with your parents' car, or you lost something you borrowed from a friend. See if you can remember how you characterized that situation when you were asked about it. Write down both the circumstance and your response. Be ready to talk us through what happened.

DAY 2: ACTIVE AND PASSIVE IN EVERYDAY LIFE, PART 2

Okay. Let's spend a little time in groups talking through what you found, and then we'll come together as a class to see what's interesting.

Student experiences and responses will likely cover the spectrum, with some students owning their fault or blame outright and others hiding or obscuring their involvement. Solicit representative examples from each group and compile a range of responses. Ask students to explain their choices—whether or not they were intentional at the time, and why.

Very interesting. I appreciate your thoughts on this topic. It seems that sometimes we "own" a situation or event by using "I" and other times we'd rather avoid taking responsibility.

Let's try this. I've got a list of situations here. See if you can come up with two very different sentences: one where you accept responsibility for what happened, and one in which you hide or obscure the cause. Ready?

- It's your job to mow the lawn, but it hasn't happened.
- Looks like you deleted your group's digital folder with drafts of your group project. Oops.
- You're helping a friend with posters for an event, but there's a big spelling error.
- You ate the last cupcake, and now someone's upset.
- Your friend confided in you, but then you told the secret to someone else.
- Your crew pranked a favorite teacher's car, but things got out of hand.
- You left a big bag of chips open, and now they're all stale.
- You didn't lock your car, and now some of your boyfriend's stuff is missing.
- You missed the final shot of the game, and the other team won by one point.

Let's talk about the different ways we can respond to these situations, either taking responsibility or trying to avoid it. I'm eager to see what you've created.

Students should have fun with these and similar situations—the idea is to safely invoke common teenage dramas that inevitably involve blame, guilt, and consequence. In considering varying ways to characterize events, students gain more control over language.

> **Great work. Do you notice any patterns with these responses? For example, when you take responsibility, do you see certain words or phrases used more often? What about when you try to hide your responsibility?**
>
> *If it's not obvious, you're looking for students to voice some of the characteristics of active and passive phrasing (e.g., the use of the past participle verb form in passive).*[45]

DAY 3: ACTIVE AND PASSIVE IN EVERYDAY LIFE, PART 3

Thanks everybody for your work in the last lesson. We're going to continue thinking through how we use language to emphasize or de-emphasize our actions and involvement in situations.

First though, I'm interested in your thoughts about a couple of words. Here's the first one: *active*. If you would, go ahead and do some freewriting about what you think of when you hear that word. *Active*.

Okay, thank you. Would anyone like to tell us about your reaction to this word?
Active should be fairly familiar to most students as a general adjective, so you should get plenty of relevant associations (e.g., sports, activities, movement, energy, etc.).

Now I'd like you to do the same for another word. Ready? That word is *passive*. Even if you're not familiar with this word, go ahead and write about what you *think* it might mean.
With luck, some students will have a working understanding of passive as a general descriptor of behavior. They may have heard the term passive aggressive or have an impression of passive behavior.[46]

I appreciate your reflections on these words. As you might have guessed, these descriptions kind of fit with the sentences you wrote yesterday. When you "owned" the situation, you portrayed yourself in an "active" way, right? Let's look at a couple of those examples.
Discuss a few of these examples.

Similarly, when you minimize your role (or made it disappear completely), you took a more "passive" posture. Here are a couple of examples from yesterday.
Again, a brief discussion.

Okay. Time for some official terms. We only have a couple of them to remember for this topic, and their names fit pretty well with what's happening with the actual language. The terms are *active voice* and *passive voice*.[47]

---

45. We don't recommend getting into deep grammatical terminology here. The next lesson introduces active and passive voice as formal labels, but that's pretty much the limit of grammar labels you might need.

46. Etymologically, *passive* derives from a root meaning *suffering or undergoing hardship*: imagine someone accepting punishment without protest as a martyr might. This de-emphasis of a subject as a "doer" in a situation maps onto *passive voice*, which does something similar grammatically.

47. While we generally feel that presentation software is overused in teaching, this might be a reasonable moment for a slide or two.

What's the difference between active and passive? Well, I think you already know because you just showed that you can do this!

We can get technical and say that active voice emphasizes the "doer" in the sentences, and passive voice de-emphasizes the "doer." Let's take a look at some examples (see Table 4.3).

Table 4.3 Examples of Active Voice and Passive Voice

Active Voice	Passive Voice
We figured out the answer to that calculus problem.	The answer to the calculus problem was figured out by us.
You should have done the laundry and dishes.	The laundry and dishes should have been done by you.
Richard Linklater directed *Dazed and Confused* in 1993.	*Dazed and Confused* was directed in 1993 by Richard Linklater.
We broke a few rules in order to finish on time.	A few rules were broken in order to finish on time.
I made some mistakes.	Mistakes were made.

Take a few minutes with a partner to look at these different versions. What patterns or characteristics do you notice?

Conduct a short discussion.

Good observations! One of the things you noticed is how the "doer" is shifted in the passive version, often to a "by" phrase (as in "by you" or "by us").

Take a look at the last two examples: the "by me" (or "by us") phrase has been left off. How do you think that changes the message of the sentence?

One way you can tell if you have a passive voice sentence is by adding "by zombies" (or whatever person or creature you prefer) to the sentence after the verb phrase. If it makes sense, you know you're dealing with passive voice. In real life, you'll never get asked to figure out if a sentence is written in an active or passive voice or not. But if you ever need to do this for a class, now you know a useful hack.

DAY 4: WHEN PASSIVE VOICE MIGHT BE APPROPRIATE

All right, all right, all right! Let's keep on keeping on.

You may have heard from teachers in the past that you should "avoid passive voice" in your writing. Anyone ever hear that advice?

Few moments for discussion.

A couple of examples might help us understand what a teacher has in mind with this recommendation.

Tell me what you notice here (see Table 4.4).

Table 4.4 Examples of Active Voice and Passive Voice

Active Voice	Passive Voice
I will use persuasive strategies in this essay to convince my audience.	In this essay, persuasive strategies will be used in order to convince my audience.
Nathaniel Hawthorne's *The Scarlet Letter* is a commentary about hypocrisy.	*The Scarlet Letter* by Nathaniel Hawthorne was written to comment on hypocrisy.

Again, a brief discussion.

Passive voice in the examples below does seem kind of flat and boring, right? And that kind of matches what some of you were saying last time. So, in general, that advice is sound. It's usually a good idea to write in active voice.

Here's a question for you: Why would we ever use passive voice? Are there other reasons to hide or de-emphasize the "doer" in a sentence (other than we don't want to be blamed for something bad that happened)? What do you think? *Students responses will vary.*

Turns out that passive voice is pretty useful in everyday spaces, especially in *what we say to others* about a situation.

Anyone have a family member in the military? Okay, great. There's a rule in the military: when your commanding officer asks you a question, you should answer directly rather than trying to hide the truth.[48] We might consider the value of this tactic in our own lives.

Let's imagine a situation in which you broke something that belongs to some-one else. Is there value in owning up to what happened? In saying, "I broke that" instead of saying, "It was broken"?

What about when something bad happened, and it was caused by someone else, and now you're trying to protect someone's feelings? Let's try this out. See if you can come up with a way to rephrase the following statements (possibly using passive phrasing) in order to protect other people.

- Jaden fumbled the ball on the last play, and we lost!
- Geri didn't save the receipts, so we can't get our money back.
- I failed the test because you didn't help me study!
- Rhett and Wyatt decided to cancel the big party.
- Abra forgot to reserve a space for the band's performance.

It can be frustrating when things don't turn out as you'd hoped. But sometimes, we can resist blaming people directly. Let's talk about how you transformed these statements. *Discussion here. Ideally, you're looking for students to identify the link between sentence structure and meaning.*

Nice work!

---

48. That is, there should be no equivocation, hedging, dissembling, or other kinds of linguistic evasion.

DAY 5: CONTEXT-SPECIFIC USE OF PASSIVE VOICE/SELF-MONITORING

In the last lesson, we practiced ways to phrase statements to protect the feelings of other people. Often, we can do that by using passive voice, right? Does anyone recall exactly how passive voice can protect people?
Discuss how passive voice minimizes one's role in a situation.

Let's talk a little bit about where we might encounter passive voice. Because it turns out, it's also pretty useful in specific real-world situations. Take a look at this example:

> Three people were injured this afternoon in an accident on Highland Avenue in Pinehurst.

Talk to me about what you notice here.
By this time, students will recognize passive phrasing; they'll also likely identify this sentence as a typical news report statement.

Take a stab at why the passive voice might be a good choice for this information. As part of that process, you might think about what an active voice version of this statement might look like.
You might ask students to ponder this for a bit, perhaps jotting down their ideas. The central idea here is that the fact that "three people were injured" is the most compelling part of the news here, rather than the accident itself (which is pretty common). It might not seem like that big of a deal, but for a news report, the idea is to lead with a hook.

Okay, good work. So, news reports are one kind of situation where we might expect passive voice. Let's look at another one.

> Tests were conducted to determine the side effects of the new medicine.

Talk to me about what you're seeing here. I'm particularly interested in why you might think the "doer" in this sentence is relatively unimportant.
Some students might recognize that in scientific research, reproducibility in experiments is a vital principle, which means that who's doing the research is less important than the research itself.

It's interesting to see how research writing minimizers the individual people who are actually doing the work.
   I have some detective work for you. I'd like you to search for signs in public places *that tell people what they can't do in that place*. I think you know what I'm talking about since these kinds of signs are just about everywhere. See what you notice about the language on these signs and come to class with some notes and examples.

DAY 6: RECAP AND EXPERIMENTATION

Okay, let's talk about what you noticed about public signage. If you have examples of signs with the words "No" in them, go ahead and write them on the board over here. If you have examples of signs telling what's not allowed, use the other board. Ready?
Students will likely record examples such as those in Table 4.5; fill in other examples as appropriate.

What do you notice about the language of these signs?[49]
Students may have much to say here. There is obvious passive voice on display in some examples. Other have what we might call a "passive spirit" to them—meaning there is no "doer" who will dole out the punishment for violating these rules; however, there is a threat of punishment. You might also point out that the language of the "no" signs (basically, "no" plus a noun form of a verb, called a gerund) can also be expressed in passive voice (and vice versa). So, "no smoking" can also be phrased as "smoking is prohibited." The bigger question might be the following . . .

A deeper question for you: What is the effect on a reader or a viewer of hiding the "doer" in these messages? How does this language affect our relationship with those in authority?
We're getting into more abstract thinking here, but we believe these ideas are important. The enactors and enforcers of these rules are missing from these signs, and the effect is to emphasize the message as unquestionable and immutable. A dialogue about the rule is not just impossible—it's nonsensical. There are no people involved at all! This is the language of compliance rather than conversation.

Who decides these kinds of rules? What if you disagree with what's stated on these signs? Does this language invite a discussion, or does it communicate something different?

Table 4.5 The Absence of a "Doer" in Public Signs

"No"-Type Signs	"You Can't Do This"-Type Signs
No smoking	Smoking not allowed
No parking / Parking by permit only	Parking prohibited—this property is patrolled
No dumping	Cameras not allowed
No skateboarding	Unauthorized persons not permitted
No loitering	Food and drink are forbidden in this area
No swimming / No fishing	Access restricted—violators will be fined
No cell phones allowed	Do not walk on the grass
No trespassing	

---

49. Yes. We know that all of these signs do not align with a strict definition of *passive*; however, they all hide the doer, which means we can call them "passive in spirit," but, truly, we don't think that you even need to get into these weeds. The point of today's conversation is to consider how the absence of a "doer" affects a message.

More discussion here. A point worth debating: is it possible to invite dialogue in all situations? Is the language of compliance just common sense in some situations? What might those be?[50]

Are more "polite" kinds of signs possible? Let's see if we can imagine some. As a follow-up, work with a partner to choose a standard prohibitory sign and see if you can create a version that acknowledges human relationships rather than hiding them. Design this new sign and be prepared to talk about it for the next class.

DAY 7: PASSIVE VOICE AND POWER, PART 1

I'm excited to see the alternate versions of signs that you've created. Who wants to start us off?

Conversation should be a part of these informal presentations. Sometimes it can be a challenge to imagine a different way of being in public. "Polite Notice" signs, such as those included below (see Figure 4.5), are one example (you can easily find more online).

Thank you for this thought-provoking work exploring what's possible with language in public.

Now that we've connected language to authority, let's keep talking about some of the implications of active and passive voice as it's used in the world. Any time we're dealing with authorities—the government, the police, the military, corporations, or anyone else with a lot of power—we may want to look closely at how language works to support or "normalize" their power.

Here are two ways to describe the same situation:

1. A man was killed today in an officer-involved shooting.
2. A police officer shot and killed a man today.

Which one should we use? What's the difference?

Students will likely have an opinion about these sentences.

Okay. Take a look at the next two sentences. Here's your task: for each statement, come up with a situation that calls for this particular language. That is, what circumstance would call for each version?

---

50. Such as situations involving danger of bodily harm. A sign reading, "Experts have determined that climbing on this structure exposes you to dangerous levels of electricity. Please don't do it!" might be burying the lede.

1. The soldiers were ordered to execute the prisoners.
2. The captain ordered the soldiers to execute the prisoners.

Figure 4.5 Polite Notice Signs

Polite Notice
Please save these spaces
for parents dropping off
or picking up children.
Thank you!

SKATE
BOARDING
IS COOL

JUST NOT
ON THIS
PROPERTY...

For the Well Being of Our Patients and Customers
We Prohibit Cell Phone Use

Thank You for Your Consideration

Figure 4.5 Continued

DAY 8: PASSIVE VOICE AND POWER, PART 2

You all are doing a great job thinking about how the language we use connects to power. We can decide to emphasize who is responsible for an action, and we can decide to hide blame.

We're all used to dealing with people or organizations that have a certain amount of power over us: parents, teachers, preachers, the police, the government, and even businesses and corporations.

But as individuals (and consumers, and citizens) we have power too. Let's look at some examples and discuss options.

- Payments received after the due date will be assessed a $35 late fee.

I'd like you to think about this statement in your groups. Where would you likely encounter it? What do you notice about the language use, and what does it suggest about power?

Aside from identifying the use of passive voice, students may have insight into context (bills and billing contracts) and impact. As with previous examples, this statement constructs a reality in which no particular individual assesses this fee: rather, it is the company or organization itself. Responsibility is not pinned on one person—someone who made a decision that you might argue with on the phone— but spread amorphously across an entity.

Interesting insights. What does this statement imply about that late fee? What options does a customer have?

Students might notice again that there are literally no people mentioned directly in this sentence. Statements of this kind obscure and minimize the power of customers, conveying settled rules rather than a circumstance open to dialogue or compromise.

Let's try this. Imagine that the company behind the statement above is considering a revision toward a more customer-friendly message.

- What might be the arguments in support of keeping this language? What benefits exist for the company?
- Try creating a new statement that uses active voice and includes references to actual people. Then consider the benefits and drawbacks of this new language.

Sometimes, it takes safe experimentation to even realize that alternative ways of communication even exist. There are no requirements that a company adopt such language, but there certainly are economic and contractual expediencies motivating such decisions. The larger an organization, the more likely it is to use "legalese" to remain efficient—language characterized by passive phrasing, a distant and formal tone, and nominalization in order to constrain responses from customers.

Great job thinking through these alternatives. Sometimes it takes risk and experimentation to realize what's possible.

Let's now consider another professional situation. Imagine that you're an employee of a business about to receive some bad news. With a partner, consider the sentence variations below.

a. The decision has been made to terminate your employment.
b. You're fired.
c. I'm firing you.

What are benefits and drawbacks of each option? Which are we likely to hear, and why?

By now, students may be attuned to how phrasing shapes meaning and context. They may be able to articulate insights such as the following.

The first statement both locates the action in the past and obscures who precisely made the decision (which is presented as something that's already happened and, thus, is not open for discussion). While "you're fired" may have some cultural cachet, it's not a common option in many organizations—why not? Most likely because it feels confrontational, even though the "doer" remains obscured. Meanwhile, adding the "doer" gets us something like statement c. This phrasing is not common and shows just how much we're accustomed to language designed to defuse confrontation and convey finality.

DAY 9: ALTERNATIVES AND OPTIONS, AKA DEMOCRACY AND POWER

By now, you all are getting quite good at noticing the connection between language and power. I appreciate that you're noticing examples of how people or organizations try to shape reality with what they say or write. It happens all the time, doesn't it? Especially when people in the public eye—celebrities, politicians, really anyone famous—make public statements about something embarrassing or legally problematic. Instead of an apology, what we sometimes hear is a "non-apology."

Check out these examples:

- I'm sorry, and I regret what I did.
- I am saddened by what happened.
- This situation is regrettable.
- Poor decisions were made.

What counts as an apology? Is there a reason why someone wouldn't want to actually own up and admit guilt?

Surely all students have some perspective on the nature of apologies, if only from firsthand experience giving and receiving them. An interesting discussion might include the sometimes-conflicting interests between personal relationships and legal liability. Many public moments of apology (or something similar) are characterized by lawyerly language use. See the final lesson in this sequence for some scenario-based work around this phenomenon.

Let's talk a bit more about leadership and language. Pretty soon—if you haven't already—you will find yourselves in positions of leadership. That means you'll have people who rely on you to both create the framework for their efforts and to protect them when things go awry. Rather than the stereotypical rule-enforcing image of a boss, good leaders are more about building teams and supporting individuals. That means using language to bring people together instead of dividing them.

Imagine that someone on your team messed up, and now the project is delayed. As the leader, you have to let your own boss know the situation. How do you handle it?

1. Henry made a mistake, so the project will be late.
2. A mistake was made, delaying the project.
3. We've run into a mistake that set us back a bit.

In your groups, see if you can trace the differences in emphasis with these options. *Students will likely have relevant insights here.*

Do you notice how statement 1 basically throws Henry under the bus?[51] Statements 2 and 3 "socialize" the mistake—they diffuse blame across the team. Is that fair? What if everyone else did a great job except him?
The specific circumstances are, of course, essential here. It really depends on the situation—we can imagine a scenario in which Henry needs to be called out, maybe because he's been consistently falling short of expectations. As a general principle, however, protecting those with less power might be the better move.

DAY 10: ACTIVE AND PASSIVE VOICE IN REALISTIC SITUATIONS

Scandals and Apologies

In teams of two, research a public apology (or a statement that passed for an apology) made by a celebrity, politician, or other person in the public eye. Locate a transcript of the apology and analyze its language. Specifically, consider the following language aspects:

- Use of active and passive voice
- Nominalized concepts and noun phrases (e.g., "this episode," "these circumstances," "what happened") rather than direct naming of people and actions

Your goal will be to assess the degree to which the apology seems legitimate based on the language it uses. Prepare a poster presentation that specifically identifies interesting language choices and demonstrates your understanding.

Your Own Apology

A few years ago, you and several friends worked on a series of unique T-shirt designs based on retro themes and classic video game culture. It never went anywhere at the time. But in college you revived the idea, pitched it to investors, and started making real money. Then—boom—you get hit with a lawsuit from your old friends, who argue that you stole their ideas.

---

51. Or "underbusses Henry," if you prefer.

The truth is, you kind of did. Part of you thinks you were justified. Those old designs were just laying around, and you had the vision to turn them into cash. But another side of you realizes that they have a point, and that they're owed an apology.

You want to apologize, but your legal team is in your ear about your liability if you "confess." Doing the right thing might mean giving up all the profit you've made and getting hit with a fine by the court as well.

What are you going to do?

You must make a public statement addressing the lawsuit and the circumstances. Choose how you want to approach this moment, and then craft your language (using passive and active voice and other tactics as appropriate) to reflect your decision.

CONCEPT #8: SEMICOLONS AND COLONS

Reasons for Teaching These Concepts

Part of helping students as writers is figuring out what they can already do and where they can grow. As we've mentioned in other sections (see **Coordinating Conjunctions**), this challenge might be conceived in terms of *functional fluency* and *rhetorical fluency*.

Young people can do some pretty advanced things with words—that's clear when you listen to them in the lunchroom or the hallway, the auditorium or the basketball court. And most students are able to demonstrate a level of functional fluency—"basic" writing and control of language—when they're asked to write for classroom purposes. The level of fluency here is obviously different for each kid: some spontaneously produce complex sentences, for instance, while others stick with simpler forms and structures. For students in the latter category, it can be difficult for teachers to focus on *what is being done well* when the student's limitations with writing may be glaringly obvious. Our attention, rather, is drawn to misspellings and misplaced commas and subject-verb disagreements, and we end up skipping over what's working: the consistent capitalization, the appropriate end punctuation, the mastery of simple and compound structures.

Maybe this seems like we're setting the bar rather low. But we think that an honest accounting of strengths (alongside weaknesses) can steer us away from pedagogical frustration and dead-end judgment ("These kids can't write, and they should have learned how by now!") in favor of practical considerations for growth and, eventually, writing proficiency ("Kai seems to understand overall beginning-middle-end organization, but the repeated sentence fragments probably mean he needs help with sentence sense").

This is where **semicolons and colons** come in.

In the grand scheme, these punctuation options can seem pretty minor. Don't we have bigger issues to address? That depends on our goals. Focusing too stringently on errors with the intent of "fixing" writing problems is bound to end poorly. We'd rather spend the lion's share of our class time building on what students can do, using new tools for making meaning.

Semicolons and colons are helpful building blocks for next-level thinking and expression. Because most students can handle simple sentences, they're ready for what these punctuation devices can do: connect sentences and sentence parts to extend our communicative range.

Key
Bold: Teacher talk
Italics: Teacher notes

DAY 1: COLONS AND SEMICOLONS? SERIOUSLY, WHO CARES?

Have you all ever seen these punctuation marks before? If you haven't, no problem. If you have, what do you think they're used for?

; :

They'll be some discussion here based on students' individual experiences and perceptions. Rather than taking a prescriptive stance and offering up rules and definitions right away, we recommend allowing students time to sort through tentative understandings (or misunderstandings) and reactions. Some may note the use of these symbols in emoticons, for instance, which might be a means of helping students remember what these symbols do as punctuation marks. You might elect to let them sort through how symbols are used in different situations, perhaps with a student recording some general "rules."

So, some of you have seen these before and know what they're called. How about this—anybody ever use this kind of punctuation when you write?

Depending on responses, this may lead to another short discussion. Why do some students avoid the colon and semicolon? For those who use one or both, what is their sense of how these tools function? What are they good for? If you can land on students explaining their own thinking and choices, great.

Okay, thank you. Some of you use these punctuation options. Some of you don't. That's absolutely okay. Here's what I'd like you to do for tomorrow's class. Just keep an eye out for these two symbols. See if you can find an example from your own life experiences that shows how they're sometimes used. If you want, you can do a little of your own research to learn more about them. That's up to you. Come to class tomorrow with any examples that you've noticed.

DAY 2: THE SEMICOLON SUPER HACK

Okay, let's see what you found when looking out for colons and semicolons.

Invite students to share their observations and impromptu research. At this point, we recommend an open approach, descriptive (what do we notice?) rather than prescriptive (that's an incorrect usage).

Let's take a closer look first at the semicolon. Remember, that's the weird one that looks like a period sitting on top of a comma.

;

If you've stayed away from the semicolon in the past, I get it. It looks strange and probably difficult to understand, like it's only for professional writers. Anyone feel that way?

But I'm gonna let you in on a secret: except for the period, the semicolon might be the easiest piece of punctuation to use. Seriously.

Here's the trick for using a semicolon.

If students have articulated this convention previously in earlier discussions, point this out.

A semicolon is used to join two sentences.

That's it. Really.

If you can write two sentences, you can use a semicolon to hook them together. Let's try it out. Grab a partner. Write two sentences, hook them together with a semicolon, and then come up to the board to show us what you did.

Students obviously have a lot of freedom here and that can sometimes be disconcerting to them. You may need to reassure them on the simplicity of this work. Yes, there are more nuances to semicolon usage, but those can be explored a bit later. Right now, it's more important that students have immediate successful practice.

In discussing the examples that students share, you may encounter some "not sentences" that have been hooked to semicolons. You have options here. If you're finding that a lot of students need help in gaining a more stable "sentence sense," this might pivot to tactics and methods to build that understanding (see Sentences and Nonsentences*).*

Otherwise, forge on with building semicolon sense with students, noting the successes in their examples. Minor constructive feedback is useful here. For instance, some students may have retained the capitalization at the head of the second sentence. In these cases, you can point out that with the semicolon, we now have a single larger sentence, which only needs capitalization at the beginning.

Great! You all nailed this.

If you can remember one guideline—a semicolon is used to join two sentences—you have the keys to using this tool. Next time, we'll talk about *why* you'd want to use this option instead of just sticking with two separate sentences.

DAY 3: PRACTICING WITH SEMICOLONS

Okay. Who remembers the guideline for using a semicolon?

Entertain responses, acknowledge understanding, and solicit a few examples.

I'm impressed! Looks like you all have a solid grasp of how semicolons work. You own it!

Now let's add a few more guidelines. These aren't hard—they're more like common sense. But let's talk about them and see what you think. Here we go.

- The sentences you join with a semicolon should be related to one another.

What do you think? This one is pretty easy since you usually don't have adjacent sentences that have nothing to do with one another. Take a look at this example.

- My father likes to fire up the barbecue during the holidays. Last year, we had smoked turkey and ribs for our Thanksgiving dinner.

Do we have two sentences here? Are they related? Can we use a semicolon?
Depending on how your students are handling these discussions, you might mention that what comes after the semicolon often provides explanation, detail, or examples of what came before. This is not a hard-and-fast rule, however, so it may be sufficient that students simply perceive a meaning-based connection.

What about this example?

- My father likes to fire up the barbecue during the holidays. Last year, everyone in our family ran the Thanksgiving half-marathon in our town.

Students will likely see the issues in focus and coherence in these two sentences, which certainly are not solved with a semicolon. The larger issue here relates to paragraphing and other higher-level organizational concerns.[52]

So clearly, the sentences we join together need to be related; otherwise, we end up with something that sounds confusing or disjointed.

Let's do a little bit of practice with using a semicolon within a paragraph. You can do this with a partner or by yourself, your choice. Your first task: write a paragraph in which you explain some strange or unconventional thing about this school to someone who's never been here. Be sure to provide enough detail so that your audience understands what you're talking about.

Once you've created this paragraph, choose two of the sentences to connect with a semicolon.

When everyone's finished, we'll look at what you created on the projector. You need to be ready to explain your choices—including why you put that semicolon where you did—so keep that in mind. Ready?

DAY 4: MORE SEMICOLON PRACTICE: JOINING SENTENCES FOR ELABORATION

Okay, last time around we were talking about how semicolons join two sentences that are related somehow. Remember the example we used?

Let's do a little more playing around with that idea. I am going to give you a sentence and a semicolon. Let's see if you can come up with a statement that would fit *after* the semicolon. Here we go.
A sample to get students started is probably a good idea.

---

52. See our grammar in context discussion in Chapter 3 for possible ways to approach that conversation.

- There's snow in the forecast for Monday night;
- My new kitten is still learning to use the litter box;
- Kyanna is applying to medical school;
- L.A. rapper Blueface just dropped a new album;

All right, let's take a look at some sentences you think would fit for each of these. *Short discussion here.*

Nice work. Let's go to the next level. This time, see if you can provide an example that *tells more about the statement before the semicolon*. Here's an example.

- Beryl is pretty well-known in the gaming community; her last Fortnite battle on Twitch had a ton of viewers.

See how the statement after the semicolon provides a specific example of how she's well known? Okay, you give it a try. You can work with a partner if you like.

- My dad always makes something weird for dinner on Wednesday nights;
- Most kids in school like Mr. Moncrief, who teaches geometry;
- Haley's taste in music is a little dark;

I'm excited to see what you came up with—let's check it out. *Have students share their sentences and explain why they added what they did.*

DAY 5: JUDICIOUS SEMICOLON USE

All right. You all are quickly becoming masters of the semicolon, and that truly puts you in the top 2–3% of student writers. You should be stoked about that.

 Most people stay away from this punctuation mark, but since you all know the secrets, that sets you apart. I hope you feel special.

 Now, take a look at this.

Getting tagged with an obnoxious nickname is never fun; when you're a teenager, however, it can seem like the end of the world. Any effort to get people to stop using a nickname like "Tubby" or "Pee Wee" or "Booger" inevitably fails; worse, such pushback may actually *increase* its use, as everyone sees how much it bothers you. My suggestion is a little counterintuitive; instead of protesting a unwanted nickname, embrace it. This tactic is like a Jedi Mind Trick; anyone using the nickname to get under your skin won't get their hoped-for reaction; in rising above with Zen-like calmness, you become the better person. Finally, remember this: getting a nickname means you're *nickname-able*; you are worth attention from others, and that's better than no attention at all.

I'm interested to hear your thoughts about this paragraph. Not necessarily what it's talking about, but the way it's punctuated. Is it working?

Discussion will ensue here. For students commenting that the writer is using too many semicolons, the natural follow-up conversation might be about the frequency and judiciousness of this tool. When is it called for? How many is too many?[53] A good rule of thumb might be limiting semicolons to one per paragraph—though even that might be overly generous.

A semicolon is a special kind of punctuation. If we employ it too often, its utility may be diluted. Saving that semicolon for an appropriate moment—perhaps when a complex idea needs extended explanation or nuance—might be a good idea.

What do you think about the following idea?

A semicolon is best used in the middle of a paragraph, rather than at the beginning or the end.

Pros and cons of this advice?

Discussion will likely ensue. Since it's useful for extending ideas, a mid-paragraph semicolon often makes sense, as that's where ideas tend to be unfolded and elaborated.

Okay. We might expect to see a semicolon in the middle of a paragraph, though it can certainly appear elsewhere.

Be on the lookout for semicolons in the wild. If you find one, bring it in, and we'll talk about it.

DAY 6: COLONS—THERE'S A HACK FOR THAT TOO

Who has a real-life example of a semicolon in use? Let's see what you got.

Brief discussion here.

Okay, semicolon pros! You now possess a powerful piece of punctuation that you can use for particular purposes.

Let's take a look at a similar tool. Just like the semicolon, this tool is pretty easy to master and gives you more power and control in your writing. Who doesn't want more power and control, amirite???

We're tackling the colon this time. Remember this thing?

●

●

So, let's start by talking about what you might already know about this punctuation tool. How have you seen this appear in writing? How do you use it, if you do?

---

53. At some point, Darren became aware of his own propensity to overuse semicolons. He traced this habit back to some rather ordinary intellectual narcissism: his thoughts were *so complex, so deep*, you see, that they needed multiple semicolons in order to be fully elaborated. Ugh.

By this point, you've ideally developed a sense of community and contribution in your classroom that invites students to share their experiences, observations, and tentative thoughts without risk. Obviously, student comments will vary here. We recommend an inductive approach—listing possible uses and guidelines, inviting feedback, charting possible consensus—before offering up standard rules. Students might also refer back to the discussion on Day 1, which is great.

All right. Here's a look at the colon in action. What do you notice?

1. My sister made varsity in three sports: basketball, softball, and volleyball.
2. If you enjoy camping and hiking, you probably understand the "no trace" policy: take only pictures; leave only footprints.
3. Amal is taking a different approach as senior class president: every weekend he leads students in a community clean-up project.
4. Of the four classic elements of hip-hop, there's one that's only indirectly connected to music: graffiti.
5. The typical Dad joke usually involves a lame pun: *How does a penguin build its house? Igloos it together.*

Following an inductive approach, the idea here is for students to discern conventional colon usages through examples. To that end, you can guide students with the following questions, perhaps working with a partner.

Based on these examples, see if you can come up with some guidelines for using a colon.

- What should come before a colon?
- What might come after a colon?
- What is a colon good for doing?

This work might take a little time; asking student groups to write their recommendations on poster paper might be a good idea. Review these tentative conclusions as a group. It's quite possible that students will arrive at the guidelines that follow.

All right. Excellent work. You all came up with some pretty accurate rules for how colons are used. Let's take a look at the details, starting with an easy hack to remember.

What comes before a colon must be able to stand as a complete sentence.[54]

This hack is pretty similar to what we learned about semicolons, right?
With a semicolon, you need sentences on both sides. With a colon, you need a sentence in front. If you forget everything else about using a colon, remembering this rule will be a big help for you.

---

54. With one kind of exception, explained in the next lesson. As a general guideline, however, the "complete sentence before the colon" is a pretty solid hack and will serve students well.

Now, the second part.

What comes after a colon can vary. It can be a sentence, a phrase, or just one word. It can be a definition, a list, an example, or something else. It depends on the situation.

So, let's sum it up: sentence in front of the colon, lots of possibilities after the colon.

DAY 7: DOUBLE-BARREL PUNCTUATION

Before we begin today and move on to specific ways to use colons thoughtfully, let's take a moment to review and clarify. Remember the rule for what comes before a colon? Let's hear it.

A sentence, right? That's true in 95% of situations. Maybe 99%. There is one circumstance that's a bit different, however, and it almost always involves the word *following***. Here are a few examples:**

- Examples of dramatic long-form TV shows include the following: *Game of Thrones*, *The Sopranos*, and *Breaking Bad*.
- The following advice is useful when traveling: always let someone know the dates and details of your trip in case of emergencies.
- Some food additions should be used sparingly, such as the following ingredients: saffron, cardamom, cloves, and vanilla.

What comes before the colon in these examples don't quite work as stand-alone sentences, do they? Be on the lookout for these quirky statements using the word *following*—**a colon might be appropriate.**

Now let's talk about *when* **and** *why* **you might use a colon. You can probably get away with never using a colon in your writing. So why use one if we don't have to? That's a reasonable question. So, what's a colon good for?**

A colon to introduce a list is a pretty common use; students might begin with this function. You'll want to get them contemplating more nuanced effects, however, so the following comparisons might help.

So, yes. Lists, most definitely.

Let's look at some options for sentences and talk about the differences.

- Amal is taking a different approach as senior class president, so every weekend he leads students in a community clean-up project.
- Amal is taking a different approach as senior class president: every weekend he leads students in a community clean-up project.

How do the structures of these two sentences affect the meaning? Why might we use the version with the colon instead of the other one?

This can be a discussion of subtle differences; understanding relatively small moves like these can help students be more intentional in how they write. Considering these questions means thinking about audience experience as a central piece of effective writing.

Arguably,[55] the first sentence expresses a cause-and-effect relationship: Amal does this work as a result of his unique commitment to the role. In the second sentence, Amal's clean-up projects are the essence of his leadership, the central (and maybe only) example.

One of our students offered a possibly helpful gloss using the shape of the colon itself: it looks and acts like two magnifying lenses, focusing our attention on the important information that follows. We like this metaphor.[56]

Nice work. When we want readers to really notice something—when we want to say "Hey, you! You need to really pay attention to this next statement!"—a colon can be pretty helpful.

Some perceptive students might also pick up on the implication of a logical conclusion that a colon suggests, as in the following example:

- The data are clear and the scientific opinions are unanimous. Everything we know leads to an inevitable conclusion: human activities are contributing to climate change.

Turns out the colon is a pretty heavy-duty piece of punctuation. You can use it to introduce a list, for sure. But you can also use it to provide an example or illustration, offer a definition, or drive home a point. Let's try to practice some of these uses. See if you can write sentences that use a colon in the following ways:

- To introduce a list
- To provide a compelling example
- To provide a definition of an unfamiliar term
- To provide a reason for an action
- To state a powerful conclusion or truth
- To shock with a single word

DAY 8: BUILDING PASSAGE-LEVEL SENSE (RHETORICAL APPROPRIATENESS AND REVISION)

Onward! You all are doing great with owning semicolons and colons. Now it's time to do a little revisioning of some of our previous work. I'd like you to take a look

---

55. Given the complexity of style and audience reception, all of these observations are arguable in the sense of being partial and context-dependent.

56. Another student compared these two dots to the double barrels of a shotgun. At least in terms of getting our attention, that comparison worked as well.

at a previous piece of your writing. Your goal is to locate an appropriate place for a semicolon or colon.

Keep in mind that these punctuation tools aren't appropriate for every kind of writing. Tell me some situation when a semicolon or colon would *not* be appropriate. *By and large, semicolons may not be a good choice for situations that call for simple, clear language: instructions, dramatic moments in narratives, or contexts when audiences don't have time.*

Great. Ready? Go ahead and revise a passage in your work to include a semicolon and a colon.

All right. Do we have a few volunteers to talk us through the changes they made, and why? *Ask students to discuss their choices and reasoning.*

Nice work, all. Now, some more targeted practice. With a partner, let's see how you handle the following. Take a look at this paragraph.

It's time for change at Brickstack High School. For too long, decisions have been made without explanation. New school rules appear as if by magic. Just last week, the student Street Art Club discovered that the designated graffiti workshop space is now suddenly off limits. The media lab hours changed without notice, severely limiting student access. And now the afterschool activities room has a sign on it reading "Standardized Testing Repository." These decisions, made with no discussion or rationale, are unacceptable.

That's why it's time for a radical change. We have a proposal. A student advisory board, made up of elected representatives, should be established. This board will take part in all discussions and decisions related to school policies and rules that affect students. We need a voice in what's happening in this space. We care about our school, and we want our time here to be meaningful and authentic. Our goal is simple. We want to move from an atmosphere of distrust and apathy to a culture of collaboration and communication.

Think about how this passage is structured and then experiment with some alternate versions. You can change specific words and phrases, but also think about the following:

- Stand-alone sentences or phrases for emphasis
- The power of colons to draw attention
- The power of semicolons to link ideas

Follow this workshopping with student examples and explanations of variations, including how their proposed changes affected meaning and impact.

DAY 9: FRIENDS IN NEED (SPEAKING FROM A POSITION OF MASTERY)

Now that you've gained some solid practice and experience with using colons purposefully, let's put these powers to use helping others!

With a partner, take on the following tasks. Your goal is to offer some advice to a friend to help them better understand semicolons and colons. Don't just point out problems or give correct answers; instead, try to give some recommendations that will help them in future situations.

1. Marley needs help. His English teacher is always telling him to "clean up his writing," but he's not sure how to do that. He's come to you for help. Take a look at Marley's writing.

   Skateboarding is not just a hobby it's a way of life. There are a lot of popular board companies Element, Zero, and Plan B among others. The thing that makes skateboarding special is the community. It's different. Skateboarders can be anyone. Punks, straightedge, slackers, nerds. Doesn't matter as long as you're dedicated to the culture. People sometimes think the skateboard scene is all drugs and crime, it's not about that at all. Stop judging other people, learn about who they are. Then pick up a board!

   Help your friend straighten out this passage. That might mean using a semicolon or colon as well as rearranging some sentences.

2. Vela is steaming. She just got her poem analysis back with a grade of 90. *Not bad*, you think, but then again, she's a straight-A student, and anything less than perfection is *just not acceptable* to her. After she calms down a little, she wants to rewrite the piece and turn it in again, and she's even asked for your help in getting those extra points. Take a look.

   T. S. Eliot's epic poem The Waste Land *is a criticism of modern life using fragmented imagery and language; by combining ancient and classical cultural references with everyday life events, Eliot reveals his theme: modern life is meaningless, the things we believe in will disappear, civilization will not save us, your iPhone is not a saving grace, the terror of defeat is looming. The challenging structure of the poem is part of its larger point; we have been trained by culture and materialism to believe that science and logic and technology and lip service to religion will somehow solve what is inevitable, that it will shelter us from difficult realizations; that we will all die, that nothing can save us, that the best of medicine and science and art will only postpone our fate; that the best we can do is reject modern values as shallow illusions and put our faith in the wordless.*

   Whoa, that's deep. And also hard to understand. It's all those long, tangled sentences. A well-chosen semicolon or colon is fine, but too many just clogs up passages. Help Vela clear out what's unnecessary, keep what's important, and say what she thinks clearly.

DAY 10: YOU OWN THESE; YOU STAND OUT

Thanks for all your hard work as we've investigated the interesting world of semi-colons and colons. Maybe it's obvious how these punctuation tools can be useful in your writing, now that you know how they work.

In a broader sense, there's another aspect we can consider in using these tools. To get us started, let's see what you think of this question: how do you think readers perceive you as a writer when they see you use a semicolon or colon well? Do you think there are any drawbacks to using semicolons or colons?

You're looking for students to demonstrate a metacognitive awareness of how punctuation might be perceived in certain situations. This is a pretty refined understanding, so if students aren't quite there, that's fine too. If students land on such considerations, great. If not, the questions and comments below might be of help.

So, here's the deal. People will judge you based on your writing, and that includes the kind of punctuation that you use. Seriously!

Let's talk about the good part first. Earlier we talked about how few students ever use semicolons or colons spontaneously in their writing because they're not sure how to use them correctly. Remember that?

Let's say you're the only student in a class who uses semicolons well. Your teacher or professor notices this punctuation choice since so few students use it (and do it correctly). What do you think the impression might be?

The idea here is that (correct) semicolon and colon use adds a level of sophistication to one's writing. It indicates a subtlety of expression, a control of a wider range of options than is typical. There are drawbacks too—we'll get to those in a second. But by and large, writing that demonstrates mastery of these sentence elements will stand out positively, especially in academic and professional contexts.

So, there it is. Semicolons and colons aren't just helpful tools. They're also indicators that *you can handle such tools well*, which means that you're probably a more accomplished writer and thinker than is typical. Is it fair that people make such judgments? Maybe, maybe not. But knowing this, you can use it to your advantage.

Now, let's talk about possible drawbacks with these punctuation tools. Any issues with using semicolons and colons?

Short discussion here.

Okay. Excellent. You're right. A semicolon or colon is not *always* the right choice. If you overuse these tools, they start to clog up your sentences. And, there's always the risk that people might think you're trying to be *too sophisticated*—you don't want to come off as a pretentious phony or smarty-pants. So, you have to be aware of your audience and the effect that your writing choices might have.

So, how do you know when to use semicolons and colons, and when not to? It really depends on the context: your topic, your audience, your purpose. You have to think about these aspects, and then you have to decide. Does a semicolon work here? Will a colon help me make these ideas clear? When you're answering these questions, you're a writer in control.

CONCEPT #9: HYPHENATED ADJECTIVES AND NOUNS

Reasons for Teaching This Concept

Hyphens can do a lot of things. According to Standardized English rules, they are used to modify nouns, connect numbers, describe words, and join words together to create a new concept. We're supposed to use them when adding certain prefixes and suffixes to words—but only in particular situations.

Like many grammar concepts, hyphens come with nuanced rules for nuanced situations. These rules can make hyphen usage daunting for the writers in your classroom. Take this example:

> *Use hyphens when the age is a noun (or a modifier directly before a noun); don't use hyphens when the age is a predicate adjective, as in, "Sharron, who is 17 years old, is competing against John, her 16-year-old brother."*

Will screwing up this rule keep you out of Harvard (if that's your jam)? We doubt it. Still, these nuanced rules are out there.

At times, you may feel the need to teach a by-the-book rule (however obscure it might be). There's nothing inherently wrong with looking at conventional rules and helping students grapple with what they mean. Our point in this book, however, is that language use is about a lot more than rules—it's about being a thoughtful and effective communicator.

Because we know that time in your classroom is precious, we don't focus on each technical rule. Instead, we show you how to teach hyphens in order to bring some glitter to your students' writing, and a little time talking about hyphenated adjectives and nouns can do just that. After all, who doesn't like reading something creative and pizzazzy from a student?

Key
Bold: Teacher talk
Italics: Teacher notes

DAY 1: WHAT DO YOU NOTICE? WHERE HAVE YOU SEEN IT?

Today we're going to start a new grammar concept. Dare I say that this particular concept can be a little "glittery"? A little fabulous even?
   Let's look at some examples and see what we notice.

1. I was shocked when Zi showed up wearing a homemade-scarf-safety-pinned-dress ensemble to prom.
2. After Carl broke up with Tamera, he knew not to show his no-good-cheating-lying face at my party.

---

3. After bowling a 300, Marek insisted on being called He-Who-Rocks-and-Rolls.
4. She created a new pie recipe and named it Coffee-Walnut-Ice-Cream Surprise.
5. The snow-ice-wind-freezing-rain debacle kept us out of school for two days!

Okay, first of all, what is the language move you see repeated in each sentence on the board? Have you ever seen this before?

Students may say "the hyphenated words" in lots of different ways, which is fine. What we call them is way less important than thinking about what they do.

If students are Harry Potter fans, they may remember that Voldemort is often referred to as You-Know-Who, particularly in the first book. They may be familiar with hyphen use in certain memes as well. Interestingly, Spider-Man creator Stan Lee added that hyphen so there'd be no confusion between Spider-Man and Superman.

At this point, you want students to agree on a term. We think hyphenated words *works well at this point, but you can certainly come up with one of your own.*

Excellent. Great discussion, everyone. Tomorrow, we're going to look at what these hyphenated words are actually doing in these sentences.

DAY 2: HYPHENS AND THE MADE-UP WORD . . .

Okay, today we're going to continue looking at hyphenated words. Let's look at our sentences from yesterday again.

1. I was shocked when Zi showed up wearing a homemade-scarf-safety-pinned-dress ensemble to prom.
2. After Carl broke up with Tamera, he knew not to show his no-good-cheating-lying face at my party.
3. After bowling a 300, Marek insisted on being called He-Who-Rocks-and-Rolls.
4. She created a new pie recipe and named it Coffee-Walnut-Ice-Cream Surprise.
5. The snow-ice-wind-freezing-rain debacle kept us out of school for two days!

How are these hyphenated words different from "normal" words? What are they doing in these sentences?

Students may notice that these are not "normal" words in the sense that you wouldn't find these words in the dictionary. They may also notice that these words are functioning as both nouns and adjectives. Of course, students may not notice any of these aspects. If that's the case, no problem. Help them along with questions that might lead them to these understandings.

Students may possibly notice things that you (or we) haven't considered. Be open to multiple thoughts and interpretations. They may stretch your understanding of hyphenated words here, so be open to the possibility!

Okay, let's think for a second here. These hyphenated words, what sentence slot[57] are they in?

Students may need support in thinking through this. You probably have taught nouns at this point, so you can use the tests of "noun-ness" to see which are acting as nouns. You can also remind students that adjectives modify nouns and that, typically, adjectives come before nouns.[58]

Good. So, we see these hyphenated words that are completely made up and that they are in noun and adjective slots, yes? Wonderful. Great work today.

DAY 3: HYPHENATED ADJECTIVES AND NEW CONCEPTS

Okay, we practiced noticing sentence slots yesterday. What sentence slot are these hyphenated words in?

1. I was shocked when Zi showed up wearing a homemade-scarf-safety-pinned-dress ensemble to prom.
2. After Carl broke up with Tamera, he knew not to show his no-good-cheating-lying face at my party.
3. The snow-ice-wind-freezing-rain debacle kept us out of school for two days!
4. Her should-be-in-the-junkyard car made her late for soccer practice.
5. We got our dog from the shelter, so he is a little-bit-of-this-and-little-bit-of-that sweetie pup.

You want to help students realize that these hyphenated words are in the adjective sentence slot.

Once they note that they are in adjective slots, you want to clarify a few points for them:

1. Hyphenated words can be replaced with one unhyphenated word: "crummy car" could replace "should-be-in-the-junkyard car." But it doesn't offer the same flair as the hyphenated word.
2. The hyphenated adjectives are not connected to the noun with a hyphen.
3. Hyphenated adjectives can create a unique "big idea." And since they are considered one big idea—one concept—they are also considered one word.
4. A hyphenated adjective can be next to an unhyphenated adjective. For example, number five has two adjectives: "a little-bit-of-this-and-little-bit-of-that" and "sweetie." We could take out either one of those words (our hyphenated adjective or our one-word adjective) and the noun phrase would make sense,

---

57. See the **Glossary** for a discussion of the **Sentence Slot**.

58. The raw truth is that few Standardized English rules are written in stone (despite what grammar and style books may dictate). Instead, *fit* or *appropriate use* governs language in action. This notion can be difficult for students to grasp, especially if they're used to a right/wrong notion of language use. There's no perfect time or place to broach this reality. Be on the lookout for opportunities as they arise.

but we cannot take out any of the words from the hyphenated word, because then the sentence wouldn't make sense.

Let's play around with hyphenated adjectives a little. Can we use hyphenated adjectives to describe these pictures? (See Figure 4.6)

(Delso, 2015)

(Morin, 2018)

(M 93, 2012)

Figure 4.6 Images to Practice Hyphenated Adjectives

Rather than putting one picture on the board at a time, we recommend putting all of the pictures on the board so students will have a variety from which to choose. If none of these images relate to your students, you can find copyright-free images on Wikimedia Commons.

Okay, everyone, here's a sentence I wrote.

His don't-mess-with-me stare made me back away.

Questions for discussion:

1. Which picture am I describing?
2. Where is my hyphenated adjective?
3. Do I connect my hyphenated adjective to my noun? (No!)
4. What other word might substitute for the hyphenated adjective?

Let's play around with this and see what you can come up with.
Once students have created their sentences, check their understanding. See "Checking Student Understanding Without Demoralizing" in the introduction to Chapter 4 for a variety of ways to do this—your choice should be dependent on your students' confidence and understanding of the concept.

Note here that students may create hyphenated nouns. If they do, that's great. That means they're beginning to understand the concept. You might want to point it out to them quickly, praise them on getting the concept, and move on. Now is probably not the time to split hairs.

Excellent job today, everyone. How cool is it that you can make up your own words by using hyphens?

DAY 4: HYPHENATED NOUNS AND NEW CONCEPTS

Remember yesterday we looked at hyphenated adjectives? Great. So, what do we remember about hyphenated adjectives?
Among other observations, students might recall the following points:

1. Hyphenated adjectives create new concepts and are considered one word (you could, if you wanted to be duller, replace the hyphenated adjective with one word).
2. They are not connected with a hyphen to the noun they modify.
3. A hyphenated adjective and an unhyphenated adjective can modify the same noun.

Excellent. Now, today we're going to look at *hyphenated nouns*. Aww, yeah.
     Here are a few sentences that you've seen before along with some you haven't—let's take a look at them.

1. After bowling a 300, Marek insisted on being called He-Who-Rocks-and-Rolls.
2. My kinda-boyfriend-kinda-friend asked me to the movies.
3. Sophia told me to meet her at the mall-corner-cafe.
4. Li created a pie recipe and named it Coffee-Walnut-Ice-Cream-Surprise.
5. His music might be considered jazz-classical-bluegrass.

Okay, just to remind ourselves. These hyphenated words, what sentence slot are they taking? Yes, that's right, they are all nouns. And you can see these hyphenated nouns can go anywhere in a sentence that a plain, ole boring noun can go, right? But what's fantastic is that these hyphenated nouns give the sentence a playful feel, and better yet, we can create ideas and images that can't be done with "regular" words.

I mean, don't we all know someone like Marek? Someone who after accomplishing something pretty cool, likes to make sure we know how awesome he is by making up his own silly nickname?

Well, these hyphenated nouns allow Marek a way to express his own sense of awesomeness. Without the hyphenated noun, the story isn't quite as memorable, right? Okay, we're going to talk about their rhetorical power a little bit more tomorrow, so let's play around right now and create some hyphenated nouns.

Like yesterday, I have some images here. Check it out (See Figure 4.7).

Here's my sentence:

Naomi's sister, a part-time-costume-designer-part-time-actor, made me this outfit.

Which picture am I describing?

If your students are as clever as ours, they'll probably try to convince you that the sentence could describe all three. If they do this, praise them for their creativity and then ask them which one is, most likely, a costume.

Okay, good. Now you all play around and see if you can create a sentence that has a hyphenated noun that describes one of these pictures.

Once students have created their sentences, check their understanding—again, your tactics here should be dependent on your students' confidence and understanding of the concept.

Excellent job today, everyone.

(Kuarum a la Fledermaus, 2007)

(Sharp, 2017)

(Touhid, 2016)

Figure 4.7 Images to Practice Hyphenated Nouns

DAY 5: WITH OR WITHOUT THEM?

Okay, today we're going back to some of our original sentences with hyphens, but they now have a partner sentence. Let's look at them.

1. I was shocked when Zi showed up wearing a homemade-scarf-safety-pinned-dress ensemble to prom.

    a. *I was shocked when Zi showed up wearing a homemade dress to prom. It was made up of a scarf and lots of safety pins.*

2. After Carl broke up with Tamera, he knew not to show his no-good-cheating-lying face at my party.

    a. *After Carl broke up with Tamera, he knew not to show up at my party. He cheats and lies.*

3. The snow-ice-wind-freezing-rain debacle kept us out of school for two days!

    a. *The storm kept us out of school for two days!*

4. Her should-be-in-the-junkyard car made her late for soccer practice.

    a. *Her old beater made her late for soccer practice.*

5. We got our dog from the shelter, so he is a little-bit-of-this-and-little-bit-of-that sweetie pup.

    a. *We got our dog from the shelter, so he is a mutt but a sweetie pup.*

Okay, so you can see that, without much work, we were able to revise these sentences to take out the hyphenated word. But what happens when we take out that hyphenated word? Let's look at the first sentence and its partner sentence closely and talk about what happened.

In this discussion, highlight that especially in this construction, hyphenated words contribute to an original style and can create a playful tone. So, we have to think of our audience for writing—will a unique style or a playful tone help or hurt our point with our readers?

You may want to discuss more than one example with the students, but you can be pretty consistent in your conversations. Hyphenated words lend themselves to alternate perspectives: of humor, irony, sarcasm, or lightheartedness.

Here are some specifics you might want to discuss:

- *Sentence 2 succinctly describes Carl and clearly conveys an attitude about him.*
- *In sentence 3, the "the snow-ice-freezing-rain debacle" is much more descriptive than "storm" and also conveys an attitude (sarcasm?) about the event. So, hyphenated words can suggest a stance toward a subject.*

- *Sentence 5 provides an example that hyphenated words demonstrate the voice of the speaker. "Mutt" is a common, everyday word; however, "a little-bit-of-this-and-little-bit-of-that" is an uncommon construction, thereby demonstrating an uncommon speaker.*

In these types of conversations, there is power in students exploring how to express ideas in new ways.

How many of these details you discuss as a class and how many you ask students to discuss in groups (and then share out) will be dependent on the students' comfort with the concept and your comfort discussing rhetorical grammar moves.

Okay, folks, excellent job today! So, you can see that hyphenated words can create a new concept in a way that regular, ole words just can't

---

DAY 6: SCENARIO TIME!

Okay! I've got a situation for you to think about.

It is unbelievable! Your little town in Florida got their first snow in 30 years, and no one knows how to drive or what to do with the six inches of snow! It is a completely new experience for everyone. You just took a walk around the neighborhood and saw some pretty ridiculous sights: people using laundry baskets as sleds; others standing on sheets of plastic and being pulled by a rope behind a four-wheeler; your neighbor's chihuahua, Sweetie-Poo, jumping through the snow since it's too deep for him to walk. This is just the experience that you've been waiting for—the story you can write that will set your application apart for the writer's residency in Fairbanks, Alaska, this summer.

You just got home from your walk where you saw all of these amazing sights. Jot down a quick paragraph describing the scene, making it vivid and interesting for a reader. Use hyphenated words to really make these images, and the larger scene of Florida snow, stand out.

DAY 7: TO HYPHEN OR NOT TO HYPHEN?

Okay, folks. So yesterday you all wrote a response to a scenario about the crazy Florida snow and all of the amazing things you saw people (and Sweetie-Poo!) doing in that snow. Today, we're going to look at how those hyphenated words change the tone of your writing.

This work can be done in any number of ways and should be dependent upon your students' comfort and understanding of the concepts.

Here's one. Have students work in groups of three to review yesterday's responses. First, ask students to switch papers with one person, then have that person choose two sentences that have hyphenated words that are particularly good or funny. Then have that second person rewrite those sentences without the hyphenated words (they may have to change the sentence significantly for this to work). Then have them switch with the third person in the group. Have the third person analyze whether or not the paragraph is better with or without the hyphenated words. Here are some guiding questions that can help students in this process:

- Is the image the author is trying to convey stronger or weaker with the hyphenated words?
- Is the narrative funnier or more entertaining with the hyphenated words than without them?
- Which one is more interesting to read? Why do you think so?
- What are some other differences you notice between versions with hyphenated words and those without?

Have a class discussion based on what the groups found. Keep in mind that you may have students argue that the hyphenated words are problematic—there were too many of them, or they made the reading difficult to process, or something similar. This is a valid argument worth discussing. Sometimes authors can lean too heavily on a grammar move (something we're all guilty of from time to time). At this point, you might also open a conversation about the pitfalls of "too many cool grammar moves" in a piece of writing.[59]

Be open to all opinions and see if you can find a rational basis for them all. Just as many thematic interpretations of Hamlet *can be valid, so might multiple interpretations of hyphenated words have merit.*

DAY 8: ACADEMIC WRITING: HOW DO WE USE THESE FANCY HYPHENS WITH FORMAL ADJECTIVES?

So the last few days we've been learning fun ways to use hyphens. Turns out that sometimes hyphens are needed for clarity too. The next two days we're going to look at some Standardized English rules for hyphen usage. Take a look at this.

- Look at the man-eating fish.
- Look at the man eating fish.

What do you notice about these two sentences?
Brief discussion here. You may need to remind students that hyphenated words can create a new concept. You want to help students understand that in the first sentence, both "man" and "eating" are combined to create one concept that modifies fish, which may

---

59. The issue here is one of judicious control and effectiveness. Some student writers may feel compelled to demonstrate *how much they can do with words* regardless of whether such extravagance is called for, in which case the challenge becomes one of moderation and audience fit.

conjure images of sharks and the like. So, "a man-eating fish" creates one particular image while "a man eating fish" creates another image: a guy sitting down for a fish dinner.

Clearly, hyphenated adjectives can really affect our understanding of a noun.

Here's where you want to introduce a couple of quick rules when considering hyphenated adjectives.

Sometimes we need to consider whether or not the adjectives need the hyphen. Here are a couple of tests. Let's say we want to conjure the image of a fish that can literally devour a person. Do we hyphenate or not?

Test 1: Can we switch the words with the sentence still having the same meaning?

Look at the eating-man fish.

Hmm . . . nope. That's sounds very odd.

Test 2: Can we drop one of the words with the sentence still having the same meaning?

Look at the man fish.
Look at the eating fish.

No. Neither of these make sense.

We have to assume, then, that we need both "man" and "eating" to talk about a "man-eating fish," which means the two words need a hyphen between them.

Let's look at some more sentences and see how the hyphen changes the meaning of the sentence.

1. (Thirty odd) students tried out for the play.

    We can say "thirty odd" students, which denotes that those thirty students are peculiar.
    Or we can say "thirty-odd" students, which means 30+ students.

2. He got a deal on a (little used) car.

    We can say "little used" car, which means that the used car is compact.
    Or we can say "little-used" car, meaning that the car has only been used for a short time.

3. The group was made up of (six foot) doctors.

    We can say "six foot" doctors, which means we have six doctors specializing in podiatry.
    Or we can say "six-foot" doctors, meaning we have a group of tall doctors.

Excellent. Let's look at a couple more examples and see if you all can figure them out—do we need hyphens or not? Make sure to use our two tests.

Those tests should be posted somewhere for students to see during this activity.

1. Marcus loved buying (old fashioned) music equipment.
2. The (long term) plan for the band was still undecided.
3. Can you imagine being the (clean up) crew for the (dog friendly) beach?

Have students discuss their answers and their reasoning behind their thinking. Students' meta-critical comments—why they're thinking what they're thinking, basically—help you understand what they know and what you may need to teach or reteach.

Excellent job, everyone.[60]

DAY 9: ACADEMIC WRITING: HYPHENS WITH FORMAL NOUNS

So today is a tricky lesson and let me tell you why. The rules that I'm going to share with you change all of the time and what one person thinks is right, another person might think is wrong. And that's the beautiful frustration of hyphenated nouns.

Let's look at what I mean. All of these words used to be hyphenated (Rabino-vitch, 2007):

- Ice cream used to be ice-cream
- Bumblebee used to be bumble-bee
- Fig leaf used to be fig-leaf
- Leapfrog used to be leap-frog
- Lowlife used to be low-life

Look at that. And what's crazier is that some of those words just dropped the hyphen and became two words and others decided to smush themselves together and become a compound word. I would like to tell you that there is a rhyme or reason for these changes, but it's just the English language marching on, evolving as times change. Sometimes, there are no logical explanations.

Turns out that there are nouns that just can't decide what they want to be, so supersmart grammar folks say they can be any of these, depending on context.

---

60. There are several other adjective-hyphen rules that we don't delve into deeply here, such as those for indicating age. If you find that your students need these lessons (meaning these types of mistakes in their writing are impeding understandability), then you can follow the same format as found in this day's lesson. We should also remember here that, typically, predicate adjectives aren't hyphenated, so we could say, "I like the dog-friendly beach," but would say, "The beach is dog friendly." (And even this rule isn't always hard and fast.) But these are exactly the kinds of weeds in which we lose students. We aren't advocating for including days eight through ten in your hyphen instruction. We just wanted to show you what it might look like if your students' writing is suffering because of hyphens. After all, there may be more pressing needs than memorizing the nebulous rules of Standardized English hyphenated adjectives.

- Water-bottle or water bottle
- Playgroup or play-group or play group
- Changing room or changing-room

So which one do you use? Well, that depends on your intention and audience. You know, those rhetorical choices. This is why we can't always just look up the answer in a grammar book: even the experts agree that sometimes, it's just up to the author, and that's you!

   Now, there are a couple of hard and fast rules about hyphenated nouns. You hyphenate some family relationships:

1. My sister-in-law just got back from a month-long vacation in Australia!
2. Ralfano told me that his great-great-grandmother was a famous writer and artist.
3. I didn't know that her father-in-law trained horses.

I'm sure you've seen this, and it is a pretty easy rule to remember, right?

   The next one can be just a little tricky, and it relates to both nouns and adjectives. Think of proper nouns, and the specific things they name. Remember, proper nouns are almost always capitalized (as in Chicago, Beyoncé, Jupiter, December, Halloween, and so on).

   When we add a prefix to a proper noun, we use a hyphen whether it is a noun or an adjective.

1. I will see you in mid-July.
2. She has a mid-July birthday.

Help students see that sentence 1 has a hyphenated noun and sentence 2 has a hyphenated adjective. However, both need to be hyphenated because the prefix is attached to a proper noun.

And someone somewhere is going to be sad if we don't at least look at the rule for ages and hyphens. Here are some examples.

1. He is an 80-year-old rock star.
2. My 16-year-old friend just got his driver's license.
3. Her mom is 40 years old.
4. The two-year-old screamed for his mother.
5. Her car is 100 years old.
6. The 25-year-old just graduated college.
7. She knows her six-year-old son will do great in school.

Okay. I've given you a bunch of sentences here. I think I've given you enough to figure out the rule—these are all used correctly. Can you look at them with a partner and figure out what the rule for hyphenated ages is?

You can provide the following as guiding questions:

- Is the age coming before or after the verb?
- Is the age modifying a noun (meaning it is an adjective)?
- Or is it a noun (remember to use our test for nouns)?

These questions should help students come to the following conclusions:

- You hyphenate an age when it is an adjective that comes directly before the noun.
- You hyphenate an age when it is a noun.
- You do not hyphenate an age when it is an adjective after the verb that describes a noun before the verb (that is, a predicate adjective).

DAY 10: SCENARIO

Let's see if you can use your hyphen powers to help out in this situation.

Your friend Marybel needs help. She's got to turn in a paper, but she's completely clueless when it comes to hyphens. She really wants you to look at her paragraph. Can you help her with her hyphens? She's going to need to know where to put them, but you also need to explain to her why they go there!

Charles Hargbough argues that the mid April break is harmful to students. He believes that first year college students need more time in the classroom and less time with spring break related activities. He is quoted as saying, "Eighteen year olds need a ready for the world confidence that only dedicated classics oriented study can bring." Hargbough insists that today's students need more book focused learning time.

Help your friend, but be sure to explain your thinking to her in ways that she'll understand.

CONCEPT #10: DASHES

Reasons for Teaching This Concept

We like dashes. Of all of the punctuation marks, dashes are the best to have at a grammar party (should such an excellent gathering come to pass). A dash slides across a wooden floor in socks and sunglasses, the center of attention, drawing all eyes.

Dashes interrupt the flow of a sentence to give the reader important information. They amplify the material around them, yelling out, "Hey! Look here! This is important and exciting stuff!"

As with any party animal, too many dashes can lead to chaos. These tools are best used in moderation—enough to turn up the volume when necessary, but not so many that we end up with mayhem.

Key
Bold: Teacher talk
Italics: Teacher notes

DAY 1: WHAT DO YOU NOTICE ABOUT THE DASH?

Okay! Today we're going to start learning about a little piece of punctuation called the dash. Let's look at some sentences together.

1. Jamie knew exactly what he wanted for his birthday—a trip to the beach!
2. There was no way that they—those mean girls from my old neighborhood—were going to ruin this day for me.
3. My cousin—the girl who won the Ironman last year—just got a scholarship to Yale.
4. Jakub's blog has over 5,000 followers—business owners, college students, and stay-at-home parents!
5. Cerie said she would pay for lunch—as if that would ever happen!

Everybody notice the dashes? Good—those lines in the sentences. Have you ever seen this piece of punctuation used before?

Students might confuse the dash with the hyphen here. That's completely okay, as it provides the opportunity to discuss the difference.[61] Such a discussion should be light—don't get too lost in the grammar weeds if this issue arises. For now, clarify and move on.

Good. This line here, this dash, is going to be our next focus. It's a pretty powerful piece of punctuation, so we'll need to learn how to use it wisely. But I think you are all up for the challenge. Tomorrow, we'll look at what these dashes are doing in these sentences.

---

61. In short, a dash joins parts of sentences, while a hyphen joins two or more words (mostly; see **Hyphenated Adjectives and Nouns** for more).

DAY 2: DASHES: HOW DO THEY WORK?

Okay, yesterday we had a quick introduction to the dash. The point was for you to recognize it and think, Oh yeah! That's a dash! Today, we're going to look at those sentences again and talk about what those dashes are actually doing.

1. Jamie knew exactly what he wanted for his birthday—a trip to the beach!
2. There was no way that they—those mean girls from my old neighborhood—were going to ruin this day for me.
3. My cousin—the girl who won the Ironman last year—just got a scholarship to Yale.
4. Jakub's blog has over 5,000 followers—business owners, college students, and stay-at-home parents!
5. Cerie said she would pay for lunch—as if that would ever happen!

Now, first of all, let's just look at where the dashes are in the sentence—they really occur in two places. Talk to a neighbor and see if you can identify those two places. *Students should note that they appear either toward the end of the sentence or separate something in the middle of the sentence.*

Let's think about how we read with these dashes. How are they different from periods or commas? Do they affect the way we read these sentences?
Guide students' thinking here. You want to help them realize that a dash is a more prominent piece of punctuation than other options. It's visually more striking, perhaps because it separates at a mid-level height in a sentence, rather than at the bottom of a line as a comma or period does. Dashes may feel like a more significant marker of separation than a period or comma. We may scan over commas and periods, but it's difficult to miss a dash.

Dashes separate parts of a sentence, which has the effect of making what comes after a dash seem more important. When two dashes "set off" a section of sentence, what's between the dashes gets extra attention.

In this discussion, you also want to guide students to see that there are no spaces around a dash. A dash is usually created with two hyphens without any spaces; word processing programs may automatically convert these into a single longer line.

At the end of class, consider building a list with students of everything you've learned about dashes. Your list might look something like this:

1. Dashes separate information.
2. What comes after a dash gets more attention.
3. With two dashes, what comes between gets extra attention.
4. *Dash-emphasized* information can come in the middle or at the end of a sentence.
5. There are no spaces around a dash.

Great job today, everyone! We'll add onto this more tomorrow.

DAY 3: DASHES THAT INTERRUPT

Okay, today we're going to start with dashes again. What have we learned about dashes?

You want to help students remember your list from yesterday.

1. Dashes separate information.
2. What comes after a dash gets more attention.
3. With two dashes, what comes between gets extra attention.
4. *Dash-emphasized* information can come in the middle or at the end of a sentence.
5. There are no spaces around a dash.

Excellent! Now, let's look at these three sentences.

1. There was no way that they—those mean girls from my old neighborhood—were going to ruin this day for me.
2. My cousin—the girl who won the Ironman last year—just got a scholarship to Yale.
3. The whole place—the elm-lined streets and brightly colored buildings—reminded me of my hometown.

These are the interrupting dashes, right? How do we know? Yes, because they interrupt the sentence with two dashes. Good.
   Now let's see what these two dashes are doing.

You'll want to help students see that, in these particular cases, the information inside the dashes renames the noun/pronoun directly before the dash.
Possible guiding questions:

- What's inside the dashes?
- Does what's inside the dashes rename anything? What does it rename?
- Remember that dashes are powerful pieces of punctuation—why might someone use dashes to set off renaming "they" or "my cousin"? Does it say anything in particular about "they" or "my cousin"? (Powerful punctuation can relate powerful feelings about something.)

Excellent. Interrupting dashes can do more than rename. Let's see what else they can do.

1. My mother—despite her unending need to be the center of attention—was quiet and respectful during my graduation.
2. Christoph and his disgusting pet snake—so gross—are never allowed over here again!
3. It was clear—through both his words and his deeds—that he was taking his new position very seriously.

These sentences still have interrupting dashes, right? But they're not renaming the noun or pronoun that comes before them. What are they doing?

In these cases, the separated information offers a "comment," a kind of commentary on the previous subject. Comments are common in movies, plays, and similar visual storytelling. A character might comment on a situation "on the side" (to another character, or even directly to the audience) using this tactic. Writers can do the same.

Dashes can also help you describe something. Let's look at these sentences:

1. My aunt—smart, kind, and generous—is coming to my graduation.
2. At the pep rally, the student audience—falling over with laughter—got a kick out of the class president's stand-up comedy.
3. The little mouse—heart thumping wildly—dove into the hole right before the cat got him.

Look at what's inside these dashes—what's going on? Yes, they're describing the noun before the dash. Good.[62]
  Let's look at all nine of those sentences together for a moment.

1. There was no way that they—those mean girls from my old neighborhood—were going to ruin this day for me.
2. My cousin—the girl who won the Ironman last year—just got a scholarship to Yale.
3. The whole place—the elm-lined streets and brightly colored buildings—reminded me of my hometown.
4. My mother—despite her unending need to be the center of attention—was quiet and respectful during my graduation.
5. Christoph and his disgusting pet snake—so gross—are never allowed over here again!
6. It was clear—through both his words and his deeds—that he was taking his new position very seriously.
7. My aunt—smart, kind, and generous—is coming to my graduation.
8. At the pep rally, the student audience—falling over with laughter—got a kick out of the class president's stand-up comedy.
9. The little mouse—heart thumping wildly—dove into the hole right before the cat got him.

Numbers 1–3 are renaming, 4–6 are commenting, and 7–9 are describing. Let's look at what's inside those dashes. Are they complete sentences? No, they're not.
  But they can be.

---

62. For our grammar nerds out there: yes, number 3 is an absolute phrase, so technically it modifies the entire sentence (rather than just the noun in front of it). These are the kind of grammatical weeds it may be best to avoid with students, at least for now.

1. Jrue promised a better Halloween costume—he was originally going to be a pirate again—and this time he came as an '80s wrestler.
2. Old Hickory—this is the tree my grandfather planted 60 years ago—is going to be cut down to make way for the new highway.

What's inside of those dashes? Are they complete sentences?
They are.

So, let's refresh what we've learned about interrupting dashes:

- Interrupting dashes can either rename, comment, or describe.

  They can do a lot of other things too, but this is a good beginning. Be wary of turning this knowledge into a formal quiz item. (What are the three things interrupting dashes can do?) The point of labeling these functions is to establish working understandings that lead to actual use.

- What comes inside of those dashes can be a complete sentence or something else.

One thing that's pretty amazing about dashes—it's hard to get them wrong. Really hard. (How excellent is that?) There are many, many ways that interrupting dashes can be used, but I think this is a good beginning point for us.

DAY 4: DASHES THAT END

Okay, yesterday we looked at dashes that interrupt. What did we learn about them?
You want to help students remember that they rename, comment, and describe, and that they can be complete or incomplete sentences. You also want to remind them that dashes are really hard to get wrong, so while we are using the labels rename, comment, *and* describe, *remind them that dashes can do just about anything.*

So, today we are going to talk about ending dashes—those dashes that come at the end of a sentence. Here are some examples we've seen before:

1. Jamie knew exactly what he wanted for his birthday—a trip to the beach!
2. Jakub's blog has over 5,000 followers—business owners, college students, and stay-at-home parents!
3. Cerie said she would pay for lunch—as if that would ever happen!

What do you notice about these sentences?
They may first notice that they all end with exclamation points and they all have dashes. They may also guess which ones are renaming, commenting, or describing. At this point, we aren't worried about right or wrong; we just want to hear their thoughts.

If students can't agree on which ones rename, comment, or describe, don't worry. The point is to get them talking about possibilities. Students could point out many variations here, but we might argue that the first example describes (What did he want?), the second renames (Who are the followers?), and the third provides a commentary.

Here are several more examples of renaming, commenting, and describing:

1. **Rename:** Ravi's band got a gig at the best venue in town—The Underground.
2. **Comment:** She said that she didn't wanted to go to the party—girl, please.
3. **Describe:** The winter scene was perfect—pristine white landscape, clear blue sky, still air.

Please remember that the point of these conversations isn't to move students to a place where you give them a dash-filled worksheet, and then ask them to label the use of dashes as renaming, commenting, or describing. The bigger point here is that students experiment with possibilities. The intent of these labels is rhetorical conversation about possibility, not testing. Emphasize through these introductory conversations that dashes are really difficult to use incorrectly.

Excellent job today, everyone! Tomorrow we're going to play around with all the things these dashes can do with some scenarios!

DAY 5: SCENARIO

You have tried and tried and *tried* to explain the drama of your family reunion to your best friend, Nur, but she just isn't getting it. Use dashes to help her understand just how drama-filled that weekend was!

(Notice you'll be able to rename, describe, and comment with this scenario!)

DAY 6: DASHES THAT MOVE SOUND AND ACTION

So, we've learned a lot about dashes.
Refresh students' memories here if needed.

Today, we're going to look at another way that writers often use dashes in their writing. To start our discussion today, let's consider some examples.

She stopped and turned around—the sound was still there—footsteps in the darkness. Then silence. In front of her—the dark hall stretching out. Then the sound came again—footsteps behind—darkness before her. She began running.

Okay. These dashes aren't really renaming, commenting, or describing, or, are they? What are they doing?
Students may notice that the dashes are moving the action along or setting up suspense; they may even suggest that the dashes connect the characters' thoughts, actions, and experiences. You may need to probe a bit to get students to this point. If they're having difficulty, go ahead and show them the version of the text below in comparison.

> She stopped and turned around. The sound was still there. Footsteps in the darkness. Then silence. In front of her, the dark hall stretching out. Then the sound came again. Footsteps behind. Darkness before her. She began running.

How are these two versions different?
Guide students' thinking here. Yes, one has dashes and the other doesn't, but what are the dashes doing? How do the periods change the mood of the text as opposed to the dashes? These dashes may indicate a forward movement of thought and action whereas the periods may suggest more hesitancy.

Let's look at another example where dashes might be a better rhetorical choice to indicate movement.

> The flakes swirled around him—so much white—so much blinding white. He reached out his hand to feel for anything. The cabin was close—straight ahead—no, wait—should he turn around and go back—to the left—right. He stopped—closing his eyes against all of the whiteness.

What are the dashes doing here?
They have a very similar effect to the first paragraph—the dashes help move the narrative along. They may signal to the reader a sense of movement (or perhaps in this case, a lack of movement and overwhelming confusion on the part of the character).

Let's look, again, at what happens to the narrative when we take out the dashes.

> The flakes swirled around him. So much white. So much blinding white. He reached out his hand to feel for anything. The cabin was close. Straight ahead. No, wait. Should he turn around and go back? To the left? Right? He stopped, closing his eyes against all of the whiteness.

Discuss the differences between these two paragraphs. You may have students who favor dash-free versions. Get them to explain their thinking. There is no right or wrong answer here. The goal is intentionality. We want students to make thoughtful rhetorical choices and be able to justify those choices—whatever they might be.

Okay, great job today, everyone. Remember that dashes are an option to help create a scene that is suspenseful, or fragmented, or confusing. Tomorrow, we'll play around with this idea a little more with a scenario.

DAY 7: SCENARIO

Remember yesterday when we learned that dashes can help create tension or show movement? Okay, today we're going to play around with that a little. See if you can use dashes to do just that in the scenario below.

As the editor for the school paper, it is your job to make sure that every article grabs students' attention. The Gothic Literature Club has put together its yearly haunted house and has invited you to experience it first so you can write an article about all of its terrors. You went last night and can't believe how terrifying it was! Now you have to describe the experience in an article.

Make sure you use dashes to convey your sense of terror, horror, and fear.

DAY 8: IS THERE SUCH A THING AS TOO MANY DASHES?

Okay, so for the past couple of days we've talked about dashes in suspenseful writing, right? We agreed that frequent dashes can be a tool for conveying emotions such as anxiety and fear.

However, when it comes to formal, academic writing, we may need to dial back the dashes.

Remember how we've been talking about how's it hard to use dashes incorrectly? Well, here's where it can happen. You can certainly use too many dashes in academic writing.

(Put this paragraph up on the board.)

Dashes—widely used and easily understood—are a powerful tool to use in writing. However—as our teacher has told us—they can be overused—especially in academic writing. We should—therefore—be careful to use them thoughtfully—so they can retain their power—rather than becoming an annoyance to the reader.

Ask students what they think about this paragraph. Students will probably notice that the use of dashes here verges on annoying. It doesn't read like a polished academic work—the dashes confuse and frustrate rather than help.

It is important to point out here that, technically, none of the uses of the dash above are wrong—but they are probably rhetorically inappropriate.

This is a good point to discuss how our readers may feel about our writing. We don't want to unintentionally confuse or frustrate an audience (which is what might happen if we wrote a paragraph like the one above). Our job as writers is to compose texts that are rhetorically thoughtful, texts that are designed to create a specific experience for readers. In academic or professional situations, that experience will often be characterized by clarity and directness of ideas rather than suspense or mystery.

Excellent. Tomorrow, we're going to talk about how you could live a lifetime as a writer and never use a dash (although I'm not sure why you would want to do that).

DAY 9: TO DASH OR NOT TO DASH?

In this lesson, we reuse sentences from previous lessons. Feel free to use student-created sentences from their scenarios.

Okay everyone, today we're going to think about whether or not we need to use dashes. Are they going to help or hurt our message?
You might need to remind students about what dashes can do.

1. Dashes can interrupt or end a sentence
2. They can rename, comment, or describe
3. They can create suspense in our writing
4. Depending on context, dashes may or may not be appropriate

Let's look at these sentences:

1. There was no way that they—those mean girls from my old neighborhood—were going to ruin this day for me.
2. Christoph and his disgusting pet snake—so gross—are never allowed over here again!
3. Jrue promised a better Halloween costume—he was originally going to be a pirate again—and this time he came as an '80s wrestler.
4. Jamie knew exactly what he wanted for his birthday—a trip to the beach!

We've talked about all of these sentences before and what the dashes are doing—but there are other pieces of punctuation that we can use! Look at these.

1. There was no way that they—those mean girls from my old neighborhood—were going to ruin this day for me.

   a. There was no way that they, those mean girls from my old neighborhood, were going to ruin this day for me!
   b. There was use no way that they (those mean girls from my old neighborhood) were going to ruin this day for me!

2. Christoph and his disgusting pet snake—so gross—are never allowed over here again!

   a. Christoph and his disgusting pet snake, so gross, are never allowed over here again!
   b. Christoph and his disgusting pet snake (so gross) are never allowed over here again!

3. Jrue promised a better Halloween costume—he was originally going to be a pirate again—and this time he came as an '80s wrestler.

   a. Jrue promised a better Halloween costume. He was originally going to be a pirate again; this time he came as an '80s wrestler.

b. Jrue promised a better Halloween costume (he was originally going to be a pirate again), and this time he came as an '80s wrestler.

4. Jamie knew exactly what he wanted for his birthday—a trip to the beach!

 a. Jamie knew exactly what he wanted for his birthday: a trip to the beach!
 b. Jamie knew exactly what he wanted for his birthday, a trip to the beach!

Focus on the dash as one choice among many and why we should use this punctuation mark with care—sometimes it is appropriate and other times it may be too much rhetorically.

You might consider the impact of each option: a colon feels more formal, parentheses feel as though the information is less vital, a semicolon tells us that there is a close connection between the two sentences, a comma is, well, commonplace. A dash—a dash announces, tells the reader that the information is significant. A dash highlights and stresses; it's powerful punctuation that should be used with care and tact.

DAY 10: SCENARIO

Today's lesson can be more metacognitive. You can have students dig into the rhetorical choices they make with dashes in this scenario (and perhaps have them revisit previous work to make sure they rhetorically approve of those choices now).

You were there and saw it all—the epic food fight in the cafeteria was amazing! But now the principal wants you to email her and tell her everything you saw. Okay. You will. But you also have to email your best friend, Adele, and tell her about the food fight!

Craft two emails, one to the principal and one to Adele, telling them about what happened. Use dashes in both emails but be thoughtful about their use.

REFERENCES

anneheathen. (2010). *Logan* [Digital]. Retrieved from www.flickr.com/photos/52066925@N00/6813687463

Bellairs, J. (1997). *The treasure of Alpheus Winterborn*. London: Puffin.

Cohen, Z., Stracqualursi, V., & Liptak, K. (2019, January 17). 4 Americans among those killed in Syria attack claimed by ISIS. *CNN*. Retrieved from https://edition.cnn.com/2019/01/16/politics/syria-attack-us-patrolled-city/index.html

Collins, S. (2008). *The hunger games*. New York: Scholastic.

Crovitz, D., & Devereaux, M. D. (2017). *Grammar to get things done: A practical guide for teachers anchored in real-world usage*. New York, NY and Urbana, IL: Routledge, NCTE.

Delso, D. (2015). *Búho nival (Bubo scandiacus), Arcos de la Frontera, Cádiz, España* [Digital]. Retrieved from https://commons.wikimedia.org/wiki/File:B%C3%BAho_nival_(Bubo_scandiacus),_Arcos_de_la_Frontera,_C%C3%A1diz,_Espa%C3%B1a,_2015-12-08,_DD_03.JPG

Do, L. (2011). *Protestors*. Retrieved from www.flickr.com/photos/56414187@N04/5640304599

Harwood, J. (2018, October 24). Deadlocked Georgia governor race tests power of voter restrictions. *CNBC*. Retrieved from www.cnbc.com/2018/10/24/deadlocked-georgia-governor-race-tests-power-of-voter-restrictions.html

Hillocks, G. (1986). *Research on written composition.* Urbana, IL: NCTE.

Khatulistiwa, B. (n.d.). *No title* [Digital]. Retrieved from https://unsplash.com/photos/RdLw6AuTH6Y

Kuarum a la Fledermaus. (2007). [Digital]. Retrieved from https://commons.wikimedia.org/wiki/File:Kustum_a_laFledermaus.png

M 93. (2012). *Bugatti* [Digital]. Retrieved from https://commons.wikimedia.org/wiki/Car#/media/File:Bugatti_Veyron_16.4_%E2%80%93_Frontansicht_(2),_5._April_2012,_D%C3%BCsseldorf.jpg

Morin, B. (2018). *Cat playing with lizard* [Digital]. Retrieved from https://commons.wikimedia.org/wiki/File:Cat_playing_with_a_lizard.jpg

NGrossman81. (2017, December 11). *How hard will Alabama Alabama? Might be one of the Alabamist Alabamings Alabama ever Alabamas. Or not* [Tweet]. Retrieved from https://twitter.com/NGrossman81/status/940390746053644288

Noden, H. R. (2011). *Image grammar: Teaching grammar as part of the writing process* (2nd ed.). Portsmouth, NH: Heinemann.

Park, L. S. (2012). *When my name was Keoko.* New York, NY: HMH Books for Young Readers.

Parke, C. (2019, January 16). Controversial "McJesus" art sculpture defended by Israel. *Fox News.* Retrieved from www.foxnews.com/world/controversial-mcjesus-art-sculture-defended-by-israel

Postman, N. (2011). *The end of education: Redefining the value of school.* New York: Random House.

Rabinovitch, S. (2007). Thousands of hyphens perish as English marches on. *Reuters.* Retrieved from www.reuters.com/article/us-britain-hyphen-1/thousands-of-hyphens-perish-as-english-marches-on-idUSHAR15384620070921?sp=true

Re, G. (2018, October 24). Pelosi, Schumer claim Trump's words "ring hollow" as he calls for unity over explosive devices. *Fox News.* Retrieved from www.foxnews.com/politics/pelosi-schumer-claim-trumps-words-ring-hollow-as-he-calls-for-unity-over-explosive-devices

Romano, T. (2000). *Blending genre, altering style: Writing multigenre papers.* Portsmouth, NH: Heinemann.

Sharp, C. J. (2017). *Hairy dragonfly* [Digital]. Retrieved from https://commons.wikimedia.org/wiki/File:Hairy_dragonfly_(Brachytron_pratense)_male_close_up.jpg

Shutdown is building a wall—at TSA airport checkpoints. (2019, January 16). *USA Today.* Retrieved from https://eu.usatoday.com/story/opinion/2019/01/16/government-shutdown-building-wall-tsa-airport-checkpoints-editorials-debates/2595651002/

Terkel, A. (2018, October 24). Fear dominates final weeks of the 2018 campaign. *Huffington Post.* Retrieved from www.huffingtonpost.com/entry/fear-2018-campaign_us_5bd08c0ee4b0d38b587ee1f8?guccounter=1

Touhid, T. A. (2016). *Monkey at Satchari national park* [Digital]. Retrieved from https://commons.wikimedia.org/wiki/File:Phayre%27s_leaf_monkey_funny_position.jpg

APPENDIX

A. GRAMMAR SHORTCUT SHEET

Grammar Concept	What It's Good For	Examples
Fragment	Creating suspense; suggesting certain states of mind (panic, confusion, anxiety, distraction); helpful with ironic or sarcastic commentary	*As if.* *I can't even.* *We can go to the park. Or not.*
Run-On	Conveying excitement, panic, overwhelming emotion; helpful with ironic or sarcastic commentary	*The football team gets new uniforms and a locker room renovation and a new stadium even though the school can't supply enough textbooks so that every student has one but yay sports amirite?*
Simple Sentence	Stating information directly; summarizing info succinctly at the beginning or end of paragraphs; emphasizing a point as a stand-alone paragraph	*Suddenly, everything changed.* *Never underestimate a North Cobb Warrior.* *My first day of high school was quite memorable.*
Compound Sentence	Establishing comparisons, relationships, and consequences; can suggest equal weight or balance between concepts; can be used to purposefully oversimplify complexity in order to present a binary choice	*We can either have a great time hanging at my house, or we can be bored over at Todd's place.* *Alabama: love it or leave it.*
Complex Sentence	Expressing nuance; acknowledging multiple views; suggesting complex ideas; inviting those with different viewpoints to consider our position	*While I respect your choice of Hardee's as a dining option, I believe that Henry's offers a more rewarding culinary experience.*
Compound-Complex Sentence	Expressing nuance; acknowledging multiple views; elaborating on complex ideas; digging deep into detail	*Even if we consider allowing students to leave school for lunch, it's still not a practical choice; the local traffic makes it impossible to return on time.*

Grammar Concept	What It's Good For	Examples
Simple Conjunctions (FANBOYS)	Establishing relationships between clauses, phrases, and words (see: **Compound Sentence**); "yet" and "nor" lend a more sophisticated tone to a contrasting view or position	*The principal said the right things at the meeting, **yet** I remain skeptical.* ***And** we don't need to mention David's reputation with women.* ***But** I digress.*
Subordinating Conjunctions (i.e., *while, although, because, since,* etc.)	Expressing nuance; acknowledging multiple views; suggesting complex ideas (see: **Complex Sentence**)	***While** I understand your position and share your concern, I still think we need to consider a change in the band's direction.* ***Although** she wasn't entirely convinced by the commercial, Ali decided to give the product a try.*
Passive (and Active) Voice	De-emphasizing the "doer" in a sentence; concealing blame, cause, or authority; emphasizing outcome, result, or impact rather than the "doer"	*"Kelly fired Jess" versus "Jess got fired."* *"A man was killed today in an officer-involved shooting" versus "Police shot and killed a man today."*
Dependent Clause	Establishing reasons; shading an assertion with conflicting perspectives; suggesting complexity	*I believe that students should be able to express themselves freely in school **though this right shouldn't interfere with learning.***
Appositive Phrase	Providing details for a noun concisely; offering a synonym that explains a noun; shaping meaning and reality depending on what details are chosen; controlling tone and implication	*"The principal, **a man of integrity and vision**, stepped onto the stage" versus "The principal, **a notorious disciplinarian**, stepped onto the stage."*
Participial Phrase	Focusing on particular details; shaping meaning and reality depending on what details are chosen; controlling tone and implication	*"**Invigorated by the routine**, the dancer awaited her score" versus "**Sweating profusely**, the dancer awaited her score."*
Absolute Phrase	Focusing on particular details; shaping meaning and reality depending on what details are chosen; controlling tone and implication	*"**Eyes darting around the room**, the accused stood before the jury" versus "**Hands clasped around a rosary**, the accused stood before the jury."*
Gerund	Shifting from action to noun; creating abstract categories for specific actions; generalizing; moving from retelling of events or statement of particulars to broader propositions	*"They should not cut down all the trees when new houses are built" versus "**Clear-cutting** should not be allowed in new developments."*

Grammar Concept	What It's Good For	Examples
Infinitive	Showing an intention ("I plan to . . . " "I intend to . . . "); explaining "why" in response to a question; repetition for rhetorical impact; suggesting future actions as a consequence of a choice, position, or proposal	*With this new law, we renew our American promise:* **to protect** *those most in need,* **to guarantee** *a bright future,* **to ensure** *that every child has a fair chance.*
Preposition	Showing relationships between/among things; offering precise direction or location; implying influence or impact when used figuratively	*Check-cashing outlets are often located* **next to** *pawn shops.* **Within** *the coach's inner circle, the rules are different.* **Behind** *every great man, there's a great woman.*
Noun/ Nominalization (See also: **Gerund**)	Naming; creating abstract categories for specific actions; generalizing; creating distance from specific examples	*"My uncle was laid off and his family is struggling" versus* *"***Labor costs** *were trimmed to maximize profits."* *"Show me that you get results, or you're fired" versus* *"***Deliverables** *are the new measure of employment security."*
Adjective/ Adjectival Phrase	Providing details about a noun; shaping meaning and reality depending on what details are chosen; controlling tone and implication	*"Jackson,* **who came to court well-dressed,** *stepped to the podium" versus* *"Jackson,* **who seemed pale and nervous,** *stepped to the podium."*
Adverb/ Adverbial Phrase	Demonstrating relationships through time, reasons, concessions, conditions, and more; shaping meaning and reality depending on what details are chosen; controlling tone and implication (see: **Dependent Clauses**)	*Can you please hand me that vase,* **carefully**? **Evidently** *Joe is more interested in baseball than biology.* *I've had* **quite** *enough fun for one evening.*
Conjunctive Adverb (*however, therefore, nevertheless, likewise, etc.*)	Pivoting or "making a turn" in one's focus, perspective, etc.; elaborating on a point; revealing complexity (see: **Compound-Complex Sentence**); communicating a more academic or sophisticated tone or persona	*I understand and appreciate your passion for speed metal;* **nevertheless**, *it's probably not appropriate in church.* *Silent sustained reading has been a success;* **therefore**, *we're going to extend time on this activity.*
Pronoun	Avoiding repetition; adding voice; suggesting community or universality; invoking a vague adversary or opponent; shaping meaning and reality; alienates or includes depending on pronoun selection (*I* versus *we*, etc.)	*"***You** *missed the game-winning shot" versus "***We** *didn't play well enough to win."* **Some** *say we should not discuss religion in schools. I disagree.*

Grammar Concept	What It's Good For	Examples
Colon	Defining, clarifying, or explaining concepts; introducing lists; announcing a point with emphasis or finality, especially with a pronoun	*Her final words will stay with me forever:* [the words] *The most important thing to remember is this:* [the thing]
Semicolon	Showing relationships between adjacent sentences; suggesting complexity; communicating a more academic or sophisticated tone or persona	*Don't let my less-than-stellar GPA fool you; my teachers know me as a dedicated team player and active volunteer.*
Dash	Emphasizing a sentence part to make a point; suggesting importance or urgency; can convey increased volume or enthusiasm	*I turned on the light—and just about lost my lunch.* *Tiana—who broke her leg just three months ago—is back in the starting lineup.*
Hyphen	Creating unique concepts through combining words; revealing idiosyncrasy; emphasizing boundary-crossing and complexity over simplicity or established labels	*My brother considers himself a* **half-jock-half-geek-all-straightedge** *kind of guy.* *I finally got to meet her* **too-shy-for-words** *boyfriend.*

B. A BRIEF GLOSSARY OF USEFUL TERMS

Grammar and Usage

Prescriptive grammar: The grammar that lives in grammar and style books, dictating the ideas of correct and incorrect language use. Largely decontextualized and rule-driven, this is the grammar familiar to most of us from traditional language instruction that focuses on memorizing and applying established rules through exercises and drills.

Descriptive grammar: Descriptive grammar seeks to describe how people actually use language in their everyday worlds. Rather than imposing prescribed universal rules as an ideal, descriptive grammar involves a process of discovery: analyzing language patterns to determine the particular rules and conventions that govern contextual language use.

Rhetorical grammar: Rhetorical grammar focuses on how language choices arve determined by context, including situation, purpose, audience, and subject. Since these elements change from context to context, a person's grammatical choices will also shift accordingly. What's appropriate in one situation won't necessarily fit in others.

Grammar: The underlying structure of a language. All language dialects have a specific grammar, because all dialects follow particular rules (see Chapter 3 for a discussion of dialectical grammar). Dialectical moves that may violate standardized usage (e.g., *Him and me went to the store*) are nevertheless following specific dialectical rules, which makes them grammatical. For a more thorough discussion of grammar, see our first book.

Usage: The socially privileged or preferred conventions of language. While grammar describes the structure of languages and dialects, usage deals with notions of correctness. When people judge language as "incorrect," they usually mean that the usage doesn't fit Standardized English conventions (as in, *Him and me went to the store*). For a more thorough discussion of the differences between *grammar* and *usage*, see our first book.

Linguistic Concepts About Grammar

Form and Function: In short, form is "what it is" and function is "what it does."

Consider the gerund: **an -ing verbal that functions like a noun**, as in "*Sneezing* is weird."

The form is *a gerund* (what it is) and the function is *acting like a noun* (what it does).

Now consider the participle, which can also be **an -ing verbal that functions instead like an adjective,** as in "*Sneezing* suddenly, he startled the class."

The form here is a participle (what it is) and the function is *acting like an adjective* (what it does).

Sometimes, a grammar concept can have the same form and function.

The *big squirrel* hid its nuts for the winter.

Here, *big* takes both the form and function of an adjective, and *squirrel* takes the form and function of a noun. But if we get creative, we can imagine *different* functions for these words.

- My grandfather likes to *squirrel* money away in secret places.
- Our team needs another *big* to really compete in the tournament.

We could get into the linguistic weeds with this one, but since this book is about grammar rather than linguistics, we'll stop here. Just remember, form is "what it is" and function is "what it does."

Known-New Contract: Sentences within passages often follow the known-new contract, meaning that known information typically comes at the beginning of a sentence and new information comes at the end of the sentence. We reference this contract throughout the book, including in **Dependent Clauses and Complex Sentences** and **Absolutes and Participial Phrases**. Following the known-new contract also helps create *cohesion*[1] in a text.

Sentence Slot: This one is going to be easier if we start with a basic sentence. Here's one, about as basic and boring as you can get.

I went to the store.

When linguists refer to *sentence slots* they are talking about concepts such as the *subject slot*, the *verb slot*, and the *object of the preposition slot*—where words can go in sentences.

Here, "I" is in the subject slot, "went" is in the verb slot, "to" is in the preposition slot, and "the store" is in the object of the preposition slot. Rather than drilling students on parts of speech (which suggests that words only occupy a single, stable category), you might ask them something like, "In this sentence, what word is in the subject slot?"

The reality is that words shift functions all the time, so an understanding of specific contextual use is more helpful. This is perhaps clearer when we look at more unorthodox language use, such as "I Ubered to the store." Ask students what part of speech "Uber" is, and they'll likely identify it as a proper noun. But the fact is, real language doesn't stay in neat little boxes.

---

1. Cohesion is the grammatical, lexical, and contextual glue that allows for the sustained exploration of ideas.

C. TEACHING LANGUAGE VARIETIES: A BRIEF ANNOTATED BIBLIOGRAPHY

Don't you just hate it when someone tells you that you should consider doing something, you're kinda keen on the idea, but then they don't help you figure out how to do that very thing? Super frustrating, right?

Well, we don't want to be those people. Throughout this book, we've talked about language varieties and the value of those varieties, and we've mentioned the importance of honoring all voices and bringing those voices into the classroom. We wanted to make sure that if such concepts are new to you, you'll have some resources that can help. Here they are. Please keep in mind that this is not an exhaustive list. But it is a place to begin.

BOOKS AND EDITED COLLECTIONS

Charity Hudley, A. H., & Mallinson, C. (2011). *Understanding English language variation in U.S. schools*. New York, NY: Teachers College Press.
Charity Hudley and Mallinson offer a great resource for understanding the rule-governed nature of various American English dialects, including African American English, Southern English, and Appalachian English. Suggestions for classroom activities are also included.

Charity Hudley, A. H., & Mallinson, C. (2013). *We do language: English language variation in the secondary English classroom*. New York, NY: Teachers College Press.
In their second book, Charity Hudley and Mallinson offer strategies to discuss language variation and ideologies with students. They begin by offering linguistic truths, and then discuss the connections between language and culture, explore how language varieties are used in literature, and finish with helping students transition to college.

Delpit, L., & Kilgour Dowdy, J. (Eds.). (2002). *The skin that we speak: Thoughts on language and culture in the classroom*. New York, NY: The New Press.
This edited collection widens the lens, featuring researchers exploring language discrimination in the classroom and authors sharing their lived experiences with language. This volume offers readers a broad understanding of how people understand, interact with, and experience language variation.

Devereaux, M. D. (2015). *Teaching about dialect variations and language in secondary English classrooms: Power, prestige, and prejudice*. New York, NY: Routledge.
Defining language ideologies in the context of power, society, and identity, Devereaux offers specific entry points to teach language in the classroom. With specific frameworks and lesson plans, teachers can both better understand language variation and ideologies as well as teach them.

Devereaux, M. D., & Palmer, C. C. (2019). *Teaching language variation in the classroom: Strategies and models from teachers and linguists*. New York, NY: Routledge.
This volume includes both teachers and linguists sharing how they approach teaching language variation and ideologies in the classroom. With lesson plans and classroom-tested ideas, this practical guide can help teachers begin implementing strategies and guiding discussions immediately.

Lippi-Green, R. (2012). *English with an accent: Language, ideology, and discrimination in the United States* (2nd ed.). New York, NY: Routledge.

A must-read for any teacher interested in discussing language ideologies in their classroom: Lippi-Green explains how language variations are perceived, discussed, and often misunderstood. She further shows how these beliefs about language differences affect larger social structures in the United States.

Reaser, J., Adger, C. T., Wolfram, W., & Christian, D. (2017). *Dialects at school: Educating linguistically diverse students*. New York, NY: Routledge.

For a broad but thorough understanding of how language varieties work in schools, this is your resource. From dialect features in student writing to teaching Standardized English to the basics of sociolinguistic research, this book will show you all the ways that language matters in our classrooms and ways we can teach it equitably.

Scott, J. C., Straker, D. Y., Katz, L. (Eds.). (2009). *Affirming students' right to their own language: Bridging language policies and pedagogical practices*. New York, NY: Routledge; Urbana, IL: NCTE.

This volume brings together linguists and educational theorists to examine how language variation and ideologies are approached on a policy level and taught on a practical level.

Wheeler, R. S., & Swords, R. (2010). *Code-switching lessons: Grammar strategies for linguistically diverse writers*. Portsmouth, NH: Heinemann.

Wheeler (a linguist) and Swords (an elementary school teacher) discuss how to use code-switching and contrastive analysis as tools to help students distinguish between home dialects and the dialect of Standardized English.

Young, V. A., Barretta, R., Young-Rivera, Y., & Lovejoy, K. B. (2014). *Other people's English: Code-meshing, code-switching, and African American literacy*. New York, NY: Teachers College Press.

An excellent introduction to code-meshing, a purposeful and rhetorically powerful move to integrate both home dialects and Standardized English in a piece of writing.[2]

FREE ONLINE RESOURCES

Free Lessons

From *Teaching Language Variation in the Classroom*. Retrieved from www.routledge.com/Teaching-Language-Variation-in-the-Classroom-Strategies-and-Models-from/Devereaux-Palmer/p/book/9781138597952

---

2. Did you notice that the Wheeler and Swords book is designed to help students distinguish between dialects and the Young, Barretta, Young-Rivera, and Lovejoy book is designed to help students combine dialects? That's because we think both are important. School cannot be a "Standardized English–only" space. If we ask students to leave their home culture at the door, we are essentially asking them to choose between mama and school, and let us tell you, mama's going to win every time.

Lessons from K-12 teachers and linguists that focus on teaching language variation and ideology. Here you will find lesson plans, PowerPoints, teacher notes, and other resources.

NC State University, Dialect Instruction. Retrieved from https://linguistics.chass.ncsu.edu/thinkanddo/dialecteducation.php
The linguistics program (faculty and students) at NC State University have created many free resources to begin teaching dialects in your own classroom, including lesson plans and documentaries.

Dictionary of American Regional English, Lesson Plans. Retrieved from http://dare.wisc.edu/resources/discovering-dare-curricula
Lessons from Kelly D. Abrams and Trini Stickle that help teachers navigate the resource of the Dictionary of American Regional English. Five days of lessons help teachers begin teaching language variation and ideology.

Good Videos to Start Thinking About Language Diversity

Three Ways to Speak English. Retrieved from www.ted.com/talks/jamila_lyiscott_3_ways_to_speak_english
Jamila Lyiscott shares her experiences in speaking her three varieties of English. In this video, we are introduced to the idea that all variations of English have value.

Where Did English come from? Retrieved from www.youtube.com/watch?v=YEaSxhcns7Y
When we understand the history of English, we can better appreciate its diversity. Through its history, English has been influenced by an overwhelming number of factors, including colonialism, wars, and slavery.

Podcasts

Lingthusiasm. Retrieved from https://lingthusiasm.com/
A podcast hosted by Gretchen McCulloch and Lauren Gawne that features episodes with titles like "Every word is a real word" (episode 25) and "What does it mean to sound black? Intonation and identity interview with Nicole Holliday" (episode 13), and "Kids these days aren't ruining language" (episode 7).

Lexicon Valley. Retrieved from https://slate.com/human-interest/lexicon-valley
From 2012–2016, the show was hosted by John Garfield and Mike Vulolo. Since 2016, it is hosted by linguist John McWhorter and considers topics such as "Strunk and White is a lot of bunk and tripe" (October 21, 2017), and "How you vanquished ye, thee, and thou" (November 1, 2016).
For more language podcasts, see this list: www.dictionary.com/e/best-podcasts-language/

Features of English Language Varieties

American English: Dialects and Variations (3rd ed.). Retrieved from www.american englishwiley.com/appendix.html

As we've mentioned throughout this book, all varieties of English follow rules just like Standardized English, and there are many linguists who have researched English varieties and coded their rules. This is a resource from linguists Walt Wolfram and Natalie Schillings (2015).

INDEX

known-new contract 29, 45; and absolutes and participles 127–128; and conjunctive adverbs 97; definition 186

language: and beliefs 4, 10, 35, 124; and contextual use 12, 13, 38, 92, 186; and diversity 33–36; and power 4, 12, 14, 15, 22, 24, 99; and power, place, and people 6, 16–17; and teaching variation 187–189; and variation 34–36
lexical categories 49, 99

mechanics 11
mentor sentences 21

naming, renaming, and power 105–108, 111–112
Netflix 28–30
news articles: and nouns 31–32; and participial phrases 32, 125, 127; and passive voice 135; and verbs 32–33
nominalization, grammar shortcut sheet 183; *see also* noun
nonsentences, teaching 49–58
noun: appositives and 115; grammar shortcut sheet 183; hyphenated nouns (*see* hyphens); nominalization 99, 112–113, 140; teaching 99–114; *see also* appositives phrase, and noun phrases; news articles, and nouns

parentheses 179
participial phrases 44; grammar shortcut sheet 182; teaching 115–128; *see also* news articles, and participial phrases
parts of speech 99, 186
passive voice: grammar shortcut sheet 182; and power 130–131, 137–141; teaching 129–143
phrases: absolute (*see* absolute phrase); appositive (*see* appositive phrase); participial (*see* participial phrases)
physics 9, 12
power *see* active voice, and power; language, and power; naming, renaming, and power; passive voice, and power; rhetorical grammar, and power; Standardized English, and power
prepositions 45, 63

prescriptive grammar: and attitude 145; definition 185
pronoun, grammar shortcut sheet 183
punctuation: colons (*see* colon); commas (*see* comma); dashes (*see* dash); hyphens (*see* hyphens); parentheses (*see* parentheses); semicolons (*see* semicolon)

reciprocal teaching and learning 6
rhetorical grammar: definition 185; and the news 31–33; and power 80, 161; and social media 30–31
run-on *see* nonsentences, teaching

scenarios: creating 39–40; teaching 47–48
semicolon: grammar shortcut sheet 184; teaching 144–155
sentence 4, 10, 25, 26, 29; grammar cheat sheet 181; teaching 49–58; *see also* complex sentence; compound-complex sentence; compound sentence; mentor sentences
sentence slot 158, 161, 186
simple sentences *see* sentence
social media 4, 12, 37, 79, 99; *see also* rhetorical grammar, and social media
society 11, 16
Standardized English 4, 11, 12, 16, 17; as a dialect 34; and dialect diversity 33–35; and power 16, 34
stress position 97, 127
subject: and the definition of sentences 49; -verb-object 11

themes 3; and grammar 22–24
thesis statements 71

usage 11, 185–186

verb 99, 103–104, 110, 118–119, 136; and the definition of sentences 49–50; and zero copula 34–35; *see also* news articles, and verbs
verbal 49–50, 52, 185